# THESAURUS OF LIBRARY AND INFORMATION SCIENCE TERMS

**Dr. Rajendra Kumbhar**
*M. Com., M. Lib. I. Sc., Ph.D.*
*Department of Library and Information Science,*
*H. P. T. Arts and R. Y. K. Science College, Nasik (Maharashtra)*

**Ess Ess Publications**
4837/24, Ansari Road, Darya Ganj,
New Delhi-110002
✆ : 23260807
Fax : 23274173
E-mail: essess@del3.vsnl.net.in
*url:http://www.essessbooks.com*

**First Published 2004**

**ISBN : 81-7000-378-4**

**Price : Rs.1200/-**



*Published by :*

**Ess Ess Publications**

4837/24, Ansari Road, Darya Ganj,
New Delhi - 110 002
Phone : 23260807
Fax : 23274173
E-mail : essess@del3.vsnl.net.in

*Laser Typesetting:*

**Mukesh Graphics**

L-2/8, DDA Market,
Mangolepuri, New Delhi
Ph. : 27924405

*Printed at :*
Print Line

# List of tables


| Table No. | Particulars |
|---|---|
| 1. | (QI) for (Spl) to [1P1] |
| 2. | Grouping of (QI) for (Spl) to [1Pl] |
| 3. | Principles used for arranging (Sp1) to [1P 1] |
| 4. | (QI) for (Spl) to [1P2] |
| 5. | Grouping of (QI) for (Spl) to [1P2] |
| 6. | Principles used for arranging (Spl) to [1P2] |
| 7. | Principles used for arranging (Sp2) to [1P2] |
| 8. | (QI) for (Spl) to [lMP1] |
| 9. | Grouping of (QI) for (Spl ) to [lMP1] |
| 10. | Principles used for arranging (Spl) to [1MP1] |
| 11. | (QI) for (Sp1) to [lMP2] |
| 12. | Principles used for arranging (Spl ) to [lMP2] |
| 13. | (QI) for (Spl) to [lE] |
| 14. | Grouping of (QI) for (Sp1 ) to [1E] |
| 15. | Principles used for arranging (Spl) to [1E] |
| 16. | (QI) for (Sp2) to [lE] |
| 17. | Principles used for arranging (Sp2) to [1E] |
| 18. | (QI) for (Spl) to [2E] |
| 19. | Principles used for arranging (Spl) to [2E] |
| 20. | Sectors allocated |

# List of Abbreviations used

| | | |
|---|---|---|
| (A1) | = | Array 1 |
| (A2) | = | Array 2 |
| (AD) | = | Alphabetical Device |
| [1E] | = | First round energy |
| [2E] | = | Second round energy |
| [1MP1] | = | First round first level matter property |
| [1MP2] | = | First round second level matter property |
| [1P1] | = | First round first level personality |
| [1P2] | = | First round second level personality |
| BT | = | Broader term |
| CC | = | Colon classification |
| (CD) | = | Chronological Device |
| CEI | = | Common energy isoiates |
| CMPI | = | Common matter property isolates |
| [E] | = | Energy |
| FC | = | Fundamental Category |
| (GD) | = | Geographical Device |
| ISR | = | Information Storage and retrieval |
| ISRS | = | Information storage and retrieval systems |
| LICs | = | Libraries and information centres |
| LIS | = | Library and information science |
| [MP] | = | Matter property |
| (ND) | = | Numerical Device |
| NL | = | Natural language |
| NLP | = | Natural language processing |

| | | |
|---|---|---|
| NT | = | Narrower term |
| (QI) | = | Quasi isolate |
| (QIs) | = | Quasi isolates |
| RT | = | Related terms |
| (SD) | = | Subject Device |
| (Sp1) | = | Speciator kind 1 |
| (Sp2) | = | Speciator kind 2 |
| Tel | = | Telescoping |
| TT | = | Top term |
| UDC | = | Universal Decimal Classification |
| UF | = | Use for |

# CONTENTS

**1:INTRODUCTION** ... 1

1.1 Problems created by Natural languages in ISR

1.1.1 Problem posed by synonyms

1.1.2 Problem posed by homonyms

1.1.3 Spelling variations

1.1.4 Singular and plural forms

1.1.5 Compound phrases

1.1.6 Scattering of related terms

1.2 Role of thesaurus in ISR

1.2.1 Standardizes writer's terms

1.2.2 Helps the information organizers in vocabulary control

1.2.3 Helps the information searchers

1.3 Scope of the present thesaurus

1.3.1 Special isolates only

1.4 Methodology / procedure

1.5 Outline of the book

**2: DEPTH CLASSIFICATION: AN OVER VIEW** ... 9

2.0 Introduction

2.1 Classification

2.1.1 Library classification

2.1.2 Need for library classification

2.2 Colon classification

2.2.1 The postulational approach

2.2.2 Postulate of Fundamental Categories

2.2.2.1 Personality

2.2.2.2 Matter
2.2.2.3 Energy
2.2.2.4 Space and Time
2.2.3 Postulates of Rounds and Levels
2.2.3.1 Postulate of Rounds
2.2.3.2 Postulate of Levels
2.2.4 Postulate of Quasi Isolate
2.2.5 Postulate of Speciator
2.2.5.1 Kinds of speciators
2.3 Depth classification
2.3.1 Meaning
2.3.2 Need of depth classification
2.3.2.1 Depth classification and documentation activities
2.3.3 Approach / methods used in the construction of depth classification schemes
2.3.4 Common isolates and depth classification schemes
2.3.5 Lengthy class numbers and depth classification scheme: a justification
2.3.6 Depth classification - dual use
2.4 Rational for selecting CC as a model for designing the present depth classification schedule
2.5 Notational system for depth classification schemes
2.6 Examples of depth classification schedules
2.6.1 Depth classification schedules of library and information science

3: THESAURUS - AN OVER VIEW ... 25

3.0 Introduction

3.1 Definitional analysis

3.1.1 Language thesaurus and information retrieval (IR) thesaurus

3.2 Natural versus controlled language

3.3 History of IR thesaurus

3.4 Thesaurus and other vocabulary control devices

3.4.1 Thesaurus and lists of subject headings

3.4.2 Thesaurus and classification schemes

3.4.3 Classification schemes and lists of subject headings

3.5 Thesaurus and post-coordinate indexing systems

3.6 Purposes of thesaurus

3.6.1 Information technology based ISRS systems and thesaurus

3.7 Thesaurus construction methodologies

3.7.1 Approaches to thesaurus construction

3.7.2 User oriented thesaurus

3.7.3 Standards and guidelines for thesaurus construction

3.7.4 Manuals for thesaurus construction

3.7.5 Use of information technology in thesaurus construction

3.7.5.1 Thesaurus management softwares

3.8 Thesaural relationships

3.8.1 The equivalence relationship

3.8.1.1 Synonyms

3.8.1.2 Lexical variations

3.8.1.3 Quasi synonyms

3.8.1.4 Factored and non-factored terms

3.8.2 The hierarchical relationship

3.8.2.1 Generic relationship

3.8.2.2 Whole-part relationship

3.8.2.3 Instance relationship

3.8.2.4 Polyhierarchical relationship

3.8.3 The associative relationship

3.9 Display methods

3.9.1 Alphabetical display

3.9.2 Systematic display

3.9.3 Graphic display

3.9.4 Screen display

3.10 Sources providing lists of thesauri

3.11 Review of existing thesauri

3.11.1 Thesauri of LIS terms

3.11.2 Thesauri covering other subject fields

**4: DEPTH CLASSIFICATION SCHEDULE OF LIBRARY AND INFORMATION SCIENCE** ... 56

4.0 Introduction

4.1 Construction methodology

4.1.1 Understanding the subject

4.1.2 Identification of sample population

4.1.3 Analysis of data

4.1.4 Recording of terms

4.1.5 Grouping of isolates

4.1.6 Grouping of speciators

4.1.7 Arrangement of isolates and their speciators

4.2 Schedule of [1P1] isolates

4.3 Arrangement of (QI) for (Spl) to [1P1]

4.4 Inverted order

4.5 Arrangement of (Sp1) to [1P1]

4.6 Schedule of [1P2] isolates

4.7 Arrangement of (QI) for (Spl) to [1P2]

4.8 Arrangement of (Spl) to [1P2]

4.9 Arrangement of (Sp2) to [1P2]

4.10 Schedule of [lMP1] isolates

4.11 Arrangement of (QI) for (Sp1) to [1MP1]

4.12 Arrangement of (Spl) to [lMP1]

4.13 Arrangement of (Sp2) to [!MP1]

4.14 Schedule of [lMP2] isolates

4.15 Arrangement of (QI) for (Spl) to [lMP2]

4.16 Arrangement of (Spl) to [lMP2]

4.17 Schedule of [lE] isolates

4.18 Arrangement of (QI) for (Sp1) to [1E]

4.19 Arrangement of (Sp1) to [1E]

4.20 Arrangement of (QI) for (Sp2) to [lE]

4.21 Arrangement of (Sp2) to [lE]

4.22 Schedule of [2E] isolates

4.23 Arrangement of (QI) for (Spl) to [2E]

4.24 Arrangement of (Spl) to [2E]

4.25 Natational system adopted

4.25.1 Telescoping array

4.25.2 Main class notation

4.25.3 Allocation of sectors

4.26 Notational consistency with Colon Classification edition seven
4.27 Testing of the depth classification schedule
4.28 Index to the depth classification schedule of library and information science
4.29 Depth classification schedule of library and information science

**5: THESAURUS CONSTRUCTION METHODOLOGY** ... **171**

5.0 Introduction
5.1 Subject field covered
5.2 Methodology adopted
  5.2.1 Procedure adopted for preparing the alphabetical thesaurus
5.3 Language of the thesaurus
5.4 Standard followed
5.5 Sources for the thesaural terms
  5.5.1 The isolate terms alone
  5.5.2 The speciator terms alone
  5.5.3 The combination of speciators with isolates
5.6 Grammatical forms of terms used
  5.6.1 Noun forms
  5.6.2 Adjectival phrases
  5.6.3 Verbs
  5.6.4 Initial articles
  5.6.5 Singular and plural forms
    5.6.5.1 Count nouns
    5.6.5.2 Non count nouns

5.6.5.3 Abstract concepts
5.6.6 Spellings
5.6.7 Acronyms
5.6.8 Parenthetical qualifiers
5.6.9 Apostrophes
5.6.10 Hyphens
5.6.11 Capitalization
5.7 Proper names of institutions
5.8 Scope notes and definitions
5.9 Compound terms
5.9.1 Citation order of compound terms
5.10 Thesaural relationships
5.10.1 The equivalence relationship
5.10.1.1 Synonyms
5.10.1.2 Terms of different linguistic origin
5.10.1.3 Acronyms
5.10.2 The hierarchical relationship
5.10.2.1 Generic relationship
5.10.2.2 Whole - part relationship
5.10.2.3 Instance relationship
5.10.3 The associative relationship
5.10.3.1 Isolates across facet
5.10.3.2 Speciators under the (QI) 'By cause' to [1MP1] isolates
5.10.3.3 Speciators under the (QI) 'By tools' to [1E] and [2E] isolates

5.10.3.4 Terms within facet

5.11 Display

5.11.1 Parts of the thesaurus

5.11.2 Reference structure

5.11.3 Alphabetization

5.11.4 Typography

5.12 Testing of the thesaurus

**6: THESAURUS OF LIBRARY AND INFORMATION SCIENCE TERMS** ... 187

REFERENCES ... 383

GLOSSARY OF THESAURUAL TERMS ... 409

INDEX ... 414

# Preface

Human beings are communicating information and knowledge through information sources since long. Information sources form the basic stock for the services to be provided by libraries and information centres. Systematic organization of information sources and or their surrogates is essential for effective retrieval. The document surrogates along with author and title are also prepared and arranged under the name of the subject. Terms (vocabularies) are used to represent the subject name in the surrogate entries. To represent subjects, objectively irrespective of space and time the vocabulary used must be controlled. Various tools like thesaurus are used to control vocabulary in information storage and retrieval systems (ISRS).

Natural language words i.e. vocabulary used in ordinary discourse can also be used for representing subjects in ISRS. However, the richness of natural language in word forms and variety affects the recall and precision performance of ISRS.

The synonyms in natural language scatter entries of documents on the same subject under different names. The homonyms need to be controlled to avoid retrieval of irrelevant information. Singulars and plurals if not controlled may also retrieve irrelevant information. Whereas, uncontrolled coordination of term result in retrieving unwanted information and missing some relevant information. A thesaurus as a vocabulary control tool provides solutions to all these problems posed by the natural language in ISRS.

The library and information science (LIS) is one of the fast developing interdisciplinary subject. Literature on this subject is increasing at exponential rate. For effective storage and retrieval of information on LIS either in hard copy format or in digital format, offline as well online, vocabulary control tool like a thesaurus was urgently needed. To fulfill this need the present thesaurus is constructed.

This thesaurus is constructed by adopting the blending of the two approaches i.e. *a priori* and posteriori approach. Further, the thesaurus is based on a specially constructed depth classification schedule of LIS terms.

The book is divided into six chapters. First chapter describes the uses of thesaurus and states the scope of the present thesaurus. Second chapter explains various concepts dealing with depth classification. It also reviews literature dealing with depth classification. Definitional analysis of thesaurus and review of literature on thesaurus is presented in the third chapter. Chapter four has two components i.e. (i) it describes in detail the methodology useful for constructing depth classification schemes based on the concept of speciators and fundamental categories and (ii) it presents the actual schedule of depth classification of LIS. Methodology adopted in constructing the present thesaurus is described in the fifth chapter. The thesaurus of LIS terms is given in the sixth chapter.

Thesaurus, its types, uses, construction methods is part of LIS curriculum. LIS courses of many universities have practicals in thesaurus construction. This book will be useful to all those who are concerned with thesaurus and thesaurus construction.

The author is indebted to all those professionals who have helped directly or indirectly in completing this. Naming them all will be a difficult task. However, the author owes special thanks to Dr. (Mrs.) A.A. Vaishnav, Professor and Head, Dept. of Library and Information Science, Dr. Babasaheb Ambedkar Marathwada University, Aurangabad for developing my interest in this topic and Professor S. Seetharama, Former Head, DRTC, Banglore, for widening my views. The author is thankful to the M/s Ess Ess Publications for bringing out this volume in very short time.

*Rajendra Kumbhar*

# 1

# INTRODUCTION

Communication is one of the basic necessities of human societies of all times. Information is communicated through various means across space and time. These means include information sources in hard copy format, audio-visual, computer readable formats, etc. Effective organization of information sources is as important as communication itself. This task of organizing information sources is entrusted to libraries and information centres.

While organizing information sources in systematic order libraries and information centres create two sets of databases. The first set consists of actual information sources, while the second set consists of entries describing information sources in the first set. The first set is usually arranged by using the call numbers, prepared according to a classification scheme. Usually three types of entries are prepared to describe the information sources. These are author entries, title entries and subject entries. The subject entries in this second set are arranged under the terms representing the subject contents of the information sources. This set of subject entries serves as subject index to the first set. The set of entries representing the subject of whole document is usually referred to as subject catalogue. Whereas, the set of subject entries referring to parts / contents of documents, such as articles in periodicals, is called subject index. In the field of library and information science (LIS) the word 'index', without any epithet mostly stands for subject index.

The steps involved in preparing both. the subject catalogue and index are same. These steps are: -

1. Analyzing contents of document and identifying its subject.
2. Translating the subject name into a standard term or phrase i.e. a subject heading.
3. Preparing and arranging the index entries under the subject heading.

The standard terms used in the index to represent the subject of the document are called index terms. They are also called as descriptors because they describe subject of the document.

The set of index terms along with rules for their selection and coordination is referred to as, 'indexing languages'. The appropriateness of index terms is of vital importance because they represent subject of both, the document and the reader's request. Thus, using the indexing language, information is stored and retrieved.

Indexing languages can be categorized into natural language (also called uncontrolled language) and controlled language (Rowley and Farrow, 2000). Controlled language is the language in which both the terms that are used to represent subjects and the process whereby terms are assigned to particular document's description are controlled. Natural language consists of terms taken from the title, abstract or text of the document. Natural language offers a great variety of terms in the form of synonyms, antonyms, homonyms, adjectival forms, etc. Thus, natural language is complex and rich in variety. These features of natural language create number of problems in information storage and retrieval (ISR).

## 1.1 PROBLEMS CREATED BY NATURAL LANGUAGE IN ISR

The richness of natural language is like a blessing in disguise as far as the business of information storage and retrieval is concerned. The richness of natural language in terms of variety itself puts forth a number of problems in ISR. These problems are:

### 1.1.1. Problems posed by synonyms

Natural language offers synonyms, i.e. various terms to represent one and the same concept or thing. The concept of 'periodicals', for example, can be represented in an index by using at least two other terms, i.e. 'journals' and 'serials'. Unless a rule is made to use one of these three terms, whenever the concept 'periodical' will be indexed, it may be indexed at different times under different terms. Similarly, the searcher may search under any one of these three terms, and if no directions found he will have only a partial retrieval.

### 1.1.2. Problems posed by homonyms

Depending upon the context, some terms have more than one meaning. 'Charging', for example, means 'issuing' in the context of circulation work. Levying fees or collecting money for library service is also called charging. If the context is not specified the information storage and retrieval system (ISRS) is bound to retrieve some irrelevant items.

### 1.1.3. Spelling variations

Different countries follow different rules for spellings. Unless some control is exercised, the variations in spellings will lead to scattering of index entries on one and the same subject.

### 1.1.4. Singular and plural forms

Natural language uses these two forms of terms to represent a single item / concept and multiples respectively. However, some terms when used as singulars connote different meaning than when used as plural. The term 'coating' for example, as singular indicates 'process' and 'coatings' i.e. the plural form indicates material. In order to avoid irrelevant retrieval appropriate term forms must be used.

### 1.1.5 Compound phrases

Some concepts can be properly represented by using compound phrases only i.e. phrases made up of two or more terms. For example, 'library school'. Regarding the compound phrases the indexer and the searcher face the problem of deciding the sequence of terms in the phrase. The terms, 'library' and 'school', can be combined in different order to get compound phrases such as:

1. Library school
2. School library

As can be seen from the given example, the different sequences connote different meanings, and so if not managed properly can affect the retrieval adversely.

### 1.1.6. Scattering of related terms

A searcher in an information retrieval system (IRS) always desires to find not just information on his subject of interest but also on its related subjects. However, the alphabetical order used for arranging entries in an index, scatters entries of related subject. A searcher looking for information on 'classification', would be interested in 'indexing' and 'cataloguing' as well, for, they also deal with information organization. However, in alphabetical arrangement the entries of these three subjects will be placed at different positions, even though they are closely related with each other.

Vocabulary control is needed to resolve these problems. Vocabulary control is standardization of indexing terms (Davis and Rush, 1979). Such standardization is achieved by selection of preferred terms. Vocabulary control helps to improve the performance of ISRS.

Lists of subject headings, classification schemes and thesauri are the prime vocabulary control tools. Of these the lists of subject headings mostly provide pre-coordinated headings and the classification schemes are basically useful in arranging documents on the shelves. Both, the lists of subject headings and classification schemes do not have adequate mechanism to show associative relations i.e. reference to related terms. Further, the classification schemes cannot bring into notice the synonyms. Thesaurus is such a vocabulary control tool, which through its relational structure and display overcomes the lacunae of the other two vocabulary control devices.

The thesaurus exercise control over synonyms by selecting a term as 'preferred term' and giving cross-reference to it from its 'non-preferred' synonym.

In thesauri the homonyms are distinguished by using parenthetical qualifiers. Problems of spelling variations and compound phrases are resolved by recommending appropriate rules for indexers and searchers. The problem of scattering of related concepts in purely alphabetical lists like the lists of subject headings is resolved by the thesaurus by listing all related terms under the descriptor along with its exact relation, such as 'broader term', 'narrower term' and 'related term'.

These features of thesaurus help the indexer and the searcher in representing the subject accurately, objectively and consistently at both, storage and retrieval stages.

LIS is one of the fast developing interdisciplinary subjects. Literature on LIS is increasing at exponential rate. For effective storage and retrieval of information on LIS, in manual, offline or online environment a vocabulary control tool is needed. Hence it was felt necessary to construct a vocabulary control tool i.e. a thesaurus of LIS terms.

## 1.2 ROLE OF THESAURUS IN ISR

There are three main agencies involved in the process of communication of information through libraries. These agencies are the writer, the information organizer (i.e. the information professional) and the end user. The thesaurus helps these agencies in selecting / using right term/s in ISR.

### 1.2.1 Standardizes writer's terms

One of the desirable objectives of thesaurus is to provide means by which the use of terms by writers in a given subject field may be standardized (Foskett, 1980). The descriptors listed in the thesaurus may help in achieving this desirable purpose. Use of standard terms by writers in the field will be beneficial to the users, as they will understand a particular subject more easily, because the subject would be described in standard terms. Use of standard terms by the writers will ultimately help the information organizers also because vocabulary control will be exercised at the origination stage itself.

### 1.2.2 Helps the information organizers in vocabulary control

The information organizers describe subjects of documents in various records such as catalogues, indexes, databases, etc. for search and retrieval of documents. Precise description of subjects of documents in such records is of vital importance from the point of recall and precision. Consistency in subject representing terms is equally important. Vocabulary control devices, such as, thesaurus help in representing subjects of documents in precise terms consistently. That is why the information organizers must use vocabulary control devices like thesaurus.

### 1.2.3 Helps the information searchers

Information about documents stored in the form of catalogues, indexes, databases, etc. may be searched by the information professionals and the end users. During the search process a query statement is prepared, which consists of terms representing user's information needs. The query statement is used for searching information from catalogues, indexes, databases, etc. The information searcher should use vocabulary control devices like thesaurus to represent his information needs. Use of thesaurus for this purpose will help to have expected recall and precision.

## 1.3 SCOPE OF THE PRESENT THESAURUS

The core subject covered by the present thesaurus is LIS. As such it lists terms related with libraries and information centres (LICs), LIS personnel, library buildings and furniture, library technologies, information sources, users, services and facilities provided by LICs, management of LICs, etc. It does not cover the fused subject 'bibliometrics'. This is because the seventh edition of CC (which is the base for the construction of the present depth classification schedule and the thesaurus) has assigned a separate class number to 'Bibliometrics'. So separated from the LIS.

The thesaurus contains 1399 terms, of these 1285 are descriptors and 114 are non- descriptors.

### 1.3.1 Special isolates only

This thesaurus is based on the specially constructed new depth classification schedule. The newly constructed depth classification schedule itself is based on a general classification scheme i.e. Colon Classification (Ranganathan, 1987). As such it enumerates only special isolates (and their speciators) related with the LIS. The schedule does not list 'space' and 'time' isolates, so also it does not list common isolates. However, certain common matter property isolates and common energy isolates appearing in the seventh edition of Colon Classification are enumerated in the newly constructed schedule as special isolates. This is done to facilitate notational structure, as is done in the Colon Classification (Ranganathan, 1987a).

## 1.4 METHODOLOGY / PROCEDURE

A brief description of the methodology / procedure followed in the construction of the classification schedule and the thesaurus based on the classification schedule is presented here. Detail description of the methodology adopted for the construction of the classification schedule and the thesaurus is presented in chapter 4 and 5 respectively.

First a faceted depth classification scheme was constructed. This scheme was based on Colon Classification edition seven. Isolates and speciators were selected by analyzing 500 assorted micro documents. The isolates and speciators were grouped facet-wise and within facet were arranged by applying various principles and canons given by Ranganathan (1989a, b, c). Notations were assigned to the arranged isolates and speciators as per the notational scheme used in the seventh edition of Colon Classification.

Using the terms from the specially constructed depth classification scheme the thesaurus of LIS terms was constructed. Various thesaural relations were established with the help of the depth classification scheme. Help of Unesco's *Guidelines for the establishment and development of monolingual thesauri* (Unesco, 1981) was also taken to decide descriptor forms, forming compound terms etc.

## 1.5 OUTLINE OF THE BOOK

This book is divided into six chapters.

1.5.1 First chapter 'introduction' explains (i) the problems posed by natural language in ISR, (ii) role of thesaurus in ISR and (iii) scope of the present thesaurus.

1.5.2 Review of literature on depth classification schemes is provided in the second chapter.

1.5.3 The third chapter presents literature review of thesaurus along with definitions of thesaurus.

1.5.4 Depth classification schedule of LIS and its index is given in chapter four.

This chapter also describes in detail the methodology adopted for the construction of depth classification schedule of LIS.

1.5.5 Chapter five gives detail description of the methodology adopted for the construction of the present thesaurus.

1.5.6 Chapter six presents the thesaurus of LIS terms.

The book is concluded with the references, glossary of thesaural terms and Index.

# 2

# DEPTH CLASSIFICATION – AN OVERVIEW

## 2.0 INTRODUCTION

Classification schemes are the tools used in classifying books and or arranging their entries in the catalogues, bibliographies, etc. The classification schemes can be categorised into two categories, i.e. broad classification schemes and depth classification schemes. This chapter aims to review literature dealing with depth classification. It also aims to explain various technical terms related with depth classification.

## 2.1 CLASSIFICATION

Etymologically the word classification has been derived from the Latin word 'classis', which means 'groups'. The Oxford English Dictionary provides meaning of classification as -

'The action of classifying or arranging in classes according to common characteristics or affinities' (Oxford, 1970). Thus classification is the process of grouping like entities and separating unlike entities.

### 2.1.1 Library classification

Library classification is the arrangement of books on the shelves or description of them in the manner which is most useful to those who read (Sayers. 1955). Ranganathan (1964b) explained library classification as a process of formulation of groups of subjects, arrangement of those groups in a helpful sequence and representing them by ordinal symbols denoting their respective position in the sequence.

### 2.1.2 Need for library classification

The number of documents produced is increasing with exponential rate. The multidimensional, infinite and dynamic nature of the universe of subject is as expected putting forth varieties of new subjects. This increase in the documents and their subjects demand increasing efforts for their systematic arrangement. Library classification is one of the important tools useful for systematic arrangement of documents on the shelves. Library classification is also useful for deriving subject headings for cataloguing and indexing purpose. It also helps to arrange the entries in the classified catalogue. Apart from these traditional uses, classification is useful in computerized catalogue (Satija, 1988) and in online systems (Svenonius, 1983), (Chan, 1995). The call number has an important role in multimedia catalogues (Ramaiah, 1998). Classification also plays a vital role in computerized information storage and retrieval (Dhyani, 1999), (Jaiswal, 1999). Such being the need and uses of library classification, experts in the LIS field have developed various library classification schemes. Colon Classification is one of the important library classification schemes.

## 2.2 COLON CLASSIFICATION

Colon Classification (CC) is the brain - child of Shiyali Ramamrita Ranganathan. It was first published in the year 1933 (Ranganathan, 1933). Till now seven editions of CC have been published. The seven editions as per their features are grouped in three groups called versions (Gopinath, 1976).

Version 1 - Rigidly faceted classification schemes: First, second and third editions of CC belong to this version. Editions of this version used only one facet indicator digit i.e. Colon (:). That is the reason it got the name Colon Classification. Editions belonging to this version gave short schedules of basic subjects, few common isolates and large number of special isolates.

Version 2- Almost freely faceted classification schemes: Fourth, fifth and sixth edition of CC belong to this version. This version is called as almost freely faceted version because it used different facet indicator digits for different facets such as:

| *Facet* | *Indicator digit used* |
|---|---|
| 1. Personality | , (Comma) |
| 2. Matter | ; (Semi colon) |
| 3. Energy | : (Colon) |
| 4. Space | . (Dot) |
| 5. Time | ' (Single inverted comma) |

Editions of this version of CC also introduced the concept of Rounds and Levels to remove the severe rigidity.

Version 3 – Freely faceted classification schemes: Seventh edition of CC (Ranganathan, 1987) published in the year 1987 represents the third version. This edition incorporates findings of dynamic theory of classification (Gopinath, 1976). Being a freely faceted classification scheme it has no rigid formula for compound subject going with the basic subject.

### 2.2.1 The postulational approach

The universe of subjects as represented by documents is multidimensional. However, the documents can be arranged on the library shelves only in linear manner. It is difficult to arrange the multidimensional universe of subjects in an uni-dimensional way. To overcome this difficulty Ranganathan resorted to the postulational approach.

'A postulate is a statement about which we cannot use either of the epithets 'right' or 'wrong'. We can only speak of a set of postulate as helpful or unhelpful' (Ranganathan. 1962). Gopinath discusses postulational approach and believes that it has provided objectivity and scientific basis to CC (Gopinath, 1986). M. M. Kashyap reviews development and impact of postulational approach (Kashyap, 1986).

### 2.2.2 Postulate of Fundamental Categories

Ranganathan has based his CC on many postulates. The postulate of fundamental categories is one of them. According to Ranganathan there are five and only five fundamental categories-viz. Time, Space, Energy, Matter and Personality, which are defined by enumeration only (Ranganathan, 1989d). The number of categories, however, differ from person to person (Seetharama, 1972). These categories being postulates have no scientific justification but are extremely useful in library classification. Ranganathan not only enumerated the fundamental categories but also recommended their sequence as PMEST. Hemalata Iyer analyzes this sequence in the context of user preferences. (Iyer, 1986). Based on the fundamental categories, Ranganathan developed the concept of facet analysis. Facet analysis is useful in designing faceted / analytico-synthetic classification schemes. Facet analysis has many more applications, which are described by Devadasan (1986). The terms representing fundamental categories may have different meanings in different subjects, however Ranganathan used them with a specific context i.e.

#### *2.2.2.1 Personality*

Personality covers manifestations of wholeness, for example, chemical compounds, plants and animals and parts of them, languages, religions, etc. The other Fundamental Categories are attributes of Personality.

Without Personality there can be no organ, constituent, attribute, action, reaction or incidence in space and time. Personality forms the basis, the host, locus of all other categories. In the main class 'library and information science' (LIS) concepts like libraries, information sources, library personnel, and users form the locus to the other fundamental categories. That is the reason these isolates belong to the fundamental category, Personality.

The fundamental category, Personality presents great difficulty in its identification. It is too elusive. It is ineffable (Ranganathan, 1989e). As it is difficult to identify the fundamental category, Personality, Ranganathan suggested the 'method of residues' for its identification.

Norman Roberts provides definitional analysis of Personality and discusses the limitations of this concept (Roberts, 1969). Foskett (1961) and Grolier (1962) provide a critical evaluation of Personality.

#### *2.2.2.2 Matter*

Since recent past name of the fundamental category Matter is replaced by Matter Property [MP]. Initially, as Ranganathan claimed this fundamental category represented materials only. Latter on two more manifestations of this category were identified, i.e. Matter Property and Matter Method. (Ranganathan, 1971). Library activities like classification, cataloguing, circulation, etc. for example, represent the property of the Personality of library. So they belonged to Matter facet. The fundamental category Matter Method mostly manifests in science and technology subjects. For example in the main class 'geology' isolates like 'mechanical, seismological' etc. manifest as Matter Method isolates. Neelameghan and Gopinath (1967) discuss the problems in grouping of [MP] isolates and solutions thereto.

#### *2.2.2.3 Energy*

The fundamental category, Energy represents action. The action may be among and by all kinds of entities- inanimate, animate, conceptual, intellectual and intuitive (Ranganathan, 1989f). In the main class 'library science' computerization, preservation, management, etc. are examples of the manifestation of the fundamental category, Energy.

*2.2.2.4 Space and Time*

The fundamental category 'Space' represents geographical area and 'Time' represents period.

**2.2.3 Postulates of rounds and levels**

Recurring manifestation of aforementioned fundamental categories is required for classifying subjects of greater intension. This need is fulfilled by postulates of rounds and levels.

***2.2.3.1 Postulate of rounds***

According to this postulate the fundamental category, Personality, Matter and Energy may manifest itself in one and the same subject more than once (Ranganathan, 1989g). Ordinarily, the fundamental categories, Space and Time may manifest only once in the last round.

***2.2.3.2 Postulate of levels***

According to this postulate the fundamental category, Personality and Matter may manifest itself more than once in one and the same round within a subject (Ranganathan, 1989g).

**2.2.4 Postulate of quasi isolate**

Name of the characteristics used to represent an isolate idea or a speciator is called quasi isolate (QI). It is so called because it does not represent a true isolate idea, e.g. the 'Personality' isolates of the main class 'Sociology' in the seventh edition of CC are first represented as (QI). These are for example, 'By age', 'By residence', etc. (Ranganathan, 1987b). Similarly in the main class 'Educational Psychology' the speciators are grouped under various quasi isolates (QIs) (Ranganathan, 1987c). Some times a particular facet may have a large number of (QIs). When the number of (QIs) is large the problem of their ranking arises. As a solution to this Neelameghan and Gopinath (1966) suggested 'Group Strategy'. Group strategy is a useful method for grouping (QIs).

### 2.2.5 Postulate of speciator

Speciator is an isolate idea used as a qualifier for an isolate or another speciator.

When a sub isolate i.e. a qualifier to an isolate, has a possibility of going with more than one isolates, it is listed as speciator, instead of chain division, e. g. the sub isolate 'computerized' can go with the isolates such as cataloguing, classification, circulation, etc. As such the sub isolate 'computerized' is listed as a speciator, only once, and can be combined with any appropriate isolate as and when needed to form class number for a compound subject.

#### *2.2.5.1 Kinds of speciators*

There are two kinds of speciators. Speciator kind 1 (Sp1) qualifies an isolate idea, e.g. 'branch' a (Sp1) may qualify the isolate 'library' in the main class LIS to represent the subject 'branch library'. The connecting symbol hyphen (-) is used to connect the speciator kind 1 to an isolate.

Speciator kind 2 (Sp2) qualifies the speciator kind 1, e.g. 'abstracting sources' is a speciator kind 1. It qualifies the isolate idea information sources. The proper name Library and Information Science Abstracts (LISA) is speciator kind 2, as it qualifies the speciator kind 1 'abstracting sources'. Speciator kind 2 are attached to speciator kind 1 by using the connecting symbol 'equal to' (=). Neelameghan and Gopinath (1973) provide meaning and use of (Sp2) through a case study.

## 2.3. DEPTH CLASSIFICATION

### 2.3.1 Meaning

To Ranganathan, depth classification is 'a scheme of

classification fitted to reach co-extensiveness and expressiveness in the classification of micro thoughts having many rounds and levels of facets and isolates of high orders in any or all of them (Ranganathan, 1957). A schedule of depth classification scheme can be developed by extending a class in general classification scheme.

### 2.3.2 Need of depth classification

All social institutions for their successful survival have to respond positively to the various social pressures. The library is a social institution. As a social institution it is pressurized to develop new techniques to organize the ever growing, diverse universe of subjects.

The human race has great passion for specialization. Increasing specialization ultimately results in the creation of documents dealing with micro thoughts. For systematic organization of documents dealing with micro thoughts depth classification schemes are needed. In another words depth classification schemes are needed to provide expressive, individualizing, unique class number to any micro thought within any number of facets and phases.

Ranganathan explains the need of depth classification in the context of research saying that 'depth classification schemes of micro subjects functions, as a link in the chain of communication needed to prevent the reversion of relay-research into research by isolated individuals (Ranganathan, 1989h).

Depth classification schemes are also needed to bring together all aspects of a subject. Need and importance of depth classification is further explained by Bhattacharyya (1969).

The need for depth classification schemes can be more precisely proclaimed as-

1. Most general classification schemes do not give adequate details for precise representation of the highly complex subjects in papers and reports that documentation must handle today.

2. Broad classification schemes do not have optimum helpful sequence.
3. The highly specialized subjects catalogued today are compound, they can be accurately designated by subject headings which combine two or more terms. Each term may be used in a great variety of combinations. So it is necessary to have complete flexibility in forming combinations. Such flexibility is provided by depth classification.

### *2.3.2.1 Depth classification and documentation activities*

**The efficiency of any information storage and retrieval system depends upon two things.**

**(i) Selecting standard terms to representing micro subjects.**

**(ii) Creating compound headings by arranging the component terms in a helpful order.**

**Any general, broad classification scheme cannot truly serve both the self- arrangement and documentation. The depth classification schemes fulfill both these requirements, for it lists micro subjects and provides rules for synthesizing the various terms representing the subject. Further a term in a compound phrase may form part of many combinations and it is only the depth classification's faceted nature, which provides complete flexibility in coordination of terms. The depth classification schemes employ more means to minimize the schedule size.**

**Such being the usefulness of depth classification, Ranganathan estimated the need for about 5000 depth classification schedules (Ranganathan, 1964c). Responding to this need, up till now about 100 depth classification schedules covering about 120 basic subjects have been constructed in India (Gopinath, 1966).**

Depth classification schedules, so far developed, mostly cover engineering and technology subject field (Gopinath, 1966). The social sciences and interdisciplinary subjects have not been paid much attention to. This is an effort to fill up this gap by constructing a depth classification schedule of LIS, an interdisciplinary subject.

### 2.3.3 Approaches / methods used in the construction of depth classification schemes

There are two basic approaches following which, a depth classification scheme / schedule can be constructed. These approaches are:

(i) **The speculative approach:** This approach is also recognized as *a priori* approach. According to this approach the classification schedule is constructed on the basis of conjecture.

(ii) **Pragmatic approach:** This approach is also called as literary warrant approach. This approach recommends that the classification schedule should be constructed by following the literary warrant.

(iii) **The blending approach:** Use of only one of the approach mentioned above may throw the classification schedule out of focus. To avoid this Ranganathan has recommended the use of 'blending method' i.e. the combination of both the above methods (Ranganathan, 1964).

Milstead (1984) provides a comparative account of the *a priori* and pragmatic approach. She writes that, 'most classifications construct pigeonholes, which are performed without reference to the subject of a particular document. Therefore documents are put into the pigeonholes "close in size to the subject". Co-extensiveness is based on the subject of individual documents while pigeonholing is based on the structure of the system.

Explanation of each step involved in the construction of depth classification scheme is provided by Ranganathan in his article published in 1964 (Ranganathan, 1964a). This is a very basic article on the subject. Neelameghan (1969) has also explained with example, the methodology to be followed in the construction of depth classification schemes.

Designing of depth classification scheme by applying the

pragmatic approach is explained by Neelameghan and Gopinath (1965) through a case study of the subject 'Diesel Engine Production Engineering'.

Neelameghan and Gopinath (1965a) present an investigative account of design methodology for depth classification scheme. They also explain the methodology of making the design work amenable to scientific method and making the work of classificationist and of the classifier more productive.

M. A. Gopinath has published a manual giving step by step instructions for the construction of depth classification scheme (Gopinath, 1986a).

B. C. Vickery has prepared a comprehensive manual providing guidance for the construction of faceted classification (Vickery, 1960).

### 2.3.4 Common isolates and the depth classification schemes

The depth classification schemes so far constructed on the basis of CC, basically give isolates of Personality facet. Few isolates of Matter [MP] and Energy [E] facet are also given. Most of the isolates of [MP] and [E] facet are believed to be common to many main classes. Methodology of searching common [MP] isolates is described by Ranganathan (1960). The seventh edition of CC provides list of common matter property and common energy isolates (Ranganathan, 1987d).

### 2.3.5 Lengthy class numbers of depth classification schemes- a justification

For representing micro subjects multiple terms are needed. For representing more components of a subject in a class number more notational symbols are needed.

Depth classification schemes endeavor to facilitate individualization of specialized subjects. This is done by representing every component of a compound subject and as a result the class number becomes lengthy. By virtue of more digits and connecting symbols the class number becomes cumbersome too.

Thus, the choice is between non-coextensive, short, easy class number provided by the general classification scheme and coextensive, lengthy class number provided by the depth classification scheme. The excellence in librarianship in general and information storage and retrieval, in particular, forces to favour the latter of the aforesaid alternatives.

### 2.3.6 Depth classification - dual use

To provide options and varieties is the 'command' of 'The great creator'; [That is why probably, the human beings are provided with two hands, two eyes etc. instead of one] and to choose the right option is the intelligence and judgement of the 'created'. Similarly, the depth classification schemes offer class numbers for specialized topics as well as for broad subjects. It is the privilege of the information organizer to choose the option, expedient to his purpose.

## 2.4. RATIONAL FOR SELECTING CC AS A MODEL FOR DESIGNING THE PRESENT DEPTH CLASSIFICATION SCHEDULE

Species of classification schemes available for selecting as a basis for designing a depth classification schedule are:

1. Purely enumerative
2. Almost enumerative
3. Almost faceted
4. Rigidly faceted
5. Freely faceted

Amongst these species of classification schemes, only the freely faceted classification scheme offers freedom in the sequence and number of facets. So only the freely faceted classification schemes can be of use in the depth classification of newly emerging micro subjects. A more detailed explanation for using a freely faceted species for designing a depth classification schedule is provided by Ranganathan (1966).

A freely faceted scheme analyzes a subject and arranges the facets available in it in a helpful sequence. It also provides rules for number building by synthesizing appropriate facets. This is why the faceted schemes are also called as analytico-synthetic classification schemes. The seventh edition of CC belongs to the freely faceted species of classification and so it is chosen as a model for designing the present depth classification schedule. In addition to this justification, the following two reasons substantiate the decision favouring CC as a model for designing the depth classification schedule.

(i) CC is based on sound theoretical foundation. It's normative principles, canons, postulates, principles of facet sequence and the various devices guide objectively in the design of depth classification (Ranganathan, 1989i).

(ii) Notational qualities: CC uses mixed notation consisting of Roman alphabets, both upper and lower case, Indo-Arabic numerals, various punctuation marks and mathematical symbols. This extensive base of the notational system provides tremendous scope for the interpolation and extrapolation through various devices. The large base of this notational system also helps to have shorter class numbers.

## 2.5 NOTATIONAL SYSTEM FOR DEPTH CLASSIFICATION

Ranganathan provides a descriptive account of notational system useful for designing a depth classification scheme. He explains it with a case study of a classification schedule of 'Push bicycle' (Ranganathan, 1972). Neelameghan and Sangameswaran (1966) explain use of array division with packet notation.

## 2.6 EXAMPLES OF DEPTH CLASSIFICATION SCHEDULES

There are about 100 depth classification schedules constructed so far, here is a select list, presented in chronological order.

1. Fatma, A. R. and Ranganathan, T. (1964). Screw production engineering: depth classification. *Library Science* 1. paper B.
2. Ranganathan, S. R., Neelameghan, A. and Gopinath, M. A. (1965). Medical microbiology: depth classification. *Library Science* 2, section G82.
3. Neelameghan, A. and Bhattacharyya, G. (1966). Locomotive production engineering: depth classification. *Library Science* 3, section P52.
4. Anjaneyulu, V. (1967). Computer production engineering: depth classification. DRTC Seminar 5. Banglore: DRTC. Paper H.
5. Neelameghan, A. (1967). Glass production technology: depth classification. *Library Science* 4. Paper L.
6. Neelameghan, A., Gopinath, M. A. and Denton, P. H. (1967). Motor vehicle production: depth classification- a demonstration. *Library Science* 4. Paper H.
7. Ravichandra Rao, I. K. and Rawat, K. (1972). Computer programming languages: depth classification version of CC. *Library Science* 9. Paper B.
8. Seetharama, S. (1973). Human digestive system: depth classification version of colon classification. *Library Science* 12. Paper A.
9. Sangameswaran, S. V. and Gopinath, M. A. (1986). Design and development of depth version of colon classification for food technology. *In* T. S. Rajgopalan. *Ed.* Ranganathan's philosophy: assessment, impact and relevance. New Delhi: Vikas. P. 257-268.

In addition to these the DRTC students, as a part of their curriculum, every year prepare depth classification schedules for various subjects.

### 2.6.1 Depth classification schedules for library and information science

In 1966 Ganesh Bhattacharyya and Maya Bhattacharyya prepared a depth classification schedule of LIS. This schedule is prepared by using the blending method i.e. the combination of the *a priori* and pragmatic approaches. The pragmatic approach included selection of over 300 assorted micro documents published during the period 1961-64. This schedule gives comprehensive list of [1P1] isolates. These are grouped under various (QIs). It also lists 11 [1P2] isolates under the (QI) 'distinctive practices'. These isolates actually belong to [MP] facet. It also lists 22 isolates under the [E] facet (Bhattacharyya and Bhattacharyya, 1966).

In 1970 Ranganathan himself prepared a brief schedule of library science giving list of isolates belonging to 'Personality', 'Matter' and 'Energy' facets. In this schedule he writes that ' the literary warrant is extending a greater variety of compound subjects in the main subject library science than what it was forty years ago. Therefore time has come to extent the schedule of the main class library science' (Ranganathan, 1970). In the recent past the revised schedule of the library science main class appeared in the seventh edition of CC (Ranganathan, 1987e).

It is the same reason, what Ranganathan expressed above, for which it was thought apt to construct an extended schedule of the main class library and information science. The present depth classification schedule of LIS lists isolates of all the three facets i.e. Personality, Matter Property and Energy. The present schedule also puts in practice for the first time, the concept of speciators as far as the subject LIS is concerned.

Ruth Daniel and J. Mills constructed a depth classification schedule for LIS. This schedule is not exactly based on the construction methodology of depth classification suggested by Ranganathan. But it is one of the exhaustive schedules on the subject so far. It is based on faceted principles and the facet formula used is:- 'End - product (user – cum – system) – materials (stock) – operations – agents – properties - space – time'. Non hierarchical notations consisting of upper case letters for facets and lower case letters for classes within them are used (Daniel and Mills, 1975).

The survey presented in this chapter indicates that the concept of depth classification is well established. The survey also indicates that no depth classification schedule is constructed covering the latest LIS literature and adopting the concept of speciators.

The thesaurus of LIS terms presented in the sixth chapter is based on depth classification schedule. After taking stock of the literature on depth classification it is apt to have a review of the literature on thesaurus, which is the scope of the next chapter.

# 3

# THESAURUS – AN OVERVIEW

## 3.0 INTRODUCTION

The objective of this chapter is to review the literature dealing with thesaurus. This is an overview of literature on information retrieval (IR) thesaurus of monolingual nature. The literature dealing with language thesaurus and multilingual thesaurus is beyond the scope of this survey.

## 3.1 DEFINITIONAL ANALYSIS

Derivationally the word thesaurus originated from the Greek language and symbolizes the concept of treasury or store- house of knowledge. The Webster's dictionary has defined thesaurus as, 'a useful literary collection or selection especially a book of synonyms and antonyms'. (Webster, 1987). The Unesco has defined the thesaurus as, 'a vocabulary of controlled indexing language formally organized so that the *a priori* relationships between concepts (e.g. 'broader' and 'narrower') are made explicit' (Unesco, 1981a). This definition lays emphasis on *a priori* relationships, which are document independent. The British Standards 5723 defines a thesaurus as, 'a means of displaying the terms in a controlled indexing language, together with indications of their apparent relationships' (British, 1979). Ajoy Kumar Roy provides definition, giving list of those whose natural language expressions are controlled. He defines thesaurus as, 'an IR thesaurus is chiefly a terminological control device for transformation of natural language (NL) expressions, used by authors, referees, publishers, indexers and users who form the various links in the information transfer chain into a more constrained system of vocabulary' (Roy, 1981). Thesaurus can also be defined functionally and structurally. Functionally a thesaurus is a terminological control device used in translating the natural language into the systems language. Structurally it is a tool consisting of controlled set of terms linked by hierarchical or associative relations, which mark any needed equivalence relations (synonyms) with terms from natural language and concentrate on a particular area of knowledge (Guinchat and Menou, 1983).

While emphasizing the standardization function Rowley (1992) defines thesaurus as, 'a compilation of words and phrases showing synonyms and hierarchical and other relationships and dependencies, the function of which is to provide a standardized vocabulary for information storage and retrieval systems'.

Emphasizing the systems which make use of thesaurus Aitchison, Gilchrist and Bawden (2000) defined thesaurus as, 'a vocabulary of controlled indexing language, formally organized so that *a priori* relationships between concepts are made explicit, to be used in information retrieval systems, ranging from the card catalogue to the Internet'. The last word in this definition indicates the potential usefulness of thesaurus in Internet information retrieval.

Davis and Rush (1979) explain the concept of vocabulary control as:

'Indexing may be thought of as a process of labeling items for future reference. Considerable order can be introduced in this process by standardizing the terms that are to be used as labels. This standardization is known as vocabulary control, the systematic selection of preferred term.

In any information storage and retrieval system (ISRS)

indexing plays an important role. An index describes subject of documents with the help of descriptors arranged in systematic order. The indexer and the user are the two main parties who have to use precise terms in indexing and searching respectively. Use of precise terms is essential for having optimum recall and precision. The indexer as well as the user in the process of information storage and retrieval (ISR) always come across variety of terms (vocabulary) representing the same concept. This vocabulary must be controlled. Vocabulary control is warranted for two reasons, i. e.

1. To promote consistent representation of subject matter by indexers, thereby avoiding the dispersion of related materials, through control (merging) of synonymous and nearly synonymous expressions and by distinguishing among homographs.
2. To facilitate the conduct of a comprehensive search by linking together terms whose meanings are related paradigmatically or syntagmatically (Lancaster, 1985).

The thesaurus is a vocabulary control device. Inversely, the vocabulary contained in thesaurus (as well as in other vocabulary control devices such as lists of subject headings, classification schemes, etc.) is called controlled vocabulary.

### 3.1.1 Language thesaurus and information retrieval (IR) thesaurus

The various thesauri available can be categorized in two broad categories, i.e. the language thesaurus and IR thesaurus. The language thesaurus is primarily a dictionary of synonyms, though structurally it may differ, to some extent, from ordinary word dictionary. Roget's thesaurus (Roget, 1987) is a classic example of language thesaurus, which, according to Vickery (1960a) is a tool for writing in English. The IR thesaurus collects terms of a subject/s and organizes in such a manner so as to bring out the relations between concepts. Thinking on the same line Schultz, quoted by Lancaster, expresses that the purpose of Roget's thesaurus is to give an author a choice of alternative words to express one and the same concept (Lancaster 1972). The IR thesaurus tends to be more prescriptive. According to Wall (1962) however, the purpose of both the above categories of thesauri is same.

## 3.2 NATURAL VERSUS CONTROLLED LANGUAGE

Another name for controlled vocabulary is controlled languages. The opposite of controlled language is natural language, which is synonymous with ordinary discourse, also called as free text. The search based on natural language is called free text search. Internet search is mostly free text search. Both of these indexing languages have their own advantages and disadvantages (Fugmann 1987). The debate over the pros and cons of natural and controlled indexing language is going on for a long period. This debate is divided into four eras by Rowley (1994). Aitchison and Gilchrist (1987) provide comparative account of natural language and controlled language. Keen and Digger (1972), Bhattacharyya (1974), Cleverdon (1966), Knapp (1982), Perez (1982), Dubois (1987), Rowley (1990), Fidel (1991, 1992), Milstead (1995), Knapp, Cohen and Juedes, (1998) wrote in favour of natural language.

Markey (1980) mentioned that free text gave higher recall and controlled terms gave higher precision. Blair and Maron (1985), Coco (1984) supported the controlled language. Milstead (1995) too believes that thesauri [controlled language] have prolonged life.

Free search is not absolutely uncontrolled, for one has to control at least synonyms and homonyms and free search is useful only for super new concepts, which are not yet formed part of terminological control devices. Because of these two reasons Henzler (1978), Ulmann (1967), Holst (1966), Lancaster (1972a) preferred hybrid systems, i.e. combination of natural and controlled languages.

## 3.3 HISTORY OF IR THESAURUS

Long back in 1878, W.F. Poole though not under the name

'thesaurus' regarded that some device of vocabulary control will be potentially useful in IR. While describing the feature of *Poole's index*, he insisted that references, additional to those in the index itself should be issued as a separate publication like Roget's thesaurus (Poole. 1878). Poole's this dream remained unaccomplished for next 81 years until first fully operational thesaurus was developed and used at Du Pont in 1959.

In modern times, it was the group of researcher at Cambridge Language Research Unit in England, who began to discuss the applicability of thesaurus concept to IR. (Joyce and Needham, 1958).

Roberts (1984) summarizing history of thesaurus mentions that in February 1947, C. N. Mooers made reference to the use of thesaurus in the context of mechanized information retrieval.

The credit for re-introducing the idea of thesaurus into the normally available professional literature goes to C. L. Bernier and E. J. Crane of Chemical Abstracts Services (Bernier and Crane, 1948).

Thinking on the idea of thesaurus Whelan (1958) recommended lattice arrangement of index terms because it provided greater freedom of conceptual connections implied by such a form. Whelan used the word 'head term' what Mooers called 'descriptors'.

It is believed that the word 'thesaurus', in print media, in the context of IR was first used by H.P. Luhn in 1959 (Kumar, Raghavendra Rao and Kamath, 1975). However, actual use of thesaurus in ISRS was started by engineering department of E. I. Du Pont Nemours and Company, USA in 1959 (Lancaster, 1972b).

From 1960 onward there were fast developments in the concept of thesaurus. During this period the thesaurus was widely adopted for vocabulary control. Initially, it was used only in manual post coordinate indexing systems, then in mechanized ISRS and now it is used even in pre-coordinate indexing systems and of course in computerized ISRS.

## 3.4 THESAURUS AND OTHER VOCABULARY CONTROL DEVICES

There are other devices like authority lists, lists of subject headings, classification schemes, etc. which, are used for the purpose of vocabulary control. To resolve the chaos of terminology of thesaurus itself, some professionals opinioned that, all the above listed vocabulary control devices should be called thesaurus (Korotkin, 1965), (Strater, 1969). Nevertheless, there exist some basic differences between these various vocabulary control devices.

### 3.4.1 Thesaurus and lists of subject headings

Charles Ammi Cutter (Cutter, 1889) in his *Rules for dictionary catalogue* gave useful rules for formulating subject headings. The famous rule was that a subject is to be entered under its most specific heading. The ALA in 1895 issued its list of subject headings (American, 1895) with the general principle that 'the heading shall be under which it is supposed that the majority of educated Americans will look, with cross references from other forms of heading'. This was followed by the first edition of *Library of Congress list of subject heading* (Library of Congress, 1911) which had made extensive use of sub headings.

List of subject headings is said to be one of the simplest forms of vocabulary control devices. Lancaster (1972c) has differentiated the thesaurus from list of subject headings on the basis of conventions and application. According to him thesaurus distinguished between Broader Terms (BT), Narrower Terms (NT) and Related Terms (RT). Whereas the lists of subject headings coupled all these together under see also references. The subject heading stands alone in alphabetical subject catalogue, whereas the thesaural descriptor is used in conjunction with other descriptors even though in itself it may already be highly pre-coordinated.

### 3.4.2 Thesaurus and classification schemes

Bates (1988) summarizes the fundamental differences between classification and the thesaurus as:

a) Indexing terms are grounded on a linguistic basis, whereas classification schemes organize conceptual categories.

b) The aim of indexing dictionaries is the exposure of durable solid words and expressions for document description, while the aim of classification schemes is the creation of absolutely distinct and incompatible conceptual categories that are exhaustive in their aggregate.

c) The classification schemes' structure, which is not evident in indexing dictionaries, is the part of realization of such accurate division of categories.

Lu (1990) however, in the process of making his own model of IR came to the opposite conclusion from those of Bates. According to Lu relationships that are merely lexical can be expressed with the structure of a classification "tree", while merely semantic relations with a structure of indexing "network".

Classification as Miller (2001) puts it, is an indexing and retrieval tool of a mono-hierarchical, mono-aspectual information system, in which every concept can be included in one or another category according to this category's aspect. Whereas a thesaurus is the same type of aid for multi-hierarchical, multi-aspectual system offering access via multiple aspect.

Weinberg (1995) provides a more detailed comparison of thesaurus and classification.

In spite of various differences between thesaurus and classification schemes there is a great compatibility between the principles followed in the construction of thesaurus and classification schemes (Gopinath and Prasad, 1975).

### 3.4.3 Classification schemes and lists of subject headings

Classification brings together related terms by careful

application of principles of division. In the lists of subject headings related terms get separated due to alphabetization. Relationships between separated headings are indicated through syndetic structure. Lists of subject headings provide pre-coordinated headings. Such headings pose two problems.

a) Problem of word order in compound headings; and

b) Lack of specificity.

Ranganathan (1945), Pettee (1946), Coates (1960) addressed these problems.

The pre-coordinated headings failed to provide access to every term in the compound heading. The sequence of terms in pre-coordinated heading may not be suitable. Solutions to these problems were presented by post-coordinate systems.

## 3.5 THESAURUS AND POST- COORDINATE INDEXING SYSTEMS

The post-coordinate indexing systems are based on the principle of entering a subject of document under isolated terms and combining these terms at the time of search. For selecting appropriate index / search term and to provide rules for coordination at searching stage the thesaurus is used.

Thesaurus has been widely adopted for vocabulary control in post- coordinate indexing systems for which it was designed (Lancaster, 1972d). It is now used in pre-coordinate systems also (Aitchison, 1982).

## 3.6 PURPOSES OF THESAURUS

According to Foskett (1980) the purposes of thesaurus are:

a) To provide map of a given field of knowledge.

b) To provide a standard vocabulary for a given subject field.

c) To provide a system of references between terms.

d) To provide a guide for users of the system.

e) To locate new concepts in a scheme of relationships with existing concepts in a way which, makes sense to users of the system.

f) To provide classified hierarchies.

g) To provide means by which the use of terms in given subject field may be standardized.

The thesaurus can also be used for generation of keyword lists which form the basis for planning, priority setting and other research management tasks (Nestsel, et.al., 1992). The thesaurus is also useful in computer assisted indexing and abstracting. Thesaurus helps in defining terms.

Thesaurus can be used for three basic purposes (Rowley and Farrow, 2000a).

1. In indexing but not in searching.
2. In searching but not in indexing.
3. In both indexing and searching.

Day by day the number of online ISR system including the Internet is increasing. The online ISR systems are making more and more information available in the full text format. The thesaurus plays vital role in retrieving relevant information from these systems (Aitchison, Gilchirst and Bawden, 2000a).

### 3.6.1 Information technology based ISRS and thesaurus

Borko (1986) claims that the use of thesaurus in ISRS will enable efficient subject search based on the inverted file of key words extracted automatically from natural uncontrolled language of the document. Austin (1986) questions this claim of Borko.

Batty (1988) explains how authors and publishers can make information more accessible [on line] by providing indexing information that uses controlled terms from a thesaurus.

Kosovac (2000) explains the usefulness of thesauri in retrieval of networked information available both, on Internet and Intranet.

## 3.7 THESAURUS CONSTRUCTION METHODOLOGIES

### 3.7.1 Approaches to thesaurus construction

Lancaster (1972e) has identified four approaches to thesaurus construction:

i) Convert an existing vocabulary; e.g. convert a list of subject headings into a thesaurus.

ii) Extract the vocabulary from an existing, more general thesaurus or develop a specialized thesaurus putting within the framework of a more general thesaurus; i.e. create a microthesaurus.

iii) Generate the vocabulary empirically [so called empirical method] on the basis of indexing a representative set of documents.

iv) Collect terms together from diverse sources, including glossaries and other publications and from subject specialists.

The third approach mentioned above is named differently by different people, e.g. inductive method (Aitchison, Gilchrist and Bawden, 2000b), bottom-up approach (Lancaster, 1985a), stalagmitic method (Wooster, 1970), literature based method (Blagden, 1968). This method was used in the construction Du Pont thesaurus (Lancaster, 1972e).

The fourth approach mentioned above is also called as committee approach, deductive method (Aitchison, Gilchrist and Bawden, 2000b), stalactitic method, top down approach (Lancaster, 1972e) and subject specialist based method (Blagden, 1968). This method was used in the construction of *Thesaurus of Engineering and Scientific Terms* (Thesaurus, 1969).

Super thesaurus construction (Stern and Rischette, 1991) and dynamic thesaurus (Rees-Potter, 1991) are new ideas which put forth the concept of universal thesaurus. From organization point of view their size, though may be a matter of concern.

The latest idea is of 'thesaurus federations' (Kramer, Nikolai and Habeck, 1997) which is a project based on development of 'switching' rules between different thesauri included in the federation.

The idea of construction of 'objective thesaurus' specially based on and meant for Internet is also emerging. Such a thesaurus, as put forth by Miller (2001a) is based on real information.

### 3.7.2 User oriented thesaurus

Most of the thesauri are constructed by considering the indexers' convenience. However, the growth of online ISR systems and users' unassisted searching have made the traditional concept of indexer oriented thesaurus obsolete (Bates, 1986). Bates suggested the construction of the so-called 'user-thesaurus'. Bates 'user thesaurus' includes:

i) A list of all terms in use in the database.

ii) Terms actually used in a given database and those that are not used.

iii) Scope notes for problems likely to be encountered by end-user.

iv) Self-explanatory names for terms or relationships and,

v) A vast entry vocabulary, geared to end-user requirements.

Bates argument is that the users' search query terms should be considered as a source for thesaurus vocabulary. This view is fully supported by Strong and Drott (1986) and Pejtersen (1980). The US National standard on thesaurus construction has also recommended construction of user thesaurus under the caption 'user warrant' (National, 1994).

A further account of developing a thesaurus based on generators (literary warrant) and user warrant is provided by Lopez-Huertas (1997).

Classaurus developed by Bhattacharyya (1982) is also a type of thesaurus. It has qualities and strength of both a thesaurus and classification. Fugmann (1990) and Devadasan (1985) reported on the automatic construction of classaurus.

### 3.7.3 Standards and guidelines for thesaurus construction

Thesaurus construction involves decisions to be taken over various aspects of thesaurus. In order to have consistency in these decisions and ultimately to have a useful thesaurus various agencies have prepared standards / guidelines. All these standards / guidelines provide prescriptions and explanations over forms of terms, formations of thesaural relationships and display of terms.

Krooks and Lancaster (1993) and Williamson (1996) have presented a detailed evaluation of principles, guidelines and standards evolved during 1959 to 1993.

Most of the individual thesauri in their introductory part provide explanations of principles, standards followed during the process of their compilations. However there exist specially prepared guidelines (Unesco, 1981) and International standard ISO–2788 (International, 1974) for thesaurus construction. The second edition of the International standard was published in 1986 (International, 1986). There also exist number of national standards for thesaurus construction, e.g. the French standard AFNOR NFZ-47-100 (Association, 1981) the British standard, BS-5723 (British, 1987), the German standard, DIN 1463 (Deutsches, 1987-1993), the US standard, ANSI / NISO Z39.19 (National, 1994). From this list of various national standards it can be noticed that there is no Indian standard for thesaurus construction.

These national standards as well as the second edition of the International Standard are based on the Unesco's guidelines for thesaurus construction (Unesco, 1981).

### 3.7.4 Manuals for thesaurus construction

In addition to the national and international standards comprehensive manuals are published, e.g. Gilchrist (1971), Soeregal (1974), Lancaster (1986), Aitchison, Gilchrist and Bawden (2000c).

General overview of thesaurus and thesaurus construction is provided by Foskett (1980a), Aitchison (1992) Gilchrist (1994, 1997), Taylor (1999), and Dextre Clarke (2001). Lancaster (1985b) has also brought out a brief manual under the General Information Programme (PGI) of Unesco. A tutorial on thesaurus construction is also available (Craven, 2001).

### 3.7.5 Use of information technology in thesaurus construction

Thesaurus construction involves intellectual and mechanical activities, e.g. selection of terms and establishment of their relations is intellectual work whereas; arranging thesaural entries is mechanical activity. Thesaurus construction and its maintenance (i.e. adding, deleting and modifying terms) is time-consuming job. To expedite the work of thesaurus construction and to improve its quality the computer and related technologies have been used since long. Experiments were carried out for testing the usefulness of computer in text analysis for thesaurus construction (Sparck Jones, 1971), (Salton, 1971). Stevens (1980) and Crouch (1990) provide a detailed account of automatic thesaurus construction. Lancaster (1986) in his book entitled *vocabulary control* devoted a full chapter to discuss the issue of automatic thesaurus construction.

Automatic thesaurus construction can be a part of automatic ISRS. In automatic thesaurus construction thesaurual relationships are mainly identified statistically (Aitchison, Gilchrist, and Bawden, 2000d). Svenonius (1986, 1987) has presented an account of development of algorithms for establishing associative relationship using co-occurrence data.

Schwanhausser (1975) and Ravichandra Rao (1975) described the procedure for the computer generation of a thesaurus from a set of descriptors manually assigned to documents.

#### *3.7.5.1 Thesaurus management softwares*

The complicated task of thesaurus construction and maintenance can now be simplified by the use of thesaurus management softwares. INDEX, PROTERM, CICADE, LIDOS, TMS, DOMESTIC, BASIC are some of the thesaurus management softwares. List and information about thesaurus management softwares along with their web address is made available by Willpower (2002).

Ritzler (1990) presents an evaluation of three thesaurus management softwares, i.e. INDEX, PROTERM and TMS.

'THESHI program', available with Unesco's Micro-CDS/ ISIS is useful in online thesaurus construction (Chowdhury, 1999). Another program available for online thesaurus construction is VOCON (Chowdhury, Neelameghan and Chowdhury, 1995). Karisiddappa and Prasad (1993) described use of the programming language PROLOG in thesaurus construction.

Milstead (1991) enumerates specifications for thesaurus construction softwares.

In order to choose appropriate thesaurus construction software from among the many available in the market there is a need of some criteria to evaluate them before purchase. Ganzmann (1990) discusses criteria for evaluation of thesaurus construction softwares.

There are others who have dealt with various aspects of thesaurus construction, e.g. Chandran (1975) has presented a case study of selection of candidate terms for thesaurus. Seetharama (1975) has explained concept representation in thesaurus by use of elemental and pre-combined descriptors. Thesaurus construction is a complicated time consuming process. Prasad, Mahajan and Thyagaragan (1975) calculate the time required for each process. Aptagiri and Prasad (1995) explain the use of Natural Language Processing (NLP) technique in grouping concepts in thesauri. Miller (1997) has illustrated the problems generally encountered during the process of thesaurus construction and methods for solving them. Once constructed, the thesaurus must be evaluated for assessing its quality. Davis and Rush (1979a) have given criteria for evaluating thesaurus.

## 3.8 THESAURAL RELATIONSHIPS

An intrinsic feature of a thesaurus is its ability to distinguish and display the relationships between terms it contains.

Broadly there can be two types of thesaural relationships (Aitchison, Gilchrist and Bawden, 2000e).

i) The micro level concerned the semantic links between individual terms. These are also called as inter-term relationships.

ii) The macro level concerned with how the terms and their inter-relationships relate to overall structure of the field.

The inter-term relationships can be of three types (Unesco, 1981b) i.e.

3.8.1 The equivalence relationship

3.8.2 The hierarchical relationship

3.8.3 The associative relationship

A critical analysis of these relationships has been made by Willets (1975), Maniez (1988) and Dextre Clarke (2000). Dextre Clarke observes that the standard rules on thesaural relationships are not always seriously applied. For this, he however, does not blame the thesaurus constructor. According to him the inconsistency appears due to pragmatic and subjective decisions about what will serve human users best.

### 3.8.1 The equivalence relationship

This is the relationship between preferred and non-referred terms. Such relationship must be paid attention to when one and the same concept is represented by different terms. The preferred term is the one, which is selected for indexing and the non-preferred terms is non-selected. However the non-preferred term also form part of an entry vocabulary directing the user towards the preferred term. Conventions used for expressing reciprocity are:

USE - *is written as a prefix to the preferred term.*

*UF*- is written as a prefix to the non-preferred term.

The equivalence relationship includes synonyms, lexical variants, quasi synonyms, and factored and non-factored terms.

**3.8.1.1 Synonyms** are terms whose meanings can be regarded as the same in a wide range of context, so that they are virtually interchangeable. Some of the common classes of synonyms are-

i) Popular names and scientific names

ii) Terms of different linguistic origin

iii) Common nouns and trade names

iv) Variant names of emergent concept

v) Current or favoured terms versus outdated term.

**3.8.1.2 Lexical variants** are different word forms for the same expression, which includes spellings, irregular plurals, direct versus indirect order, abbreviated forms, etc.

**3.8.1.3 Quasi synonyms** are also known as near synonyms. Quasi synonyms are generally regarded as different in ordinary usage but treated as though they are synonyms. Quasi synonyms include terms having significant overlaps, e.g. Gifted people / genius.

**3.8.1.4 Factored and non-factored terms:** Many a times compound terms are formed to express a concept. But the second, third term in the compound phrase may also be of significance. Such compound terms are factored and cross-references are provided from the compound term to the element used in the combination.

### 3.8.2 The hierarchical relationship

This relationship shows levels of super ordination and subordination. The super ordinate terms represent a class or whole and subordinate terms refer to its member and parts. Conventions used to express reciprocity are:

*BT* (i.e. broader term) is written as a prefix to the super ordinate term

*NT* (i.e. narrower term) is written as a prefix to subordinate term

This relationship helps in locating broader / narrower concepts. This feature of thesaurus (i.e. hierarchical relationship) distinguishes itself from unstructured lists. Through this relationship only a thesaurus helps to improve recall and precision performance. Indirectly, it also helps to clarify the scope of the term.

Terms forming part of chain in a systematic part usually display hierarchical relations. However, not all terms indented under a term in a systematic display will be hierarchically related to the one at the level above. They may be associatively related too (Bean, 1998).

The hierarchical relationships cover four situations i.e.

### *3.8.2.1 Generic relationship*

It identifies the link between a class or a category and its member or species. According to the *Unesco guidelines* (Unesco, 1981c) this relationship may be identified by using the convention:

*BTG* used for broader term generic

*NTG* used for narrower term generic

### *3.8.2.2 Whole-part relationship*

This relationship covers limited range of situations where the name of a part implies the name of its possessing whole serving as the super ordinate term.

There are four main classes of this type of relationship.

i) System and organs of a body
ii) Geographical locations
iii) Discipline or field of discourse
iv) Hierarchical social structure

### *3.8.2.3 Instance relationship*

This relationship identifies links between a general category of things or events, expressed by a common noun and an individual instance of that category. the instance then forming a class-of-one. which is represented by a proper name.

#### *3.8.2.4 Polyhierarchical relationship*

Some concepts can belong, on logical grounds to more than one category at the time. They are then said to possess polyhierarchical relations.

### 3.8.3 The associative relationship

This relationship is found between terms, which are closely related conceptually but not hierarchically and are not members of the equivalence set. Associatively related terms are known as 'related terms' (RT). The Unesco guideline identifies following two kinds of terms to be linked by the associative relationship (Unesco, 1981d).

i) Those that belong to the same category:These are the terms that relate to siblings with overlapping meaning such as boats and ships.

ii) Those that belong to different categories. Number of criteria for identification of this type of relationship are recommended (Unesco, 1981e), e. g.

   a) An operation and its agent

   b) An action and the product of the action, etc.

Aitchison and her co-authors believe that this relationship is less easy to define (Aitchison, Gilchrist and Bawden, 2000f). Biswas and Smith (1989) emphasize importance of associative relationship. Molholt (1996) has pointed weaknesses in establishing this relationship in many existing thesauri.

Willets (1975) discussed nature of associative relationship and methods for its establishment.

Efforts are made by Perreault (1965), Neelameghan (1975) and Rajan (1975) to list categories that cover associative relationship. Sparck Jones (1971) has claimed that it is possible to establish associative relationship using computer.

The present book describes a more concrete solution to the problem of establishment of associative relationship. It reveals that depth classification schedules are very useful in this task, as the isolates across facet represent associative relationship. Speciators also help to establish associative relationship.

## 3.9 DISPLAY METHODS

The thesaurus differentiates itself from other vocabulary control devices on account of display also. The terms and their relationships are displayed in various ways in a thesaurus. The *Unesco guidelines* (Unesco, 1981f) identifies three types displays, i.e.

a) Alphabetical display
b) Systematic display
c) Graphic display

### 3.9.1 Alphabetical display

It is most common form of display. It organizes all indexing terms in single alphabetical order. The *Unesco guidelines* (Unesco, 1981f) has given list and order of ancillary items to be provided along with the terms in the alphabetical thesaurus. It has also provided the prefix conventions to be followed. These are -

1. Scope notes or definitions
2. *UF* references to non-preferred equivalent term/s
3. *TT* references to top terms, if necessary
4. *BT* references to broader terms
5. *NT* references to narrower terms
6. *RT* references to related terms

Use of *BT1, BT2 / NT1, NT2* to indicate multi level hierarchies is also prescribed by the *Unesco guidelines* (Unesco, 1981f). These conventions are used in the CAB thesaurus (CAB, 1999).

The Root (British, 1985) thesaurus has used different mathematical symbols instead the *BT/NT* conventions. In multilingual thesauri such symbols help to resolve the language barrier.

In order to make the second, third terms in the compound heading a lead term the permuted index display is also used (Aitchison, 1996).

### 3.9.2 Systematic display

The thesaurus, which has systematic display, always has two parts i.e. a systematic part and an alphabetical part. The systematic part provides an overall structure or macro classification (International, 1986). The systematic part may be displayed in various ways such as-

(a) Broad subject groups: e.g. Thesaurus of ERIC description (Thesaurus, 1995).

(b) Faceted classification based thesaurus, known as thesaurofacet (Aitchison, Gomersall and Ireland, 1969).

### 3.9.3 Graphic display

Two-dimensional figures may be used to display indexing terms and their inter-relationships. The graphic display is always supported by alphabetical listings. Importance of graphical displays in thesaurus is elaborated by Rolling (1965).

The *Unesco guidelines* (Unesco, 1981f) has identified two types of graphic displays i.e. tree structure and arrowgraph. Terminograph is another form of thesaural display, which is also called as 'box charts'. This form of display is used by the SPINES thesaurus (SPINES, 1976).

### 3.9.4 Screen displays

A number of thesauri are now available on line. These thesauri display the thesaurual entries on the computer screen. Song (2000) discusses the pros and cons of screen display and suggests methods for improving the screen display.

## 3.10 SOURCES PROVIDING LISTS OF THESAURI

Lists of existing thesaurus are made available in *Knowledge Organization* (ISKO), Aslib's *Current Awareness Abstract* (Aslib) and *Thesaurus Guide* (Thesaurus, 1992). Aslib (2002) and international clearing-house at University of Toronto in Canada hold stock and information on thesauri.

There are various web sites, which provide lists of thesauri available in both the format i.e. in hard copy format and online, e.g.

1. *http://www.darmstadt.gmd.de/~lutes/thesauri.html*
2. *http:// www.willpowerinfo.co.uk.thesbibl.html*
3. *http://www.lub.lu.se.metadata/subject-help.htm*
4. *http://www.fit.qut.edu.au/InfoSys/middle/cont_voc.html*
5. *http://www.fbi.fh-koeln.de/labour/bir/thesauri_new/indexen.html*

**Many thesauri are now available on the Internet, however searching and getting the exactly needed thesaurus on the Internet is not an easy task. To make this task easier a hyper linking tool for searching thesauri is developed (Johnson and Cochrane, 2000).**

## 3.11 REVIEW OF EXISTING THESAURI

### 3.11.1 Thesauri of LIS terms

**In past efforts have been made to construct thesaurus of LIS terms. Gilchrist et.al. (1973), of the Classification Research Group, constructed, *A compressed term index language for library and information science*. Schultz (1978) compiled a similar tool.**

ASIS (1998) thesaurus of information science and librarianship. is one of the two recently constructed thesauri on

LIS. It has hierarchical listing which is supported by alphabetical thesaurus and rotated KWIC index.

Recently, Satoshi Yoshida has constructed thesaurus of LIS terms in Japanese language. (Yoshida, 1993). It is based on articles listed in Annual Bibliography of Library science, a supplement to Annals of Japan Society of Library Science. Used the deductive method for compilation and followed the *Unesco guidelines* and the ISO standard. It has systematic part and alphabetical display. In systematic display entries are arranged under 10 facets i.e. libraries, users, library staff, materials, primary operations, common operations, theories, place, periods and form.

### 3.11.2 Thesauri covering other subject fields

Jaster, J. and others (Jaster, 1962) stated that many efforts have not been made to compile thesaurus based on classification scheme. They were also of the opinion that classification based thesaurus would require extra retrieval efforts than using the classification scheme. They doubted about the depthness of the existing classification schemes, for, many of them were not able to give coextensive class numbers, particularly for subjects contained in the micro documents published in the form of articles. Dahlberg (1966) echoed similar criticism.

Despite these criticisms abundant literature is found which advocates and shows that many thesauri have been constructed based on classification schemes.

Model (1966) made an appeal for the use of Universal Decimal Classification (UDC) for construction of thesaurus. Verona (1964) supported Model by saying that the thesaurus construction is a stupendous task and the use of UDC for this purpose will help to construct the thesaurus with least efforts. However she also mentioned that the terms used and the shallow coverage of the scheme will pose certain problems. Experiment was carried out at the All-Union Research Institute of the former USSR, for investigating the possibility of using the UDC for thesaurus construction (FID, 1967).

Wadington (1958) constructed amplified version of Colon Classification. Based on this scheme he constructed a thesaurus. Meyer (1965) also advocated the use of faceted classification for the construction of thesaurus. Bauer (1967) while advocating the use of faceted classification for the construction of thesaurus suggested that it would help to overcome the weaknesses of the enumerated classification scheme and coordinated indexing.

Some thesauri covering other subject fields are:

**Alcohol and other drugs thesaurus** (NIAAA. 2000).

It has 11323 descriptors. It is published in four volumes i.e.

1. Quick hierarchy
2. Annotated hierarchy
3. Alphabetical index
4. Annotated alphabetical list.

The volume of quick hierarchy shows all descriptors in a logical arrangement. It is a listing of all descriptors in thesaurus without any annotations. Each descriptor has a term number printed on its left.

The volume of annotated hierarchies arranges all descriptors in logical order. Each descriptor has term number. The hierarchical level is expressed through typography and indentation.

History note is a feature of this thesaurus. It provides historical information with respect to the descriptor, such as the year in which the descriptor was introduced, changed etc.

To indicate the synonymous and quasi-synonymous term it uses ST (i.e. Synonymous Term) as against the USE convention.

The alphabetical index is KWOC index that shows multiword terms under each of its constituent word. The index term is followed by their number in the hierarchy. Annotated alphabetical list shows each term only once.

**Archaeological Objects Thesaurus** (RCHME / EH. 1997).

This thesaurus deals with terms referring to archaeology. It includes 2164 terms of which 1653 are preferred terms and 511 non-preferred terms.

The preferred terms included are selected from simple object names and authority lists submitted by members of Archaeology Objects Working Group of Royal Commission on the Historical Monuments of English and English Heritage.

The thesaurus display comprises two parts. The first is systematic part showing a hierarchical display of preferred terms under the class name.

There are 24 class names, which are arranged alphabetically. The class name is not a part of hierarchy term. It is used as a way of grouping terms together into particular theme of disciplines, e.g. agriculture, sports and games.

The second part is a full alphabetical display showing preferred and non- preferred terms, with scope notes and the relationships for each term.

**Art and Architecture Thesaurus** (Art, 1994)

It includes 1,25000 terms. These are related with art, architecture, decorative arts, culture and archival material. The coverage ranges form antiquity to the present and the scope is global.

The hierarchical relationship is shown under seven facets (categories) such as physical attribute facet, style and period facet. They are further sub divided into 33 sub facets such as colour, conditions, etc. The facets are conceptually organized in a scheme that proceeds from abstract to concrete.

The conceptual framework of facets and hierarchies is designed to allow a general classification scheme for art and architecture however it has not used notations.

**Australian Pictorial Thesaurus** (Australian, 2000)

It lists about 15000 terms. It arranges non-abstract topic terms hierarchically under categories such as events and activities. Terms for abstract ideas and concepts are arranged following DDC.

**Thesaurus of ERIC descriptors** (Thesaurus. 1995)

This thesaurus lists terms in the field of education. It has three parts, i.e.

1. An alphabetical list of descriptors shows the relationship of each descriptor to the other terms.
2. Rotated descriptor display shows relationship among compound descriptors containing a common word.
3. Descriptor group displays descriptors alphabetically, under 52 groups. Each descriptor in this group is assigned a three digit numerical code.

**Information Retrieval Thesaurus of Education Terms** (Information, 1968) is another thesaurus, constructed on the basis of classification schedule. The thesaurus has three parts.

1. An alphabetical word list.
2. A faceted (classified) array. In this part there are 17 main groups, each group is further divided into number of subgroups. The introduction to the thesaurus states that, (a) all facets and their subdivisions are to be mutually exclusive, and (b) division of facets has not been made on any abstract set of principles, but purely on functional basis.
3. A permuted list of descriptors. This part is intended to show the relationship among multi worded descriptors having a common word.

**The INSPEC Thesaurus of terms for physics, electronics, computers and control** (INSPEC, 1979) has two parts i.e. alphabetical part and hierarchical display.

Alphabetical part is the main part which lists in a single alphabetical order all terms both preferred and non-preferred. Bold type is used to indicate preferred terms. Cross-references or lead-in terms are shown in medium types.

The hierarchical part collects the individual terms scattered throughout the main (alphabetical) part and displays them in families or hierarchies under top terms (TT) of the hierarchy.

**Intelligent Transportation System Thesaurus** (ITS thesaurus, 2000)

This thesaurus lists terms in the field of transportation and it contains 625 key words. It is used for searching the PATH database. It is prepared by using the NISO Z39.19 standard.

In the hierarchical part of the thesaurus terms are arranged facetwise which groups closely related terms. It is a classified list, so it starts with class number. Upper and lower case Roman alphabets are used as notations. It does not use the usual BT/NT conventions to show these relations but shows them through class number and indentations. But the other two relations indicating feature i.e. UF and RT are included in this part. The RT's are provided with parenthetical class number, e.g.

Bcf Data transmission systems

Bcfe Electronic data interchange.

UF LDI

RT Logistics (Pny)

This is a specialty of this thesaurus, as most of the thesauri in their classified part do not show RT.

Another section is alphabetical list of postable terms supported by class numbers.

**Macrothesaurus** was published by Organization for Economic Cooperation and Development (OECD, 1972). It covers the subject field of social sciences. It is titled as Macrothesaurus because it is derived from several microthesauri and it endeavors to incorporate all of their terms in one single framework, which would be acceptable to all of the original compilers. Each institute can take those parts of interest to itself, develop them more fully if necessary for its own purposes within the overall framework, and use the remainder to deal with the ever-present problem of 'marginal fields'. In the Macrothesaurus terms are grouped under 19 facets which represent various subject areas. Based on this thesaurus many microthesauri have been developed one such example is European (1991) Education Thesaurus.

Another thesaurus having the classification base was published by American Psychological Association (American, 1977) i.e. **Thesaurus of Psychological Index Terms**. This thesaurus is used for indexing the terms in the Psychological Abstract. This thesaurus has three parts.

1. Relationship section: This is alphabetical listing of terms, which actually works as thesaurus.
2. Rotated alphabetical term section: This section includes terms having several words, listed in alphabetical sequence under each word in turn.
3. Postable terms and terms code section: This section gives index to the terms in the thesaurus part along with the terms it gives code numbers used by the Psychological Abstracts.

**ROOT Thesaurus** (British, 1981) has been produced by British Standards Institution. It covers terms related with engineering. It is in the form of a subject display with a complementary alphabetical list. The subject display is the principal part of the thesaurus as it gives the greatest assistance to the user by displaying terms in a complete subject context rather than in alphabetical sequence. The alphabetical list is derived automatically from the subject display by using computer.

The abbreviations BT, NT etc. which are common in many thesauri are specific to English language. Since the ROOT thesaurus has been designed for multilingual applications, these abbreviations have been replaced by symbols, which are linguistically neutral. Some such symbols are:

| *Symbol* | *Meaning* |
|---|---|
| > | Broader term |
| < | Narrower term |
| - | Related term |

**Seattle City Clerk's Thesaurus** (Seattle, 1996)

This thesaurus is designed for indexing and retrieval of documents filed with the Seattle City Clerk's Office. It lists terms related with activities of city government, e.g. public works, transportation, housing, etc. Geographical concepts are also listed.

The thesaurus has two main parts i.e. classified and alphabetical. The classified part displays a hierarchical arrangement of broader and narrower terms and shows conceptual scheme used in classifying document. Each term in this part is prefixed by notation. Geographical names are excluded from this part.

In the alphabetical part authorized terms are printed in bold and include all the usual thesaurual relations. Notations support each authorized term. This notation helps to find the location of a term in the classified part.

A very comprehensive, three volume, **'SPINES thesaurus'**, (SPINES, 1976) having a specialty in the display method is produced by Unesco. It lists terms related with science and technology. The third volume of this thesaurus is devoted to 'Terminological Graphic Display'. There are 34 displays showing, in two dimensions, all the terms in the thesaurus in their various contexts of meanings and relationships. Each right hand page shows term in a central box, with lines joining it to its related terms in the same hierarchy as their central term, but they also indicate synonymous terms not used. On the verso of each page there are explanatory notes on how to use the displays. This page also lists all the RTs, which relate to the central term (or Top Term) on the recto of each page.

**The Thesaurus of Engineering and Scientific Terms: TEST** (Thesaurus, 1969), is one of the largest and best-known thesaurus.

It covers wide range of subjects. This thesaurus is the result of a cooperative efforts between 'The Engineers Joint Council and the Department of Defense of the United States'. This thesaurus has four main parts i.e.

1. Thesaurus of Terms: This gives alphabetical list of terms. (Letter – by – letter).
2. Permuted Index: This arranges multi-worded terms in permuted order. The KWOC format is used to display the terms. Index words that are themselves descriptors appear in boldface italics. Terms that are 'USE' references rather than descriptors are preceded by a centered dot (.). This index tends to group generically related terms.
3. Subject Category Index: Gives list of subjects with subject category numbers. There are 22 major subject groups. Each group is represented with four-digit notation. In the thesaurus part the notation of the appropriate group is given for each descriptor. It is arranged alphabetically by the subject heading. Under main category the sub-category subject headings are also arranged alphabetically without considering their associations.
4. Hierarchical Index: It displays descriptor families based on the BT / NT references as shown in the 'Thesaurus of Terms' section. Only those descriptors from the 'Thesaurus of Terms', which have no 'Broader Terms' and two or more levels of 'Narrower Terms' are selected as main entries. If a descriptor belongs to two or more separate descriptor families it will appear in each at its proper hierarchical level.

**Thesaurofacet** (Aitchison, Gomersall and Ireland, 1969) of the English Electric Company is another example of classification based thesaurus. This is a faceted classification and thesaurus covering engineering and related scientific, technical, and management subjects. For constructing the thesaurus 'thesaurus forms' were made out for each concept which was to feature in the classification schedule. The 'forms' contained information about the terms which could not easily be expressed in the schedules – namely synonyms and near-synonyms terms, related terms in different subject areas; and broader and narrower terms in class other than the one selected as the location for the terms in the schedules. The thesaurus is united with the schedule as a result the terms in Thesaurofacet appear twice, in different guises, once in the thesaurus and once in the schedule, the link between the two locations being the notation or the class number. At each location different information is given about the term; the two parts of the system are complementary, and if consulted apart are incomplete.

A unique approach was adopted in the construction of this thesaurus i.e. in more than half of the subject areas the thesaurus forms were developed first and the classification schedules were derived from these. In the remaining cases a tentative classification schedule was constructed first and the thesaurus details for the constituent terms were listed later.

Both the approaches had their merits; but the 'thesaurus before schedule' approach had the advantage of giving a more detailed picture of the concept to be classified, including, at times, definitions, a choice of synonyms and word forms, related terms and possible alternative hierarchies. Whichever of the two main approaches was adopted it was found that the interaction of classification and thesaurus approach resulted in a clearer picture of the nature of a concept and its place in the system.

A similar thesaurus called Unesco thesaurus (Unesco, 1977) covering the field of education, science, social science, culture and communication is published by Unesco. It is in two volumes. First volume contains the introduction, the categories, the permuted index and the hierarchical display of terms. Second volume contains the alphabetical part of the thesaurus. The Unesco thesaurus was compiled originally by preparing an unstructured list of terms based on the Macrothesaurus, which was drafted in 1973/74 and circulated to many institutions, particularly in the UN family. As a result of this process, a new version was prepared and the final version contains nearly 8500 terms in all. There is a very good introduction, as one would expect from Jean Aitchison.

The depth classification schedule forms the basis for the construction of the present thesaurus. The next chapter presents the depth classification schedule of LIS along with its index and in-depth explanation of the methodology adopted for the construction of the schedule.

# 4

# DEPTH CLASSIFICATION SCHEDULE OF LIBRARY AND INFORMATION SCIENCE

## 4.0 INTRODUCTION

The aim of this chapter is to describe the methodology used in the construction of depth classification schedule of LIS. This chapter also includes the depth classification schedule and its index. The present book is a thesaurus of LIS terms. In order to have a systematic presentation of the subject, first a depth classification schedule was constructed. The newly constructed schedule is a depth classification version of Colon Classification edition seven (Ranganathan, 1987) for the main class 'library and information science' (Ranganathan, 1987e). Based on this newly constructed schedule the thesaurus is constructed.

## 4.1 CONSTRUCTION METHODOLOGY

In 1964 Ranganathan suggested a methodology for construction of depth classification schedules (Ranganathan, 1964a). This methodology was adopted in constructing the present classification schedule.

Depth classification schedule can be constructed by using two different methods or by their combination. The two methods are speculative and pragmatic.

### a) Speculative method

In speculative method the isolate and speciator terms to be listed in the classification schedule are conjectured by the compiler on the basis of his knowledge of the subject field and his experience. However, the classification schedules based purely on conjecture may prove to be out of focus, because the isolates listed and their sequence may not satisfy various canons and principles of helpful sequence.

### b) Pragmatic method

In this method the classification schedule is constructed on the basis of 'principle of literary warrant' (Hulme, 1911-12), i.e. the isolate and speciator terms are gathered by analyzing the current literature of the concerned subject. However, the schedule based purely on the pragmatic approach may exclude some of the non-current but essential isolates and speciators. So, Ranganathan suggested the use of the combination of pragmatic and speculative methods, which he called as blending method (Ranganathan, 1964).

The present schedule was constructed by using the blending method. Majority of the isolate / speciator terms representing the LIS field were collected by reading the literature on the subject. Subjects not encountered in the literature referred to, were listed by applying the speculative approach. The depth classification schedule was constructed by adopting the procedure and steps recommended by M. A. Gopinath in his *Manual* on construction of depth classification schedules (Gopinath, 1986a). The steps given by M. A. Gopinath for the construction of depth classification schedule are -

4.1.1 Understanding the subject:

4.1.2 Identification of sample population

4.1.3 Analysis of data

4.1.4 Recording of terms

4.1.5 Grouping of the isolates

4.1.6 Grouping of speciators

4.1.7 Arrangement of isolates and their speciators

4.1.8 Assigning notations

**4.1.1 Understanding the subject**

To construct a thesaurus and classification schedule, the constructor must have adequate knowledge of the subject concerned. Highways and byways of LIS were understood by reading and referring to a large number of Indian and foreign documents available in various forms. Reading and browsing the literature on the subject helped in understanding the various facets of the subject.

**4.1.2 Identification of sample population**

For constructing the present depth classification schedule 500 assorted micro documents were analyzed. This was done to have representative sample and to avoid duplication. Micro documents only were analyzed, as they deal with the subject in depth. As such a schedule based on micro documents ultimately proves helpful in classifying macro documents also. The micro documents analyzed were articles published in various documents. Following is an illustrative list of the documents, from which the micro documents were analyzed.

1 Full text periodicals available in the hard copy format: IASLIC Bulletin, ILA Bulletin, Journal of Documentation, International Cataloguing and Bibliographic Control, Knowledge Organization, Library Quarterly, Library Trends, Program.

2. Periodicals available on the Internet.

3. Seminar, conference, festschrift and workshop volumes: ILA, IASLIC, DRTC, and CALIBER.

4. Abstracting periodicals: LISA.

The sample selection was such, so as to have adequate representation of both Indian and foreign literature. In order to satisfy the principle of literary warrant the actual micro documents were analyzed. To satisfy the canon of currency the literature published during the year 1994 to 1999 was analyzed.

### 4.1.3 Analysis of data

As far as possible the full text of the micro document was read, so as to have sufficient understanding of the contents. However, to have wider coverage, some data was collected from the abstracting sources also. The micro documents were analyzed by applying Ranganathan's fundamental categories (Ranganathan, 1989d). During the analysis the terms were identified as isolates belonging to various facets and their levels, i.e.

i) First round first level personality [1P1]. First round second level personality [1P2].

ii) First round first level matter property [1MP1] and first round second level of matter property [1MP2]

iii) First round of energy [1E] and second round of energy [2E].

Terms representing speciator of kind 1 (Sp1) and speciator kind.2 (Sp2) were also identified.

Micro documents were analyzed to get isolates going with the first three facets of the PMEST, i.e. Personality, Matter Property and Energy. These three facets always represent special isolates going with different main classes. The micro documents were not analyzed for identifying isolates going with the other two facets i.e. space and time, as their isolates lead to common isolates going with more than one main class.

### 4.1.4 Recording of terms

Four by 6-inch cards were used to record the results of the analysis. Each card contained information such as:

i) Serial number in the right hand top corner.

ii) The subject string or the feature heading: This included the name of main class, isolate and speciator terms. Connecting symbols of the respective facets were used to separate isolates of each facet, whereas the hyphen (-) and the equal to (=) punctuations separated the (Sp1) and (Sp2) respectively.

iii) The focus: In this part the bibliographical details of the micro document were recorded. This included – name of the author (s), title of the micro document, host document along with its volume number, issue number, date and page numbers.

iv) Annotations: Whenever the title failed to express the subject contents of the micro document an annotation was added to decipher the subject of the micro document.

**Recording of terms: sample entry**

| |
|---|
| *320* |
| *2, A : w – b = 1* |
| *Ls, Library > Academic : Evaluation – Availability = Textbook* |
| *Mitchell, E. S., Radgord, M. L. and Hegg, J. L.* |
| *Book availability: academic library assessment.* |
| *College and Research Libraries 55(1) Jan. 1994: 47-55.* |
| *Evaluates academic libraries by applying the criteria of Availa*bility of textbooks. |

There were some micro documents, which contained information on more than one subject. For such micro documents more than one entries were prepared. This is why there were 590 entries for the 500 micro documents analyzed.

### 4.1.5 Grouping of isolates

The isolates belonging to different facets were scattered throughout the 590 entries. These isolates were noted down facet-wise.

### 4.1.6 Grouping of speciators

The speciators too, were grouped facet-wise.

### 4.1.7 Arrangement of isolates and their speciators

The logic used for the arrangement of the isolates belonging to different facets and their speciators is explained in section 4.2 to 4.24.

## 4.2 SCHEDULE OF [1P1] ISOLATES

The Personality facet covers the core concept of any main class. In the main class library and information science, 'Library' is the core concept. So the types of libraries were listed as the isolates in the first round first level of personality facet [1P1]. While arranging the various types of libraries the general to specific sequence was maintained. So the general libraries such as libraries of international organizations, clubs, public were listed first followed by academic libraries which were followed by the special libraries. Next in the sequence are hybrid and digital libraries. These were arranged by following the Principle of later in time (Ranganathan, 1989j). Next in the list are the research libraries. Next to research libraries notations for subject libraries are provided. Notations for specific research libraries and subject libraries are to be got by the Subject Device. Considering the warrant of literature on digital libraries preference was given to the digital libraries over research and subject libraries. Followed by subject libraries the isolate 'other' is provided for other types of special libraries for which class numbers should be constructed by adding notations of appropriate speciators of [1P1] to the notation 'P' for 'other libraries'.

The institutions analogous to libraries but developed after libraries were listed next. These included, information centre, information analysis centre, translation centre, referral centre and information system. The class numbers of these centre's and systems too can be extended by using the Subject Device.

## 4.3 ARRANGEMENT OF (QI) FOR (Sp1) TO [1P1]

Total 53 speciators were identified belonging to the various isolates of [1P1] facet. These 53 speciators belong to 12 (QIs) as shown in table 1.

*Table 1. (QI) for (Sp1) to [1P1]*

| *S/N* | *(QI)* |
|---|---|
| 1 | By name |
| 2 | By system of organization |
| 3 | By purpose |
| 4-6 | By specialization |
| 4 | By user |
| 5 | By information source |
| 6 | By organizing authority |
| 7 | By service area |
| 8 | By status |
| 9 | By size |
| 10 | By accessibility |
| 11 | By approach |
| 12 | By service |

The ubiquitous Wall-Picture- Principle usually proved helpful in arranging the various (QIs) in a helpful sequence. However when the number of quasi isolates is large, the application of Wall–Picture-Principle becomes difficult and time-consuming. As a solution to this difficulty Neelameghan and Gopinath (1966) suggested the use of 'Group Strategy'

According to the Group Strategy the various (QIs) of a specific facet should first be grouped in certain groups by considering their affinity. The groups so formed should then be arranged in a helpful sequence by applying the Wall-Picture-Principle.

In the present case, as indicated by table 1 the number of quasi isolates to be arranged was 12. This number was considerably large so they were arranged by applying the Group Strategy.

The 12 (QIs) were grouped in three groups. These groups were formed by sensing affinity among the (QIs). Each group was given a name. These groups were then arranged in a helpful sequence by applying the Wall-Picture-Principle to a pair of group at time. The groups formed are given table 2.

*Table 2. Grouping of (QI) for (Sp1) to [1P1]*

| *S/N* | *Name of the Group* | *(QI) Number* |
|---|---|---|
| 1. | Personality co-related | 1 to 7 |
| 2. | Attribute co-related | 8 to 11 |
| 3. | Energy co-related | 12 |

## 4.4 INVERTED ORDER

As per the 'Principle of Inversion' (Ranganathan, 1989b) the order of (QI) in the schedule should be inverted. That is why the order of (QI) listed in table 1 was inverted in the schedule. So the schedule of (Sp1) to [1P1] begins with the (QI) 'By service'. All other facet's speciators too were listed in the schedule by applying the Principle of Inversion.

## 4.5 ARRANGEMENT OF (Sp1) TO [1P1]

The individual speciators under each of the (QI) were arranged by using the appropriate Principle of Helpful Sequence (Ranganathan, 1989j). Help was also taken of some Canons and Devices for having a helpful sequence of the speciators. Table 3 enumerates the Principles, Canons and Devices used in arranging the speciators belonging to each of the (QI) of [1P1] facet.

*Table 3. Principles used for arranging (Sp1) to [1P1]*

| *S/N* | *(QI)* | *Principles/Canons/Devices used in arranging the individual speciators* | *Illustration* |
|---|---|---|---|
| 1. | By service | Principle of later in evolution | Free, Mobile |
| 2. | By approach | Principle of increasing complexity | Automated, networked |
| 3. | By accessibility | Principle of increasing complexity | Closed access, Open access |
| 4. | By size | Principle of increasing quantity | Small, Large |
| 5. | By status | Principle of top-downwards | Central, Branch |
| 6. | By service area | Principle of spatial contiguity | International, National |
| 7. | By organizing authority | Principle of later in evolution | Private, Government |
| 8. | By specialization (By information source) | Canon of canonical sequence | Textbook<br>Periodicals |
| 9. | By specialization (By user) | Canon of canonical sequence | Prisoner<br>Blind |
| 10. | By purpose | Principle of later in evolution | Service, Profit making |

| *S/N* | *(QI)* | *Principles/Canons/Devices used in arranging the individual speciators* | *Illustration* |
|---|---|---|---|
| 11. | By system of organization | Principle of later in evolution | Centralized<br>Decentralized |
| 12. | By name | Principle of alphabetical sequence | Andhra University<br>Pune University |

## 4.6 SCHEDULE OF [1P2] ISOLATES

This schedule consists of organs of library. These include library personnel, building, furniture, library technology, information sources, users, and sections of library. The concept behind these organs will not be operative unless the concept of 'library' is conceded. So the organ isolates have been listed as second level personality [1P2].

There were 120 isolates belonging to [1P2] facet. The logic of their arrangement is:

To carry out the day to day work of the library, the library personnel are needed, so it was listed as the first isolate in the [1P2] facet. To stock the reading material, and for the administrative work the building, furniture and equipments are required, so they were listed next to the personnel. Then when the building is ready, the furniture is acquired the library need to have reading material so the next isolate listed was 'information source'. Adequate literary warrant was also noticed on the various forms of 'information' i.e. data, information, knowledge and intellectual property. These components were enumerated as chain divisions to information source. The ultimate motto of the library organization is to serve the reading community, so the next isolate listed was 'user'. For the purpose of administrative convenience the library is divided into various sections, these sections were listed as the last component in the [1P2] facet.

## 4.7 ARRANGEMENT OF (QI) FOR (Sp1) TO [1P2]

There were 319 speciators of kind 1 belonging to [1P2] isolates. These 319 speciators belong to 29 (QI) as given in table 4.

*Table 4. (QI) for (Sp1) to [1P2]*

| *S/N* | *(QI)* |
|---|---|
| 1. | By name |
| 2. | By mode of production |
| 3. | By subject |
| 4. | By kind |
| 5. | By dependent work |
| 6. | By standard |
| 7. | By sex |
| 8. | By physical abnormality |
| 9. | By value |
| 10. | By quality of mental appeal |
| 11. | By occupation |
| 12. | By membership status |
| 13. | By nature of appointment |
| 14. | By union status |
| 15. | By social status |
| 16. | By race |
| 17. | By status in family |
| 18. | By mode of exposition |
| 19. | By script |
| 20. | By edition |
| 21. | By agency of production |
| 22. | By material written upon |
| 23. | By size |
| 24. | By type of binding |
| 25. | By limit to circulation |
| 26. | By mode of procurement |
| 27. | By access |
| 28. | By area |
| 29. | By age |

These 29 (QIs) were grouped in nine groups as shown in table 5.

*Table 5. Grouping of the (QI) for (Sp1) to [1P2]*

| *S/N* | *Name of the group* | *(QI) Number* |
|---|---|---|
| 1 | Personality associated | 1 |
| 2 | Thought associated | 3 |
| 3 | Pre-exposition consideration associated | 4 to 17 |
| 4 | Exposition associated | 18 to 20 |
| 5 | Embodiment associated | 21 to 24 |
| 6 | Post-embodiment consideration | 25 to 26 |
| 7 | Energy associated | 27 |
| 8 | Space co-related | 28 |
| 9 | Time co-related | 29 |

These groups and the (QIs) in each group were arranged by applying the Group Strategy.

The (QI) 'By mode of production' was ranked as the second (QI) on the basis of the interpretation of the Wall- Picture Principle in the light of the 'Law of Parameter' (Neelameghan and Desai, 1963).

## 4.8 ARRANGEMENT OF (Sp1) TO [1P2]

The individual speciators were ranked in a helpful order by using the appropriate Principles, Canons and Devices. Table 6 illustrates these Principles, Canons and Devices used for ranking the speciators.

*Table 6. Principles used for arranging (Sp1) to [1P2]*

| *S/N* | *(QI)* | *Principles/Canons/Devices used in arranging the individual speciators* | *Illustration* |
|---|---|---|---|
| 1. | By age | Principle of latter in evolution | Old, Current |
| 2. | By country of origin | a) First speciator by Principle of literary warrant | Remote |
| | | b) Speciators 2 to 7 by Principle of increasing quantity | Rural, Metro |
| | | c) Speciators 8 to 11 by Principle of spatial contiguity | International National |
| | | d) Last three speciators by Principle of away from position | Inland Foreign |
| 3. | By access | a) First three speciators by Principle of canonical sequence | Free Fee based |
| | | b) Remaining speciators by principle of latter in evolution | Offline |
| 4. | By mode of procurement | Principle of literary warrant | Purchase Exchange |
| 5. | By limit to circulation | Principle of increasing complexity | In print Classified |
| 6. | By type of binding | Principle of latter in evolution | Handbound Clip |
| 7. | By size | Principle of increasing quantity | Pamphlet, Giant sized |

| *S/N (QI)* | *Principles/Canons/Devices used in arranging the individual speciators* | *Illustration* |
|---|---|---|
| 8. By material written upon | Principle of latter in evolution | Stone Plastic |
| 9. By agency of production | Principle of increasing complexity | Private Government |
| 10. By edition | Principle of increasing complexity | First, Pirated |
| 11. By script | Canon of scheduled mnemonic | As in Language Isolate table of CC |
| 12. By mode of exposition | Canon of scheduled mnemonic | As in Language Isolate table of CC |
| 13. By family status | Principle of latter in time | Unmarried, Married |
| 14. By race | Principle of canonical sequence | Tribe, Ethnic |
| 15. By social status | Principle of canonical sequence | Awarded, Prisoner |
| 16. By union status | Principle of canonical sequence | Non-unionized, Unionized |
| 17. By nature of appointment | Principle of decreasing complexity | Temporary Permanent |
| 18. By membership status | Principle of decreasing complexity | Registered Unregistered |
| 19. By occupation | Principle of canonical sequence | Generalized, Specialist |
| 20. By quality of mental appeal | Principle of increasing complexity | Intellectual Reluctant |

| *S/N (QI)* | *Principles/Canons/Devices used in arranging the individual speciators* | *Illustration* |
|---|---|---|
| 21. By value | Principle of increasing complexity | Spiritual, Information |
| 22. By physical abnormality | Principle of increasing complexity | Patient Blind |
| 23. By sex | Principle of canonical sequence | Female, Male |
| 24. By standard | Principle of increasing complexity | Children, Adult |
| 25. By dependant work | Principle of later in evolution | Adoption Filming |
| 26. By kind | Principle of later in evolution | Macro-documents Patents |
| 27. By subject | Subject device | Library Science |
| 28. By mode of production | Principle of later in evolution | MSS, Digital information sources |
| 29. By name | Principle of alphabetical sequence | Andhra-University |

## 4.9 ARRANGEMENT OF (Sp2) TO [1P2]:

There were few qualifiers, which qualified the (Sp1) to [1P2]. These were called as speciators of kind 2 (Sp2) to [1P2]. They represented specific names of concepts or things. As they represented specific names they were arranged by using the Principle of Alphabetical Sequence, as illustrated in table 7.

*Table 7. Principles used for arranging (Sp2) to [1P2]*

| S/N | (QI) | Principle used in arranging specific speciator | Illustration |
|---|---|---|---|
| 1. | By name | Principle of alphabetical sequence | LISA<br>Texincon |

## 4.10 SCHEDULE OF [1MP1] ISOLATES

The schedule of [1MP1] consists of isolates, which are properties of the 'Personality' isolates. There were total 251 isolates in the [1MP1] facet. The first group of isolates in this fundamental category was the isolates, which represent general properties. As such they resembled with the schedule of Common Matter Property Isolates (CMPI) given in the seventh edition of Colon Classification. (Ranganathan, 1987d). The sequence of these isolates is analogous to the sequence of Main Classes of Colon Classification, edition seven.

Next in the sequence were listed the Matter Property isolates directly related with library. It begin with the isolate of 'Collection development', the natural first activity within the library routines. This is followed by other housekeeping operation's isolates, such as, classification, cataloguing, etc.

The isolates of housekeeping operations are followed by the isolates of library services. It begins with circulation goes through reference, information to translation services and concludes with the maintenance work.

## 4.11 ARRANGEMENT OF (QI) FOR (Sp1) TO [1MP1]

There were 202 speciators belonging to [1MP1] facet. These were associated with five different (QIs) as shown in table 8.

*Table 8. (QI) for (Sp1) to [1MP1]*

| *S/N* | *(QI)* |
|---|---|
| 1. | By name |
| 2. | By purpose |
| 3. | By type |
| 4. | By information storage and retrieval (ISR) properties |
| 5. | By cause |

The (QIs) given in table 8 were grouped in two groups as shown in table 9. The groups were arranged by applying the Wall-Picture-Principle.

*Table 9. Grouping of (QI) for (Sp1) to [1MP1]*

| *S/N* | *Name of the group* | *(QI) Number* |
|---|---|---|
| 1. | Personality associated | 1 to 3 |
| 2. | Property associated | |
| | (2) Library Science associated | 4 |
| | (A) Science associated | 5 |

As indicated in table 9 the first group covers Personality associated (QIs) i.e. 'by name', 'by purpose' and 'by type'. The second group covers Matter Property associated (QIs). This group represents two (QIs) i.e. 'by information storage and retrieval associated properties' and 'by cause'. Their sequence was based on main class sequence in the Colon Classification edition seven.

The sequence of (QIs) within the first group was decided by using the Wall – Picture-Principle. The (QIs) in the second group were arranged by applying the sequence of main classes in Colon Classification edition seven e.g. library science followed by science.

## 4.12. ARRANGEMENT OF (Sp1) TO [1MP1]

Speciators of kind 1 belonging to the various (QIs) of [1MP1] facet were ranked in helpful sequence by applying the appropriate Principles of Helpful Sequence. Table 10 lists principles used for ranking the (Sp1) to [1MP1].

*Table 10. Principles used for arranging (Sp1) to [1MP1]*

| S/N | (QI) | Principles used in arranging the individual speciators | Illustration |
|---|---|---|---|
| 1. | By cause | Principle of canonical sequence | Water, Insects |
| 2. | By ISR properties | Principle of canonical sequence | Plane of work Subject |
| 3. | By type | Principle of canonical sequence | Computerized, Centralized |
| 4. | By purpose | Principle of canonical sequence | Research, Information sources |
| 5. | By name | Principle of alphabetical sequence | Blaizline |

## 4.13 ARRANGEMENT OF (Sp2) TO [1MP1]

The three speciators of kind 2 to [1MP1] deal with names, so they were arranged by using the Principle of Alphabetical Sequence.

## 4.14 SCHEDULE OF [1MP2] ISOLATES

There were 29 isolates belonging to the second level of Matter Property i.e. [1MP2]. As most of the isolates were same as the isolate in [1MP1] their sequence was retained as in [1MP1]. Additional isolates were added at the appropriate places making the sequence helpful.

## 4.15 ARRANGEMENT OF (QI) FOR (Sp1) TO [1MP2]

Total 14 speciators of kind 1 belonging to [1MP2] were

identified. These belong to three (QI) as listed in table 11. Their sequence was decided by applying the Wall-Picture-Principle.

*Table 11. (QI) for (Sp1) to [1MP2]*

| *S/N* | *(QI)* |
|---|---|
| 1. | By name |
| 2. | By agency |
| 3. | By type |

## 4.16 ARRANGEMENT OF (Sp1) TO [1MP2]:

The individual speciators belonging to the three (QIs) listed in table 11 were ranked by using the principles shown in table 12.

*Table 12. Principles used for arranging (Sp1) to [1MP2]*

| *S/N* | *(QI)* | *Principles used in arranging the individual speciators* | *Illustration* |
|---|---|---|---|
| 1. | By type | Principle of canonical sequence | Computerized |
| 2. | By agency | Principle of canonical sequence | Librarian, Teacher |
| 3. | By name | Principle of alphabetical sequence | ALA, ISO |

## 4.17 SCHEDULE OF [1E] ISOLATES

Total 66 isolates belonging to the Fundamental Category 'Energy' were identified. These isolates almost resemble to the 'Common Energy Isolates' (CEI) given in the Colon Classification edition seven (Ranganathan, 1987d). These isolates were arranged on the analogy of CEI. The sub divisions of the isolates were arranged by applying the Wall-Picture Principle. There were number of sub-isolates belonging to the 'Management' isolates within this facet. These sub-isolates were arranged by following the schedule of the main class '8 -Management' of Colon Classification edition seven.

## 4.18 ARRANGEMENT OF (QI) FOR (Sp1) TO [1E]

Total 13 speciators belonging to the [1E] facet were identified. These belong to four (QIs) as listed in table 13.

*Table 13. (QI) for (Sp1) to [1E]*

| S/N | (QI) |
|---|---|
| 1. | By type |
| 2. | By method |
| 3. | By influencing factor |
| 4. | By tools |

These (QIs) were arranged by applying the Wall-Picture-Principle in general and the recommendations by Ranganathan given in the seventh edition of Colon Classification (Ranganathan, 1987f) in particular. The (QI) for (Sp1) to [1E] were grouped by following the sequencing criteria given in table 14.

*Table 14. Grouping of (QI) for (Sp1) to [1E]*

| S/N | Sequencing criteria | (QI) Number |
|---|---|---|
| 1. | Attribute associated | 1 |
| 2. | Method associated | 2 |
| 3. | Agent associated | 3 |
| 4. | Instrument associated | 4 |

## 4.19 ARRANGEMENT OF (Sp1) TO [1E]

There were number of speciators belonging to the (QI) 'by tools'. These speciators were first grouped into four groups and these groups were arranged in general to specific sequence. So in this sequence first comes the group of speciators covering tools based on Common Matter Property associated concepts. Followed by this are the speciators covering concepts associated with the main class '2 - Library Science'. The third group of speciator covers the tools associated with the main class '8 - Management' and finally there are speciators covering the concepts associated with the main class 'D - Engineering' i.e. instrument associated properties. In another words these tools were arranged by applying the sequence of main classes.

The Principles used for ranking the individual speciators of kind 1 under each of the (QI) of [1E] facet are listed in table 15.

*Table 15. Principles used for arranging (Sp1) to [1E]*

| *S/N (QI)* | | *Principles used in arranging the individual speciators* | *Illustration* |
|---|---|---|---|
| 1. | By tools: | | |
| 1.1 | By common matter property associated tools | Principle of canonical sequence | Waiting time, Images |
| 1.2 | By library associated Tools | Principle of canonical sequence | Title page, Classification |
| 1.3 | By management associated tools | Principle of canonical sequence | Cost, Cost-effectiveness |
| 1.4 | By information technology associated tools | Principle of later in evolution | Audio cassette, Barcode |
| 2. | By influencing factor | Principle of canonical sequence | Epistemology, Librarian |
| 3. | By method | Principle of canonical sequence | Adequate-light, Fumigation |
| 4. | By type | Principle of canonical sequence | Quantitative, Statistical |

## 4.20 ARRANGEMENT OF (QI) FOR (Sp2) TO [1E]

There were six speciators of kind 2 belonging to [1E]. These belong to three (QI) as shown in table 16.

*Table 16. (QI) for (Sp2) to [1E]*

| *S/N* | *(QI)* |
|---|---|
| 1. | By name |
| 2. | By version |
| 3. | By type |

These (QIs) were arranged by using Wall-Picture-Principle.

## 4.21 ARRANGEMENT OF (Sp2) TO [1E]

The six speciators of kind 2 to [1E] were arranged by adopting the principles given in table 17.

*Table 17. Principles used for arranging (Sp2) to [1E]*

| ***S/N (QI)*** | | ***Principles used in arranging the individual speciators*** | ***Illustration*** |
|---|---|---|---|
| 1. | By type | Principle of canonical sequence | Textbook, Digital |
| 2. | By version | Principle of alphabetical sequence | Arabized, IDA |
| 3. | By name | Principle of alphabetical sequence | ACRL, NUCSSI |

## 4.22 SCHEDULE OF [2E] ISOLATES

During the construction of present depth classification schedule it was observed that most of the isolates of [1E] facet manifest in the second round of 'Energy' [2E] also. So the [1E] isolates are to be used as [2E] isolates also. To avoid redundancy the schedule of [1E] was not reproduced as schedule of [2E]. Instead the instruction 'same as schedule of [1E]' is given under the caption 'schedule of [2E] isolate'.

## 4.23 ARRANGEMENT OF (QI) FOR (Sp1) TO [2E]

The speciator kind 1 belonging to the [2E] isolates were associated with three (QIs), as enumerated in table 18. These (QIs) were arranged by applying the Wall-Picture-Principle and Ranganathan's recommendations (Ranganathan, 1987f).

*Table 18. (QI) for (Sp1) to [2E]*

| S/N | (QI) |
|---|---|
| 1. | By type |
| 2. | By method |
| 3. | By tool |

## 4.24 ARRANGEMENT OF (Sp1) TO [2E]:

The individual speciators of kind 1 belonging to [2E] were arranged as per the principles mentioned in table 19

*Table 19. Principles used for arranging (Sp1) to [2E]*

| S/N (QI) | Principles used in arranging the individual speciators | Illustration |
|---|---|---|
| 1. By tools: | | |
| 1.1 By library associated tools | Principle of canonical sequence | Title page Classification |
| 1.2 By management associated tools | Principle of canonical sequence | Cost, Cost effectiveness |
| 1.3 By information technology associated tools | Principle of later in evolution | Audio Barcode |
| 1.4 By psychology associated tools | Principle of canonical sequence | Humour |

| | | | |
|---|---|---|---|
| 2. | By method | Principle of alphabetical sequence | Conjoint analysis. Contingent valuation |
| 3. | By type | Principle of canonical sequence | Security |

The speciators belonging to the (QI) 'by library associated tools', 'by management associated tools' and 'by information technology associated tools' for [2E] were same as that of speciators of (QIs) of [1E]. So in the schedule instead of repeating the schedule of (Sp1) to [2E] the instruction 'same as (Sp1) to [1E]' is given. Where as the speciators of kind 1 under the (QI) 'by psychology associated tools', 'by method' and 'by type' were the speciators going with [2E] isolates only. So they were listed under the respective (QIs) in the schedule.

## 4.25 NOTATIONAL SYSTEM ADOPTED

The notation is defined as 'system of ordinal numbers used to represent the classes in a scheme for classification (Ranganathan, 1989k). The notations used in bibliographic classification are broadly categorised into two categories i.e. pure and mixed notation. The pure notation consists of single set of symbols e.g. only Indo-Arabic numerals. The mixed notational system consists of more than one set of symbols, e.g. Indo-Arabic numerals as well as Roman upper and lower case alphabets. These notational systems have their own merits and demerits.

CC since its first edition has used the mixed notational base. The present schedule is based on CC edition seven and so it too uses the mixed notational base.

The notational symbols used in the present schedule include–

1. Roman upper case alphabets (except I, O, and Z)
2. Roman lower case alphabets (except i, l, o and z)
3. Indo-Arabic numerals (1 to 9 and 0)
4. Punctuation marks (Comma, Semicolon, Colon, Dot, Inverted Comma etc.)

5. Circular brackets, 'equal to' (=) sign, and hyphen (-)

### 4.25.1 Telescoping array

The concept of telescoping array (Ranganathan, 1989*l*) was put forth to effect economy in notation and thereby in the class number. In the present classification schedule telescoping arrays were used in [1P1] and [1P2] facets.

### 4.25.2 Main class notation

This schedule of depth classification of LIS is based on the seventh edition of CC. As such the notation '2' assigned in the seventh edition for Library and Information Science main class was retained in this newly constructed depth classification schedule.

### 4.25.3 Allocation of sectors

In order to make the CC's notations hospitable and to keep the class number as short as possible Ranganathan used the concepts of Zones and Sectors (Ranganathan, 1989m).

While assigning sectors the frequency of manifestation of the subjects was considered. Efforts were made to assign single or two digit notations to frequently occurring isolates, e.g. most of the documents in LIS discuss subjects in relation with a specific type of library. So the type of libraries in this schedule were assigned either single or two digit notations.

Table 20 gives data on sectors allocated to isolates in different facets and their speciators.

*Table 20. Sectors allocated*

| S/N | FC (QI) to FC | | Sectors allocated |
|---|---|---|---|
| 1. | [1P1] Isolates (Sp1) to [1P1] | | (S-1), (S-91) and (S-A) |
| | 1. | By service | (S-a) |
| | 2. | By approach | (S-a) |
| | 3. | By accessibility | (S-a) |
| | 4. | By size | (S-a) |
| | 5. | By status | (S-a) |
| | 6. | By service area | (S-1), (S-91) |
| | 7. | By organizing authority | (S-A) |
| | 8-9 | By specialization | (S-A) |
| | 8. | By information source | (S-A) |
| | 9. | By user | (S-A) |
| | 10. | By purpose | (S-A) |
| | 11. | By system of organization | (S-A) |
| | 12. | By name | (S-A) |
| 2. | [1P2] Isolates Speciator kind 1 to [1P2] | | (S-a), (S-1), (S-A) |
| | 1. | By age | (S- a) |
| | 2. | By area | (S-a) |
| | 3. | By access | (S-a) |
| | 4. | By mode of procurement | (S-zA) |
| | 5. | By limit to circulation | (S-zA) |
| | 6. | By type of binding | (S-zA) |
| | 7. | By size | (S-0a) |
| | 8. | By material written upon | (S-0a) |
| | 9. | By agency of production | (S-01) |
| | 10. | By edition | (S-01) |
| | 11. | By script | (S-0A) |
| | 12. | By mode of exposition | (S-0A) |

| *S/N* | *FC (QI) to FC* | *Sectors allocated* |
|---|---|---|
| 13. | By status in family | (S-1) |
| 14. | By race | (S-1) |
| 15. | By social status | (S-9a) |
| 16. | By union status | (S-9a) |
| 17. | By nature of appointment | (S-9a) |
| 18. | By membership status | (S-9a) |
| 19. | By occupation | (S-9a) |
| 20. | By quality of mental appeal | (S-9za) |
| 21. | By value | (S-9za) |
| 22. | By physical abnormality | (S-9za) |
| 23. | By sex | (S-9za) |
| 24. | By standard | (S-91), (S-991) |
| 25. | By dependent work | (S-9A) |
| 26. | By kind | (S-9A), (S-9Za) (S-A) |
| 27. | By subject | (S-A) |
| 28. | By mode of production | (S-A) |
| 29. | By name | (S-A) |
| (Sp2) to [1P2] | | |
| 1. | By name | (S-A) |
| 3. [1MP1] Isolates | | (S-a), (S-za), (S-01), (S-1), (S-9a), (S-9A) |
| (Sp1) to [1MP1] | | |
| 1. | By cause | (S-a) |
| 2. | By information storage and retrieval properties | (S-zA), (S-1), (S-91) |
| 3. | By type | (S-A) & (S-Za) |
| 4. | By purpose | (S-Z1) |
| 5. | By name | (S-ZA) |
| (Sp2) to [1MP1] | | |
| 1. | By name | (S-A) |

| S/N FC (QI) to FC | | Sectors allocated |
|---|---|---|
| 4. [1MP2] Isolates | | (S-1), (S-A), (S-Z1) |
| (Sp1) to [1MP2] | | |
| 1. | By type | (S-a) |
| 2. | By agency | (S-1) |
| 3. | By name | (S-A) |
| 5. [1E] Isolates | | (S-a), (S-1), (S-91) |
| (Sp1) to [1E] | | |
| 1. | By tools | (S-a) to (S-zA) |
| | By CMP associated tools | (S-a) |
| | By library associated tools | (S-za) |
| | By management associated tools | (S-z1), (S-z91) |
| | By information technology associated tools | (S-zA) |
| 2. | By influencing factor | (S-1) & (S-9a) |
| 3. | By method | (S-9A) |
| 4. | By type | (S-A) |
| (Sp2) to [1E] | | |
| 1. | By type | (S-1) |
| 2. | By version | (S-1) |
| 3. | By name | (S-A) |
| 6. [2E] Isolates | | (S-a), (S-1), (S-91) |
| (Sp1) to [2E] | | |
| 1. | By tools | (S-za), (S-z1), (S-z91), (S-zA), (S-A) |
| | By library associated tools | (S-za) |
| | By management associated tools | (S-z1) (S-z91) |
| | By information technology associated tools | (S-zA) |

| | By psychology associated tools | (S-A) |
|---|---|---|
| 2. | By method | (S-A) |
| 3. | By type | (S-A) |

## 4.26 NOTATIONAL CONSISTENCY WITH COLON CLASSIFICATION EDITION SEVEN

This depth classification schedule is based on CC. As such efforts were made to have consistency in the notations of isolates belonging to various facets in this schedule and the schedule of LIS given in the seventh edition of CC. However this consistency is not cent percent because the present depth classification schedule has many new isolates which were not there in the schedule of LIS given in the seventh edition of CC. Insertion of new isolates at appropriate position is as important as that of the notational consistency. So the notations of some isolates in this schedule differ from the notations of LIS isolates in the seventh edition of CC. Such deviation in notations also appears between the notations in this schedule of [1MP1] isolates and [1MP2] isolates. This is for want of logical arrangement and sequence of notational zones.

## 4.27 TESTING OF THE DEPTH CLASSIFICATION SCHEDULE

Using the newly constructed depth classification schedule the 590 entries were classified. The class number was written on the first line of each entry. The entries were then arranged in classified order. The order of entries was found satisfactory.

Section 4.28 presents index to the depth classification schedule and section 4.29 presents the depth classification schedule. Using this depth classification schedule the thesaurus of LIS terms is constructed which is presented in the sixth chapter.

## 4.28 INDEX TO THE DEPTH CLASSIFICATION SCHEDULE OF LIBRARY AND INFORMATION SCIENCE

**Note:**

1. The terms enumerated in the depth classification schedule are listed in this index. However terms listed as illustrations, which are further to be got by (AD), (ND), (SD) etc. in the schedule, are not listed in this index.
2. The number given against each term in the index is preceded by the abbreviation of the name of the appropriate Fundamental Category or speciator e.g. [1P1], (Sp1).
3. In case the same term appears in more than one facet, speciator then their numbers in the index are separated by semicolon.

| | |
|---|---|
| Abridged | (Sp1) to [1P2], 03n |
| Edition | (Sp1) to [1MP1], 3A |
| Abridgement | (Sp1) to [1P2], 9B |
| Absenteeism | [1MP1], ze |
| Abstract | (Sp1) to [1P2], 9B1 |
| Abstracting | [1MP1], 9E1 |
| Periodical | (Sp1) to [1P2], B5 |
| Section | [1P2], K2 |
| Abstractor | [1P2], k2 |
| Academic | (Sp1) to [1MP1], S |
| Library | [1P1], A |
| Access | [1MP1], 9g2 |
| Accessibility | [1MP1], c |
| Accession | |
| Number | (Sp1) to [1MP1], 7A |
| Part of book number | (Sp1) to [1MP1], zT24 |
| Part of criticism number | (Sp1) to [1MP1], zT291 |
| Register | [1MP1], 4a |

Accessioning [1MP1]. 4
  Section [1P2], D2
Accompanying material (Sp1) to [1MP1], 62
Account section [1P2], U
Accountability [1MP1], p
Accounting [1E], 8T : [2E], 8T
Acquisition [1MP1], 3
  Section [1P2], D
Aesthetic (Sp1) to [1MP2], d
Adaptation (Sp1) to [1P2], 9A
Adequate light (Sp1) to [1E], 9A
Adhesive (Sp1) to [1MP1], N
Added entry (Sp1) to [1MP1], 82
Administration section [1P2], T
Administrative report (Sp1) to [1P2], E1
Adolescent (Sp1) to [1P2], 93
Adult (Sp1) to [1P2], 94
Advance copy (Sp1) to [1P2], d
Advanced (Sp1) to [1P2], 997
Adverse condition (Sp1) to [1MP1], s
Affiliating university [1P1], D2
Almanac (Sp1) to [1P2], Ag
Almost enumerative [1MP1], 511
Almost faceted [1MP1], 551
Alphabetic thesaurus [1MP1], 9B34
Alphabetical device (Sp1) to [1MP1], zK7
Alphabetico-classed [1MP1], 6p
Alphabetization [1MP1], 6x
Alternative title (Sp1) to [1MP1], 23
Altrafiche (Sp1) to [1P2], R331
Analysis [1E], v : [2E], v

| | |
|---|---|
| Analytical | |
| Bibliography | (Sp1) to [1P2], Ak2 |
| Entry | (Sp1) to [1MP1], 825 |
| Analytico synthetic | [1MP1], 53 |
| Anteriorising | (Sp1) to [1MP1], zB11 |
| Anxiety | [1MP1], zg |
| Aperture card | (Sp1) to [1P2], R34 |
| Application | [1E], a ; [2E], a |
| Phase relation | Sp1) to [1MP1], zH5 |
| Appointment | [1E], 8D13 ; [2E], 8D13 |
| Approval method | [1MP1], 233 |
| Aqueous de-acidification | (Sp1) to [1E], 9J1 |
| Archive | (Sp1) to [1P2], 9995 |
| Areas | (Sp1) to [1MP1], 91 |
| Art | (Sp1) to [1P2], 0r94 |
| Article | (Sp1) to [1P2], BA |
| Artificial intelligence | (Sp1) to [1E], zN ; (Sp1) to [2E], zN |
| Assistant | (Sp1) to [1P2], 9r |
| | (Sp1) to [1MP1], 166 |
| Atlas | (Sp1) to [1P2], An |
| Attitude | [1MP1], zh |
| | [1MP2], N |
| Audio cassette | |
| Information source | (Sp1) to [1P2], R4111 |
| Technology | [1P2], 711 |
| | (Sp1) to [1E], zD1; (Sp1) to [2E], zD1 |
| Audio information source | (Sp1) to [1P2], R411 |
| Audio visual | |
| Information source | (Sp1) to [1P2], R41 |
| Technology | [1P2], 71 |
| | (Sp1) to [1E], zD ; (Sp1) to [2E], zD |

| | |
|---|---|
| Auditing | [1E], 8U : [2E], 8U |
| Author | (Sp1) to [1MP1], 1 |
| Abstract | (Sp1) to [1P2], 9B11 |
| Analytical entry | (Sp1) to [1MP1], 8251 |
| Catalogue | [1MP1], 6j |
| Entry | (Sp1) to [1MP1], 821 |
| Authorized | (Sp1) to [1P2], 03c |
| Authority control | [1MP1], 9B1 |
| Auto abstract | (Sp1) to [1P2], 9B12 |
| Automated | (Sp1) to [1P1], f |
| Automatic | (Sp1) to [1E], 9D |
| Automation | [1E], m ; [2E], m |
| Availability | [1MP1], b |
| | (Sp1) to [1E], b |
| Awarded | (Sp1) to [1P2], 9a |
| Backlog | (Sp1) to [1MP1], Zg |
| Banned | (Sp1) to [1P2], 03f |
| Basic class | (Sp1) to [1MP1], zA4 |
| Bark | (Sp1) to [1P2], 0j |
| Barcode | (Sp1) to [1E], zK ; (Sp1) to [2E], zK |
| Batten | [1MP1], 9C21 |
| Behavioural | (Sp1) to [1MP1], R |
| Bias phase relation | (Sp1) to [1MP1], zH2 |
| Bibliographic | (Sp1) to [1MP1], D |
| Control | [1MP1], 9t |
| Database | (Sp1) to [1P2], R423 |
| Description | [1MP1], 6T |
| | (Sp1) to [1MP1], 1*Z |
| Exchange format | [1MP1], 6U |
| Service | [1MP1], 9s |
| Standards | [1MP1], 6TA*Z |

| | |
|---|---|
| Bibliographer | [1P2], e |
| Bibliography | (Sp1) to [1P2], Ak |
| Bilingual thesaurus | [1MP1], 9B32 |
| Binding | [1MP1], 9J |
| Section | [1P2], S |
| Bio-bibliography | (Sp1) to [1P2], Aj1 |
| Biography | (Sp1) to [1P2], Aj |
| Biological | (Sp1) to [1MP1], f |
| Blanket ordering | [1MP1], 3a1 |
| Blind | (Sp1) to [1P2], 9zq |
| Bond | (Sp1) to [1P2], 0r3 |
| Book | (Sp1) to [1P2], 9R |
| Catalogue | [1MP1], 6c1 |
| Number | (Sp1) to [1MP1], zT2 |
| Pocketing | [1MP1], 433 |
| Register | (Sp1) to [1E], zk ; (Sp1) to [2E], zk |
| Shelf | [1P2], 5e1 |
| Supporter | [1P2], 5t |
| Trolley | [1P2], 5n |
| Branch | (Sp1) to [1P1], t |
| Broadcast lecture | (Sp1) to [1P2], 9W2 |
| Brochure | (Sp1) to [1P2], 9Zj2 |
| Broken order | [1MP1], 9H21 |
| Browne | [1MP1], 8b2 |
| Budgeting | [1E], 8R ; [2E], 8R |
| Building | [1P2], 1 |
| Calendered | (Sp1) to [1P2], 0r93 |
| Call number | (Sp1) to [1MP1], zT |
| Card catalogue | [1MP1], 6c3 |
| Cartoon | (Sp1) to [1P2], 0K |
| CAS | [1MP1], 9D |

| | |
|---|---|
| Catalogue | [1MP1], 6c |
| | (Sp1) to [1E], ze ; (Sp1) to [2E], ze |
| Cabinet | [1P2], 5q |
| Card drawer | [1P2], 5q1 |
| Card tray | [1P2], 5s1 |
| Code | [1MP1], 6A |
| With abstract | [1MP1], 6s |
| With annotation | [1MP1], 6r |
| Cataloguer | [1P2], g |
| Cataloguing | [1MP1], 6 |
| Section | [1P2], E2 |
| CCF | [1MP1], 6U2 |
| CD-DA | [1P2], 74e |
| CD-I | [1P2], 74f |
| CD-R | [1P2], 74g |
| CD-ROM | |
| Database | (Sp1) to [1P2], R421 |
| Technology | [1P2], 74d |
| | (Sp1) to [1E], zH ; (Sp1) to [2E], zH |
| CD-RW | [1P2], 74h |
| CD-XA | [1P2], 74j |
| Central | (Sp1) to [1P1], s |
| Government | (Sp1) to [1P1], B1 |
| Centralized | (Sp1) to [1P1], K |
| | (Sp1) to [1MP1], Zb |
| Chain indexing | [1MP1], 9C11 |
| | (Sp1) to [1E], 5 |
| Chair | [1P2], 5m |
| Change | [1E], j : [2E], j |
| Charging | [1E], e : [2E], e |
| Tray | [1P2], 5s2 |

| | |
|---|---|
| Charitable institution | [1P1], 6 |
| Chart | (Sp1) to [1P2], 0G |
| Cheap | (Sp1) to [1P2], 03h |
| Chief | (Sp1) to [1P2], 9t |
| Children | (Sp1) to [1P2], 91 |
| Chinese | (Sp1) to [1P2], 0r92 |
| Chronological | (Sp1) to [1MP1], zK3 |
| Circular | (Sp1) to [1P2], 9Zj1 |
| Circulation | [1MP1], 8 |
| Section | [1P2], G |
| System | [1MP1], 8b |
| Citation | [1MP1], 9C41 |
| Indexing | [1MP1], 9C4 |
| City | (Sp1) to [1P1], 7 |
| Class | (Sp1) to [1MP1], zA |
| Class number | (Sp1) to [1MP1], zT1 |
| Classic | (Sp1) to [1P2], 9994 |
| Classification | [1MP1], 5 |
| | (Sp1) to [1E], zc ; (Sp1) to [2E], zc |
| Scheme | [1MP1], 5A |
| Section | [1P2], E1 |
| Classified | (Sp1) to [1P2], zP |
| Catalogue | [1MP1], 6q |
| Classifier | [1P2], f |
| Clay | (Sp1) to [1P2], 0g |
| Clip | (Sp1) to [1P2], zYa |
| Clipping | [1MP1], 9D4 |
| Closed access | (Sp1) to [1P1], k |
| Cloth | (Sp1) to [1MP1], P |
| Binding | (Sp1) to [1P2], zX |
| Information source | (Sp1) to [1P2], 0p |

| | |
|---|---|
| Club | [1P1], 5 |
| Code book | (Sp1) to [1P2], 9Zk |
| Cold | (Sp1) to [1MP1], f2 |
| Collaborator | (Sp1) to [1MP1], 16 |
| Collation | (Sp1) to [1MP1], 6 |
| Collection | |
| Development | [1MP1], 2 |
| Number | (Sp1) to [1MP1], zT3 |
| College | [1P1], C |
| Comic | (Sp1) to [1P2], 0L |
| Commentary | (Sp1) to [1P2], 9BD |
| Commentator | (Sp1) to [1MP1], 164 |
| Commercial | (Sp1) to [1P2], 0224 |
| | (Sp1) to [1MP1], V |
| Committee | [1E], 81 ; [2E], 81 |
| Commitment | [1MP1], n |
| Common | |
| Energy isolate | (Sp1) to [1MP1], zB13 |
| Isolate | (Sp1) to [1MP1], zB1 |
| Matter property isolate | (Sp1) to [1MP1], zB12 |
| Communicate | [1E], 7 ; [2E], 7 |
| Community | [1P1], 96 |
| Compact arrangement | [1MP1], 9H22 |
| Shelf | [1P2], 5e4 |
| Comparison | (Sp1) to [1MP1], zH3 |
| Compatibility | [1MP1], m |
| | (Sp1) to [1E], h |
| Competency | [1MP1], j |
| Compiler | (Sp1) to [1MP1], 162 |
| Complexity | [1MP2], K |
| Composite book | (Sp1) to [1P2], 9V |

| | |
|---|---|
| Compound class | (Sp1) to [1MP1], zA7 |
| Computer | [1P2], 73 |
| | (Sp1) to [1E], zG ; (Sp1) to [2E], zG |
| Section | [1P2], L |
| Computer output microform | (Sp1) to [1P2], R35 |
| Computerization | [1E], m1 ; [2E], m1 |
| Computerized | (Sp1) to [1P1], f1 |
| | (Sp1) to [1MP1], H |
| Concordance | (Sp1) to [1P2], Ab1 |
| Condensation | [1MP1], 9E |
| Conference | (Sp1) to [1P2], 0222 |
| | (Sp1) to [1MP1], 123 |
| Conservation | [1E], 3 ; [2E], 3 |
| Consolidation | [1MP1], 9E2 |
| Consortium | [1MP1], 012 |
| Construction | [1E], k ; [2E], k |
| Consultancy | [1MP1], 9d |
| Contents | (Sp1) to [1MP1], j |
| Page | [1MP1], 9D2 |
| Controlled language | [1MP1], 9A12 |
| Controlling | [1E], 8P ; [2E], 8P |
| Cooperation | [1MP1], 011 |
| Cooperative | (Sp1) to [1P1], M |
| | (Sp1) to [1MP1], Za |
| | (Sp1) to [1E], W |
| Copy number | (Sp1) to [1MP1], zT27 |
| Copyright | (Sp1) to [1P2], zK |
| | [1MP1], 03 |
| Core | (Sp1) to [1MP2], g |
| Corporate | |
| Author | (Sp1) to [1MP1], 12 |

| | |
|---|---|
| Information source | (Sp1) to [1P2], 02 |
| Corporation | (Sp1) to [1P1], B5 |
| Correspondence section | [1P2], V |
| Cost | [1MP1], zu |
| | [1MP2], S |
| | (Sp1) to [1E], z96 : (Sp1) to [2E], z96 |
| Effectiveness | (Sp1) to [1E], z961 |
| | (Sp1) to [2E], z961 |
| CPM | (Sp1) to [1E], z92 ; (Sp1) to [2E], z92 |
| Creation | [1E], b ; [2E], b |
| Creative | (Sp1) to [1P2], 9zc |
| Creativity | [1MP1], k |
| Criticism number | (Sp1) to [1MP1], zT28 |
| Cultural institution | [1P1], 7 |
| Current | (Sp1) to [1P2], b |
| Decentralized | (Sp1) to [1P1], L |
| Damage | [1MP1], zy |
| Data | [1P2], A1 |
| Database | (Sp1) to [1P2], R42 |
| De-acidification | (Sp1) to [1E], 9J |
| Debate | (Sp1) to [1P2], 9Zb |
| Decision support system | (Sp1) to [1E], z8 ; (Sp1) to [2E], z8 |
| Definitiveness of answer | (Sp1) to [1E], r |
| Degree college | [1P1], C1 |
| Deemed university | [1P1], D3 |
| Delay in supply | (Sp1) to [1E], T |
| Delinquent | (Sp1) to [1P2], 9d |
| Delivery time | (Sp1) to [1E], n |
| Deluxe | (Sp1) to [1P2], 03k |
| Demand | [1MP1], zp |
| Departmental | (Sp1) to [1P1], u |

| | |
|---|---|
| Depository | (Sp1) to [1P1], H |
| Depression | (Sp1) to [1MP1], k |
| Depth | |
| Cataloguing | [1MP1], 6b |
| Classification | [1MP1], 58 |
| Deputy | (Sp1) to [1P2], 9s |
| Designing | [1E], y : [2E], y |
| De-subscribing | [1MP1], 3h |
| Deterioration | [1MP1], u |
| Development | [1E], 2 |
| Device | (Sp1) to [1MP1], zK |
| Dictionary | (Sp1) to [1P2], Ab |
| Difference phase relation | (Sp1) to [1MP1], zH4 |
| Digest | (Sp1) to [1P2], 9B4 |
| Digital | |
| Information source | (Sp1) to [1P2], R4 |
| | (Sp2) to [1E], 2 |
| Library | [1P1] , J |
| Digitization | (Sp1) to [1E], 9E |
| Directory | (Sp1) to [1P2], Ah |
| Discount | [1MP1], zv |
| | [1MP2], T |
| Discussion | (Sp1) to [1P2], 9Za |
| Discussion groups | (Sp1) to [1P2], y2 |
| Display of new arrivals | [1MP1], 9D7 |
| | (Sp1) to [1E], 9K |
| Distribution | [1E], 8V24 ; [2E], 8V24 |
| District | (Sp1) to [1P1], 6 |
| | (Sp1) to [1P1], B4 |
| Divisional | (Sp1) to [1P1], 5 |
| Doctoral | (Sp1) to [1P2], 995 |

| | |
|---|---|
| Do it yourself | (Sp1) to [1P2], 9Zh |
| Document delivery | [1MP1], 8n |
| Donations | [1P2], x2 |
| Dramatization | (Sp1) to [1P2], 9L |
| Drawing | (Sp1) to [1P2], 0r5 |
| Drinking water | (Sp1) to [1MP1], T |
| Duplication | (Sp1) to [1MP1], m |
| DVD | [1P2], 74k |
| Ease of use | (Sp1) to [1E], u |
| Edition | (Sp1) to [1MP1], 3 |
| Editor | (Sp1) to [1MP1], 161 |
| Effect | [1E], g ; [2E], g |
| Efficiency | [1MP1], q |
| | [1MP2], G |
| Electronic | (Sp1) to [1MP1], G |
| Publishing | (Sp1) to [1E], 7 |
| Elementary | (Sp1) to [1P2], 996 |
| E-mail | (Sp1) to [1E], zX ; (Sp1) to [2E], zX |
| Emotional | (Sp1) to [1P2], 9zb |
| Empty digit | (Sp1) to [1MP1], zR12 |
| Empty-emptying digit | (Sp1) to [1MP1], zR14 |
| Emptying digit | (Sp1) to [1MP1], zR13 |
| Encyclopaedia | (Sp1) to [1P2], Ac |
| Endowment | [1P1], 91 |
| Energy | |
| Facet | (Sp1) to [1MP1], zE3 |
| Isolate | (Sp1) to [1MP1], zB21 |
| Entry | (Sp1) to [1MP1], 8 |
| Enumerative | |
| Classification | [1MP1], 51 |
| Device | (Sp1) to [1MP1], zK6 |

| | |
|---|---|
| Ephemera | (Sp1) to [1P2], 9992 |
| Epistemology | (Sp1) to [1E], 8 |
| Ethnic | (Sp1) to [1P2], 7 |
| Evaluation | [1E], w ; [2E], w |
| Service | [1MP1], 9E4 |
| Examination paper | (Sp1) to [1P2], G |
| Exchange | (Sp1) to [1P2], zB |
| | [1MP1], 3c |
| Exhibition | (Sp1) to [1E], 9M |
| Catalogue | (Sp1) to [1P2], Ak411 |
| Section | [1P2], Q |
| Expectation | [1MP1], zn |
| Expert system | (Sp1) to [1E], zQ ; (Sp1) to [2E], zQ |
| Expert's suggestion | [1MP1], 232 |
| Extension activities | (Sp1) to [1E], 9L |
| Facet | (Sp1) to [1MP1], zE |
| Faceted | [1MP1], 55 |
| Facility | [1MP1], zq |
| Fanciful title | (Sp1) to [1MP1], 25 |
| Feasibility study | [1E], r3; [2E], r3 |
| Fee | [1P2], x3 |
| | [1MP1], zt |
| | [1MP2], Q |
| Fee based | (Sp1) to [1P1], b |
| | (Sp1) to [1P2], v |
| Female | (Sp1) to [1P2], 9zr |
| Festschrift | (Sp1) to [1P2], 9V2 |
| Fill rate | (Sp1) to [1E], p |
| Finance | [1P2], x |
| Financial | (Sp1) to [1MP2], j |
| | (Sp1) to [1E], Q |

| | |
|---|---|
| Fine | [1P2], x4 |
| | [1MP2], R |
| Fire | (Sp1) to [1MP1], d2 |
| Floppy disk | [1P2], 74c |
| Foreign | (Sp1) to [1P2], t |
| Form | (Sp1) to [1MP1], zT22 |
| | [1MP2], U |
| Form class | (Sp1) to [1MP1], zV |
| Formation mode | (Sp1) to [1MP1], zA2 |
| Formula | (Sp1) to [1P2], Af |
| Foreign organization | [1P1], 3 |
| Free | (Sp1) to [1P1], a |
| | (Sp1) to [1P2], u |
| Freely faceted | [1MP1], 57 |
| Full text database | (Sp1) to [1P2], R424 |
| Full time | (Sp1) to [1P2], 9m |
| Fumigation | (Sp1) to [1E], 9H |
| Function | [1MP1], d |
| Furniture | [1P2], 5 |
| Game theory | (Sp1) to [1E], z931 |
| | (Sp1) to [2E], z931 |
| Gazetteer | (Sp1) to [1P2], Am |
| Generation | [1E], d ; [2E], d |
| Geographical | (Sp1) to [1MP1], zK4 |
| General phase relation | (Sp1) to [1MP1], zH1 |
| Generalist | (Sp1) to [1P2], 9x2 |
| Geographic information system | (Sp1) to [1E], zS; (Sp1) to [2E], zS |
| Giant | (Sp1) to [1P2], 0d |
| Gift | (Sp1) to [1P2], zC |
| | [1MP1], 3e |

| | |
|---|---|
| Glass | (Sp1) to [1P2], 0t |
| Globe | (Sp1) to [1P2], 0M |
| Glossary | (Sp1) to [1P2], Ab2 |
| Government | |
| Author | (Sp1) to [1MP1], 121 |
| Library | (Sp1) to [1P1], B |
| Information source | (Sp1) to [1P2], 021 |
| Graduate | (Sp1) to [1P2], 992 |
| Grants | [1P2], x1 |
| Graph | (Sp1) to [1P2], 0E |
| Graphic | |
| Abstract | (Sp1) to [1P2], 9B13 |
| Thesaurus | [1MP1], 9B36 |
| Grey | (Sp1) to [1P2], zH |
| Guidebook | (Sp1) to [1P2], Ap |
| Guideline | [1MP2], C |
| | (Sp1) to [1E], c |
| Half | |
| Cloth | (Sp1) to [1P2], zX1 |
| Leather | (Sp1) to [1P2], zV1 |
| Title | (Sp1) to [1MP1], 22 |
| Hand-bound | (Sp1) to [1P2], zQ |
| Handmade | (Sp1) to [1P2], 0r1 |
| Hard cover | (Sp1) to [1P2], zT |
| Hardware | [1P2], 731 |
| Heading | (Sp1) to [1MP1], 911 |
| Heating | [1P2], 3 |
| Higher | |
| Salary | (Sp1) to [1E], 9d |
| Secondary school | [1P1], B21 |
| Historical bibliography | (Sp1) to [1P2], Ak1 |

Holding [1MP1], 42
[1MP2], W
Home page (Sp1) to [1P2], y12
(Sp1) to [1E], zW12
(Sp1) to [2E], zW12
House periodical (Sp1) to [1P2], B3
HTML (Sp1) to [1MP1], M
Human being (Sp1) to [1MP1], n
Hybrid [1P1] , H
Idea plane (Sp1) to [1MP1], zA*ZZ
Identification [1E], f ; [2E], f
ILL [1MP1], 8m
  Personnel [1P2], h
Illiterate (Sp1) to [1P2], 95
Illustrated (Sp1) to [1P2], 03m
Illustrator (Sp1) to [1MP1], 165
Image database (Sp1) to [1P2], R426
Images (Sp1) to [1E], w
Impact [1E], h ; [2E], h
Imprint (Sp1) to [1MP1], 5
Improvement [1E], 4 ; [2E], 4
Inaugural lectures (Sp1) to [1P2], 9W1
Indicator (Sp1) to [1MP1], zR15
Index (Sp1) to [1P2], 9H
Index to the schedule (Sp1) to [1MP1], zW
Indexer [1P2], k1
Indexing [1MP1], 9A
  Language [1MP1], 9A1
  Periodical (Sp1) to [1P2], B4
  Section [1P2], K1
India (Sp1) to [1P2], 0r8

| | |
|---|---|
| Indicative abstract | (Sp1) to [1P2], 9B14 |
| Influence phase relation | (Sp1) to [1MP1], zH6 |
| Information | [1P2], A2 |
| | (Sp1) to [1P2], 9zm |
| | (Sp1) to [1MP1], B |
| Analysis centre | [1P1], S1 |
| Broker | [1P2], k4 |
| Centre | [1P1], S |
| Extraction | [1MP1], 9g5 |
| Personnel | [1P2], k |
| Retrieval | [1MP1], 9g4 |
| Section | [1P2], K |
| Seeking behaviour | [1MP1], zj |
| Service | [1MP1], 9f |
| Source | [1P2], A |
| | (Sp1) to [1MP1], Z2 |
| | (Sp1) to [1E], 2 |
| Storage and retrieval | [1MP1], 9g |
| Systems | [1P1], V |
| Technology | [1P2], 7 |
| | (Sp1) to [1E], zA ; (Sp1) to [2E], zA |
| Informational | (Sp1) to [1P1], F |
| Informative abstract | (Sp1) to [1P2], 9B15 |
| In-house | (Sp1) to [1P2], s1 |
| Inland | (Sp1) to [1P2], s |
| In-print | (Sp1) to [1P2], zE |
| Insect | (Sp1) to [1MP1], f1 |
| In-service | (Sp1) to [1E], P |
| Inspiration | (Sp1) to [1P2], 9zk |
| Institution | (Sp1) to [1P2], 022 |
| | (Sp1) to [1MP1], 122 |

| | |
|---|---|
| Insuring | [1E], 93 ; [2E], 93 |
| Intellectual | (Sp1) to [1P2], 9za |
| Intellectual property | [1P2], A4 |
| Intellectual property right | [1MP1], 04 |
| Internal audit | (Sp1) to [1E], z5 ; (Sp1) to [2E], z5 |
| International | (Sp1) to [1P1], 1 |
| | (Sp1) to [1P2], n |
| International organization | [1P1], 2 |
| Internet | (Sp1) to [1P2], y |
| | (Sp1) to [1E], zV ; (Sp1) to [2E], zV |
| Internet based service | (Sp1) to [1MP1], L |
| Inter subject phase relation | (Sp1) to [1MP1], zH92 |
| Interview | [1E], 8D11 ; [2E], 8D11 |
| With author | (Sp1) to [1E], 9T |
| Isolate | (Sp1) to [1MP1], zB |
| Interview | (Sp1) to [1P2], 9Zc |
| Intra array phase relation | (Sp1) to [1MP1], zH94 |
| Intra facet phase relation | (Sp1) to [1MP1], zH93 |
| ISBN | (Sp1) to [1MP1], 71 |
| ISO 9000 | (Sp1) to [1E], z95 ; (Sp1) to [2E], z95 |
| ISSN | (Sp1) to [1MP1], 72 |
| Issuing | [1MP1], 8d |
| Job analysis | [1E], 8B ; [2E], 8B |
| Job design | [1E], 8C ; [2E], 8C |
| Job dissatisfaction | [1MP1], zd |
| Job satisfaction | [1MP1], zc |
| Junior | (Sp1) to [1P2], 9p |
| Junior college | [1P1], C1 |
| Kardex | [1MP1], 473 |
| Keyword indexing | [1MP1], 9C3 |
| Knowledge | [1P2], A3 |

| | |
|---|---|
| | [1MP1], g |
| Based system | (Sp1) to [1E], zP ; (Sp1) to [2E], zP |
| KWAC | [1MP1], 9C33 |
| KWIC | [1MP1], 9C31 |
| KWOC | [1MP1], 9C32 |
| Labeling | [1MP1], 432 |
| Lack of | |
| Confirmed prices | (Sp1) to [1E], S |
| Library awareness | (Sp1) to [1MP1], a |
| User participation | (Sp1) to [1E], R |
| Ladder | [1P2], 5p |
| LAN | (Sp1) to [1E], zY ; (Sp1) to [2E], zY |
| Language | (Sp1) to [1MP1], g |
| Isolate | (Sp1) to [1MP1], zB14 |
| Irt book number | (Sp1) to [1MP1], zT21 |
| Large | (Sp1) to [1P1], r |
| Leading | [1E], 8L ; [2E], 8L |
| Leaf | (Sp1) to [1P2], 0m |
| Learned periodical | (Sp1) to [1P2], B1 |
| Leather | (Sp1) to [1P2], zV |
| | (Sp1) to [1MP1], Q |
| Lecture | (Sp1) to [1P2], 9W |
| | (Sp1) to [1E], 9Q |
| Ledger paper | (Sp1) to [1P2], 0r4 |
| System | [1MP1], 8b1 |
| Legal deposit | (Sp1) to [1P2], zD |
| | [1MP1], 3f |
| Legislation | [1MP1], 02 |
| Lending | (Sp1) to [1P1], d |
| Letter | (Sp1) to [1P2], 9Ze |
| Letter by letter | [1MP1], 6x1 |

| | |
|---|---|
| Librarian | [1P2], d |
| | (Sp1) to [1MP2], 11 |
| Library | [1P1], 1 |
| Edition | (Sp1) to [1P2], 03j |
| Handbook | (Sp1) to [1E], zm ; (Sp1) to [2E], zm |
| Of Congress List of Subject heading | [1MP1], 9B21 |
| Rule | [1MP1], 8a |
| Technology | [1P2], 7*Z |
| | (Sp1) to [1MP1], e |
| Week | (Sp1) to [1E], 9N |
| Lighting | [1P2], 2 |
| Limited | (Sp1) to [1P2], 03g |
| Cataloguing | [1MP1], 6a |
| List of addition | [1MP1], 9D1 |
| List of subject heading | [1MP1], 9B2 |
| Literate | (Sp1) to [1P2], 97 |
| Literature search | [1MP1], 9u |
| Local | (Sp1) to [1P1], B7 |
| | (Sp1) to [1P2], r |
| Location | [1P2], 11 |
| Long range reference tools | [1MP1], 9a3 |
| Loose leaf | (Sp1) to [1P2], zR |
| Loss | [1MP1], zx |
| In transit | (Sp1) to [1E], U |
| Machine bound | (Sp1) to [1P2], zS |
| Magnetic disk | [1P2], 74b |
| Magnetic tape | [1P2], 74a |
| Main | |
| Class | (Sp1) to [1MP1], zA1 |

| Term | Notation |
|---|---|
| Entry | (Sp1) to [1MP1], 81 |
| Maintenance | [1MP1], 9H |
| Majority | (Sp1) to [1P2], 9c |
| Male | (Sp1) to [1P2], 9zs |
| Management | [1E], 8 ; [2E], 8 |
| By objective | (Sp1) to [1E], z7 ; (Sp1) to [2E], z7 |
| Principles | (Sp1) to [1E], z1 ; (Sp1) to [2E], z1 |
| Manuscript | (Sp1) to [1P2], M |
| Map | (Sp1) to [1P2], 0F |
| Map cases | [1P2], 5h |
| MARC | [1MP1], 6U1 |
| | (Sp1) to [1E], zg ; (Sp1) to [2E], zg |
| MARC 21 | [1MP1], 6U12 |
| Market segmentation | [1E], 8V1 ; [2E], 8V1 |
| Marketing | [1E], 8V ; [2E], 8V |
| | (Sp1) to [1E], z2 ; (Sp1) to [2E], z2 |
| Mix | [1E], 8V2 ; [2E], 8V2 |
| Married | (Sp1) to [1P2], 2 |
| Mass de-acidification | (Sp1) to [1E], 9J2 |
| Matter | |
| Facet | (Sp1) to [1MP1], zE4 |
| Isolate | (Sp1) to [1MP1], zB22 |
| Material isolate | (Sp1) to [1MP1], zB221 |
| Method isolate | (Sp1) to [1MP1], zB223 |
| Property isolate | (Sp1) to [1MP1], zB222 |
| Measuring | [1E], x ; [2E], x |
| Medical facility | (Sp1) to [1E], 9f |
| Medium | (Sp1) to [1P1], q |
| Membership of institute | [1MP1], 3d |
| Metadata | [1MP1], 6V |
| Metal | (Sp1) to [1P2], 0f |

Metatags [1MP1], 6V1
Metropolitan (Sp1) to [1P1], 91
(Sp1) to [1P2], m
Metal furniture [1P2], 5b
Microcard (Sp1) to [1P2], R32
Microfiche (Sp1) to [1P2], R33
Microfilm (Sp1) to [1P2], R31
Microform (Sp1) to [1P2], R3
Microform reader [1P2], 7221
Microforming (Sp1) to [1E], 9G
  Service [1MP1], 9F2
  Technology [1P2], 722
Minority (Sp1) to [1P2], 9b
Misappropriation [1E, 8S ; [2E], 8S
Misinformation (Sp1) to [1MP1], b
Mixed notation (Sp1) to [1MP1], zRb
Mnemonic (Sp1) to [1MP1], zU
Mobile (Sp1) to [1P1], e
Modular [1P2], 13
Monitoring [1E], 8N ; [2E], 8N
Monolingual thesaurus [1MP1], 9B31
Moral (Sp1) to [1P2], 9zg
Motivation [1E], 8M ; [2E], 8M
Multidisciplinarity (Sp1) to [1E], 9a
Multilingual thesaurus [1MP1], 9B33
Multimedia
  Database (Sp1) to [1P2], R422
  Technology (Sp1) to [1E], zJ ; (Sp1) to [2E], zJ
Multi volume (Sp1) to [1P2], 9T
Mutilation (Sp1) to [1MP1], q
Multiple series (Sp1) to [1MP1], 42

| | |
|---|---|
| Municipality | (Sp1) to [1P1], B6 |
| Musical works | (Sp1) to [1P2], 9N |
| Narration | (Sp1) to [1P2], 9Zd |
| National | (Sp1) to [1P1], 2 |
| | (Sp1) to [1P2], p |
| National library | [1P1], 97 |
| Natural | |
| Disaster | (Sp1) to [1MP1], d |
| Language | [1MP1], 9A11 |
| Language processing | (Sp1) to [1E], zR ; (Sp1) to [2E], zR |
| Need | [1MP1], zm |
| | [1MP2], P |
| Neo-literate | (Sp1) to [1P2], 96 |
| Newark | [1MP1], 8b3 |
| Network | [1P2], 77 |
| | (Sp1) to [1E], zT ; (Sp1) to [2E], zT |
| Networked | (Sp1) to [1P1], f11 |
| Networking | [1E], m11 ; [2E], m11 |
| Newspaper | (Sp1) to [1P2], B7 |
| | (Sp1) to [1E], za ; (Sp1) to [2E], za |
| Newsprint | (Sp1) to [1P2], 0r2 |
| News release | (Sp1) to [1P1], 9Zj3 |
| N-gram | (Sp1) to [1E], zj ; (Sp1) to [2E], zj |
| Non book material | (Sp1) to [1P2], R |
| Non circulation | (Sp1) to [1MP1], r |
| Non professional | [1P2], r |
| Non registered | (Sp1) to [1P2], 9v |
| Non unionized | (Sp1) to [1P2], 9f |
| Non verbal | (Sp1) to [1E], E |
| Notational | |
| Digit | (Sp1) to [1MP1], zR1 |

| | |
|---|---|
| Plane | (Sp1) to [1MP1], zR*Z |
| System | (Sp1) to [1MP1], zR |
| Notification | [1MP2], X |
| Novelisation | (Sp1) to [1P2], 9M |
| Numeric database | (Sp1) to [1P2], R425 |
| Obsolescence | [1MP1], t |
| | (Sp1) to [1MP1], w |
| Offline | (Sp1) to [1MP1], J |
| Offset | (Sp1) to [1P2], 0r7 |
| One person | [1P1], G |
| Online | (Sp1) to [1P2], x |
| | (Sp1) to [1MP1], K |
| OPAC | [1MP1], 6c4 |
| Open access | (Sp1) to [1P1], n |
| Open university | [1P1], D4 |
| Operation research | (Sp1) to [1E], z93 ; (Sp1) to [2E], z93 |
| Operational | (Sp1) to [1E], K |
| Opinion | [1MP1], za |
| | [1MP2], M |
| Ordering | [1MP1], 3a |
| Section | [1P2], D2 |
| Organization | [1E], 83 ; [2E], 83 |
| Organizational | (Sp1) to [1MP1], W |
| | (Sp1) to [1E], H |
| Orientation | [1MP1], 9b1 |
| Out of print | (Sp1) to [1P2], zF |
| Outsourcing | [1E], 91; [2E], 91 |
| Overdue | [1MP1], 8f |
| Oversize | (Sp1) to [1P2], 0c |
| Oxford | (Sp1) to [1P2], 0r91 |
| Pagination | (Sp1) to [1MP1], 61 |

| | |
|---|---|
| Palm leaf | (Sp1) to [1P2], 0n |
| Pamphlet | (Sp1) to [1P2], 0a |
| Paper | (Sp1) to [1P2], 0r |
| Paperback | (Sp1) to [1P2], zU |
| Papyrus | (Sp1) to [1P2], 0k |
| Patent | (Sp1) to [1P2], K |
| Paraprofessional | [1P2], b |
| Parent | (Sp1) to [1P2], 5 |
| Participative | (Sp1) to [1E], L |
| Partial comprehension | (Sp1) to [1MP1], zA3 |
| Part-time | (Sp1) to [1P2], 9k |
| Partially open access | (Sp1) to [1P1], m |
| Patient | (Sp1) to [1P2], 9zp |
| Performance | [1MP1], r |
| | [1MP2], H |
| Periodical | (Sp1) to [1P2], B |
| Section | [1P2], J |
| Shelf | [1P2], 5e2 |
| Permanent | (Sp1) to [1P2], 9j |
| Personal author | (Sp1) to [1MP1], 11 |
| Personality | |
| Facet | (Sp1) to [1MP1], zE5 |
| Isolate | (Sp1) to [1MP1], zB23 |
| Personnel | [1P2], a |
| | (Sp1) to [1MP1], p |
| | (Sp1) to [1MP2], 1 |
| PERT | (Sp1) to [1E], z91 ; (Sp1) to [2E], z91 |
| Phase relation | (Sp1) to [1MP1], zH |
| Philosophy | [1MP2], 1 |
| Photocopied | (Sp1) to [1P2], Q1 |
| Photocopying | (Sp1) to [1E], 9F |

Service [1MP1], 9F1
Technology [1P2], 721
Photographic (Sp1) to [1P2], 0r6
Physical layout [1P2], 12
Title page (Sp1) to [1E], zb1; (Sp1) to [2E], zb1
Physical processing [1MP1], 43
Physical processing section [1P2], E3
Picture (Sp1) to [1P2], 0J
Pirated (Sp1) to [1P2], 03d
Place of publication (Sp1) to [1MP1], 51
Plan (Sp1) to [1P2], 0H
Plane of work (Sp1) to [1MP1], zA*Z
Planning [1E], 82 ; [2E], 82
Irt Marketing [1E], 8V21; [2E], 8V21
Plastic
Binding (Sp1) to [1P2], zW
Furniture [1P2], 5c
Information sources (Sp1) to [1P2], 0s
PMEST (Sp1) to [1E], zd ; (Sp1) to [2E], zd
Policy [1MP2], 4
(Sp1) to [1E], e
Political (Sp1) to [1P2], 9zj
(Sp1) to [1E], F
POPSI [1MP1], 9C12
Popular (Sp1) to [1P2], 9993
Popular periodical (Sp1) to [1P2], B2
Post coordinate [1MP1], 9C2
Post-graduate (Sp1) to [1P2], 993
College [1P1], C3
Post-master (M.Phil.) (Sp1) to [1P2], 994
PPBS [1E], 8R1 ; [2E], 8R1

| | |
|---|---|
| Pre-prints | (Sp1) to [1P2], c |
| Practice book | (Sp1) to [1P1], 9Zm |
| PRECIS | [1MP1], 9C14 |
| Precision | [1MP1], 9g42 |
| | (Sp1) to [1E], k |
| Pre coordinate | [1MP1], 9C1 |
| Pre-school children | (Sp1) to [1P2], 921 |
| Prescribed | |
| Edition | (Sp1) to [1P2], 03e |
| Textbook | (Sp1) to [1P1], 9Zg1 |
| Preservation | [1E], 1 ; [2E], 1 |
| Section | [1P2], R |
| Pre-university | (Sp1) to [1P2], 98 |
| Prevention | [1E], 5 ; [2E], 5 |
| Pricing | [1E], 8V22 ; [2E], 8V22 |
| Primary school | [1P1], B1 |
| Principle | [1MP2], 3 |
| Printed | (Sp1) to [1P2], P |
| Printer | [1P2], 75 |
| Printout | [1MP1], 9F3 |
| Private sector | (Sp1) to [1E], 9j |
| Privatization | [1E], 92 ; [2E], 92 |
| Problem | [1E], q ; [2E], q |
| Programme | [1MP2], 7 |
| Programming language | (Sp1) to [1E], zL*Z |
| | (Sp1) to [2E], zL*Z |
| Promotion | [1E], 8V23 ; [2E], 8V23 |
| Proper housing | (Sp1) to [1E], 9C |
| Proposal | [1MP2], 6 |
| | (Sp1) to [1E], g |
| Provision | [1MP2], D |

| | |
|---|---|
| Prisoner | (Sp1) to [1P2], 9e |
| Private | |
| Circulation | (Sp1) to [1P2], zN |
| Library | (Sp1) to [1P1], A |
| Information source | (Sp1) to [1P2], 01 |
| Privatization | [1E], 92 |
| Proceeding | (Sp1) to [1P2], B8 |
| Production | [1E], c ; [2E], c |
| Professional | [1P2], c |
| Profit making | (Sp1) to [1P1], J |
| Promotion | [1E], 8V23 |
| | (Sp1) to [1E], 9c |
| Prompt book | (Sp1) to [1P2], 9P |
| Prospectus | (Sp1) to [1P2], F |
| Protection | [1E], 6 ; [2E], 6 |
| Public lending right | [1MP1], 05 |
| Public | |
| Library | [1P1], 95 |
| Material | (Sp1) to [1P2], 9Zj |
| Relation | [1E], 8V231 ; [2E], 8V231 |
| Sector | (Sp1) to [1E], 9k |
| Publicity | [1E], 8V232 ; [2E], 8V232 |
| Publisher | (Sp1) to [1MP1], 52 |
| Purchase | (Sp1) to [1P2], zA |
| | [1MP1], 3b |
| Pure notation | (Sp1) to [1MP1], zRa |
| Qualification | [1MP1], f |
| Qualitative | (Sp1) to [1E], J |
| Quality | [1MP2], F |
| Quantitative | (Sp1) to [1E], A |
| Queuing theory | (Sp1) to [1E], z932 |

| | |
|---|---|
| | (Sp1) to [2E], z932 |
| Query formulation | [1MP1], 9g1 |
| Rare | (Sp1) to [1P2], zG |
| Readers advisory | [1MP1], 9a4 |
| Readers request | [1MP1], 231 |
| Reading | |
| Aloud | (Sp1) to [1E], 9S |
| Habit | [1MP1], zk |
| Room | (Sp1) to [1P2], zM |
| | (Sp1) to [1MP1], U |
| Section | [1P2], N |
| Ready reference service | [1MP1], 9a2 |
| Recall | [1MP1], 9g41 |
| | (Sp1) to [1E], j |
| Re-cataloguing | [1MP1], 6w |
| Re-classification | [1MP1], 5U |
| Recording of periodical | [1MP1], 47 |
| Recovery | [1MP1], 8g |
| Recreational | (Sp1) to [1P1], G |
| Recruitment | [1E], 8D1 ; [2E], 8D1 |
| Redesigning | [1E], y1; [2E], y1 |
| Reference interview | [1MP1], 9a1 |
| Question | [1MP1], 9a11 |
| Library | (Sp1) to [1P1], c |
| Personnel | [1P2], j |
| Section | [1P2], H |
| Service | [1MP1], 9a |
| Source | (Sp1) to [1P2], A |
| Referral centre | [1P1], U |
| Service | [1MP1], 9c |
| Regional | (Sp1) to [1P1], 3 |

Regional organization [1P1], 4
Register method [1MP1], 471
Registered (Sp1) to [1P2], 9w
Registration of membership [1MP1], 8c
Relative index (Sp1) to [1MP1], zW1
Reluctant (Sp1) to [1P2], 9zd
Remote (Sp1) to [1P2], e
Renewal [1MP1], 3j
[1MP1], 8h
[1MP2], Y
Report (Sp1) to [1P2], E
Report generation capacity (Sp1) to [1E], v
Reprint (Sp1) to [1P2], 03b
Reprograph (Sp1) to [1P2], Q
Reprographic service [1MP1], 9F
Technology [1P2], 72
Reprography section [1P2], K4
Request (Sp1) to [1MP2], c
Research (Sp1) to [1P2], 998
(Sp1) to [1MP1], Z1
[1E], r ; [2E], r
Cubicles [1P2], P
In progress [1MP1], 9D3
Institution (Sp1) to [1P2], 0221
Library [1P1], K
Reservation [1MP1], 8j
Reserved (Sp1) to [1P2], zL
Resource sharing [1MP1], 01
Retirement benefits (Sp1) to [1E], 9g
Retrieval (Sp1) to [1MP1], E
Retention [1E], 8E ; [2E], 8E

| | |
|---|---|
| Retrospective | (Sp1) to [1P2], a |
| Conversion | [1MP1], 6W |
| Return | [1MP1], 8e |
| Review | (Sp1) to [1P2], 9C1 |
| Reviewing | [1MP1], 9E3 |
| Periodical | (Sp1) to [1P2], |
| Revised | (Sp1) to [1P2], 03a |
| Right temperature | (Sp1) to [1E], 9B |
| Role | [1MP1], e |
| | [1MP2], E |
| Rolling shelf | [1P2], 5e3 |
| Routing | [1MP1], 8k |
| | [1MP1], 9D5 |
| Running title | (Sp1) to [1MP1], 24 |
| Rural | (Sp1) to [1P1], 93 |
| | (Sp1) to [1P2], f |
| Salary | [1MP1], zs |
| Saleable | (Sp1) to [1MP1], Y |
| Satisfaction | [1MP1], zb |
| Scanner | [1P2], 76 |
| Scheduled | (Sp1) to [1MP1], zU3 |
| School | |
| Library | [1P1], B |
| Children | (Sp1) to [1P2], 92 |
| SDI | [1MP1], 9D6 |
| Search | [1MP1], 9g3 |
| | [1MP2], Z1 |
| Interface | (Sp1) to [1E], x |
| Sear's list of subject headings | [1MP1], 9B22 |
| Secondary school | |

| | |
|---|---|
| Children | (Sp1) to [1P2], 923 |
| Library | [1P1], B2 |
| Section | [1P2], C |
| See also entry | (Sp1) to [1MP1], 8242 |
| See entry | (Sp1) to [1MP1], 8241 |
| Selection | (Sp1) to [1P2], 9E |
| | [1MP1], 21 |
| | [1E], 8D12 ; [2E], 8D12 |
| Section | [1P2], D1 |
| Tool | [1MP1], 23 |
| Selective cataloguing | [1MP1], 6a2 |
| Self charged | (Sp1) to [1MP1], Ze |
| Seminal | (Sp1) to [1MP1], zU1 |
| Senior | (Sp1) to [1P2], 9q |
| Librarian | (Sp1) to [1MP2], 111 |
| Series | (Sp1) to [1MP1], 4 |
| Service | (Sp1) to [1P1], E |
| | [1MP1], 7 |
| Shared author | (Sp1) to [1MP1], 14 |
| Sheaf catalogue | [1MP1], 6c2 |
| Shelf | [1P2], 5e |
| Shelf arrangement | [1MP1], 9H2 |
| Shelf list | [1MP1], 6v |
| Shelving | [1MP1], 9H1 |
| Short | |
| Communication | (Sp1) to [1P2], H |
| Title | (Sp1) to [1MP1], 21 |
| Simple book | (Sp1) to [1P1], 9U |
| Simplified cataloguing | [1MP1], 6a1 |
| Single | |
| Author | (Sp1) to [1MP1], 13 |

| | |
|---|---|
| Series | (Sp1) to [1MP1], 41 |
| Volume | (Sp1) to [1P2], 9S |
| Size | (Sp1) to [1MP1], 63 |
| Skill | [1MP1], h |
| Skin | (Sp1) to [1P2], 0q |
| Slanted abstract | (Sp1) to [1P2], 9B16 |
| SLIC | [1MP1], 9C13 |
| Slide | (Sp1) to [1P2], R2 |
| Small | (Sp1) to [1P1], p |
| Social | (Sp1) to [1P2], 9zh |
| | (Sp1) to [1E], V |
| Software | [1P2], 732 |
| | (Sp1) to [1E], zM*Z |
| | (Sp1) to [2E], zM*Z |
| Space | [1P2], 14 |
| Facet | (Sp1) to [1MP1], zE2 |
| Isolate | (Sp1) to [1MP1], zB16 |
| Special | |
| Edition | (Sp1) to [1P2], 03p |
| Isolate | (Sp1) to [1MP1], zB2 |
| Library | [1P1], F |
| Specials | (Sp1) to [1MP1], zA5 |
| Specialist | (Sp1) to [1P2], 9x1 |
| Specific index | (Sp1) to [1MP1], zW2 |
| Specification | (Sp1) to [1P2], J1 |
| Spiral | (Sp1) to [1P2], zY |
| Spiritual | (Sp1) to [1P2], 9zf |
| Stack room section | [1P2], M |
| Stamping | [1MP1], 431 |
| Stand | [1P2], 5g |
| Cassette | [1P2], 5g3 |

| Term | Class number |
|---|---|
| CD | [1P2], 5g4 |
| Display | [1P2], 5g1 |
| Newspaper | [1P2], 5g2 |
| Standard | (Sp1) to [1P2], J |
| | [1MP1], a |
| | [1MP2], A |
| | (Sp1) to [1E], a |
| Number | (Sp1) to [1MP1], 7 |
| Standardization | [1E], 84 ; [2E], 84 |
| State | (Sp1) to [1P1], 4 |
| | (Sp1) to [1P1], B2 |
| | (Sp1) to [1P2], q |
| Statistical | (Sp1) to [1E], B |
| Statistics | (Sp1) to [1P2], Ae |
| Status | [1MP1], s |
| | [1MP2], J |
| Stock rectification | [1MP1], 9H81 |
| Stock verification | [1MP1], 9H8 |
| Stone | (Sp1) to [1P2], 0e |
| Storage technology | [1P2], 74 |
| Store section | [1P2], W |
| Story telling | (Sp1) to [1E], 9R |
| Strategic | (Sp1) to [1E], M |
| Strategy | [1MP2], 5 |
| | (Sp1) to [1E], f |
| Student | [1P2], B1 |
| Style | (Sp1) to [1MP1], h |
| Subject | (Sp1) to [1MP1], A |
| Analytical entry | (Sp1) to [1MP1], 8253 |
| Catalogue | [1MP1], 6m |
| Coverage | (Sp1) to [1E], s |

| | |
|---|---|
| Device | (Sp1) to [1MP1], zK5 |
| Entry | (Sp1) to [1MP1], 823 |
| Heading | (Sp1) to [1E], 4 |
| Library | [1P1] , N |
| Subscribing | [1MP1], 3g |
| Substantive digit | (Sp1) to [1MP1], zR11 |
| Summary | (Sp1) to [1P2], 9B3 |
| Supplement | (Sp1) to [1P2], 9G |
| Number | (Sp1) to [1MP1], zT26 |
| Survey | (Sp1) to [1P2], 9C |
| Symposium | (Sp1) to [1P2], 9V1 |
| Synopsis | (Sp1) to [1P2], 9B2 |
| System analysis | (Sp1) to [1E], z6 ; (Sp1) to [2E], z6 |
| Systematic | |
| Bibliography | (Sp1) to [1P2], Ak3 |
| Mnemonic | (Sp1) to [1MP1], zU2 |
| Systems | (Sp1) to [1MP1], zA6 |
| Table | [1P2], 5k |
| Technical | (Sp1) to [1MP1], F |
| Processing | [1MP1], 5*Z |
| Report | (Sp1) to [1P2], E2 |
| Section | [1P2], E |
| Technological | (Sp1) to [1E], C |
| Teletranslation | [1MP1], 9G1 |
| Temporary | (Sp1) to [1P2], 9h |
| Terminology | (Sp1) to [1MP1], zM |
| Textbook | (Sp1) to [1P1], 9Zg |
| | (Sp2) to [1E], 1 |
| Textual | (Sp1) to [1MP1], C |
| Theft | [1MP1], 8v |
| Theory | [1MP2], 2 |

| | |
|---|---|
| Thesaurus | [1MP1], 9B3 |
| | (Sp1) to [1E], zh ; (Sp1) to [2E], zh |
| Thesaurofacet | [1MP1], 9B35 |
| Thesis | (Sp1) to [1P2], D |
| Three card | [1MP1], 472 |
| Time | |
| Facet | (Sp1) to [1MP1], zE1 |
| Isolate | (Sp1) to [1MP1], zB15 |
| Title | (Sp1) to [1MP1], 2 |
| Analytical entry | (Sp1) to [1MP1], 8252 |
| Catalogue | [1MP1], 6k |
| Coverage | (Sp1) to [1E], t |
| Entry | (Sp1) to [1MP1], 822 |
| Page | (Sp1) to [1E], zb ; (Sp1) to [2E], zb |
| Town | (Sp1) to [1P2], j |
| TQM | (Sp1) to [1E], z94 ; (Sp1) to [2E], z94 |
| Tracing | (Sp1) to [1MP1], 912 |
| Trade | |
| Association library | [1P1], 92 |
| Bibliography | (Sp1) to [1P2], Ak4 |
| Catalogue | (Sp1) to [1P2], Ak41 |
| Literature | (Sp1) to [1P2], C |
| Union library | [1P1], 93 |
| Traditional | (Sp1) to [1MP1], Zf |
| Translation | |
| Centre | [1P1], T |
| Section | [1P2], K3 |
| Transparency | (Sp1) to [1P2], R1 |
| Translator | [1P2], k3 |
| | (Sp1) to [1MP1], 164 |
| Trainee | (Sp1) to [1P2], 9n |

| | |
|---|---|
| Training | [1E], 8D2 ; [2E], 8D2 |
| Translation | |
| Service | [1MP1], 9G |
| Information source | (Sp1) to [1P2], 9J |
| Tray | [1P2], 5s |
| Treatise | (Sp1) to [1P2], 999i |
| Trend report | (Sp1) to [1P2], 9C2 |
| Tribe | (Sp1) to [1P2], 6 |
| Trust | [1P1], 8 |
| Turnover | [1MP1], zf |
| Twenty four hour open | (Sp1) to [1P1], j |
| Typed | (Sp1) to [1P2], N |
| Undergraduate | (Sp1) to [1P2], 991 |
| Undersize | (Sp1) to [1P2], 0b |
| Uniformed title | (Sp1) to [1MP1], 26 |
| UNIMARC | [1MP1], 6U11 |
| | (Sp1) to [1E], zg1 ; (Sp1) to [2E], zg1 |
| Union catalogue | [1MP1], 6u |
| | (Sp1) to [1E], zf ; (Sp1) to [2E], zf |
| Unionized | (Sp1) to [1P2], 9g |
| University | |
| Library | [1P1], D |
| Information source | (Sp1) to [1P2], 0223 |
| Uniterm | [1MP1], 9C22 |
| Unmarried | (Sp1) to [1P2], 1 |
| Unpublished | (Sp1) to [1P2], zJ |
| Urban | (Sp1) to [1P1], 92 |
| | (Sp1) to [1P2], h |
| Use | [1MP1], zw |
| Study | [1E], r2 : [2E], r2 |
| User | [1P2], B |

| | |
|---|---|
| Study | [1E], r1 ; [2E], r1 |
| User education | [1MP1], 9b |
| Vacancy | [1E], 8D ; [2E], 8D |
| Value added | (Sp1) to [1MP1], X |
| Vellum | (Sp1) to [1P2], 0q1 |
| Ventilation | [1P2], 4 |
| Verbal | (Sp1) to [1E], D |
| Mnemonic | (Sp1) to [1MP1], zU4 |
| Plane | (Sp1) to [1MP1], zM*Z |
| Versification | (Sp1) to [1P2], 9K |
| Vertical file | [1P2], 5r |
| Video cassette | |
| Information source | (Sp1) to [1P2], R412 |
| Technology | [1P2], 712 |
| | (Sp1) to [1E], zD2; (Sp1) to [2E], zD2 |
| Village | (Sp1) to [1P2], g |
| Virtual | [1P1], J1 |
| Vocabulary control | [1MP1], 9B |
| Volume number | (Sp1) to [1MP1], zT25 |
| Waiting time | (Sp1) to [1E], m |
| Water | (Sp1) to [1MP1], d1 |
| WAN | (Sp1) to [1E], zU ; (Sp1) to [2E], zU |
| Web based service | (Sp1) to [1MP1], L1 |
| | (Sp1) to [1MP2], a |
| Webliographer | [1P2], e1 |
| Web page | (Sp1) to [1P2], y11 |
| | (Sp1) to [1E], zW11; |
| | (Sp1) to [2E], zW11 |
| | (Sp1) to [2E], zW11 |
| Web site | (Sp1) to [1P2], y1 |
| | (Sp1) to [1E], zW1 |

| | |
|---|---|
| | (Sp1) to [2E], zW1 |
| Weeding | [1MP1], 9M |
| Why question | [1MP1], 9a111 |
| Wood | |
|     Furniture | [1P2], 5a |
|     Information source | (Sp1) to [1P2], 0h |
| Word by word | [1MP1], 6x2 |
| Working condition | [1MP1], zr |
| WWW | (Sp1) to [1E], zW ; (Sp1) to [2E], zW |
| Year | (Sp1) to [1MP1], zT23 |
| | (Sp1) to [1MP1], 63 |
| Yearbook | (Sp1) to [1P2], Ad |
| ZBB | [1E], 8R2 ; [2E], 8R2 |

## 4.29 DEPTH CLASSIFICATION SCHEDULE OF LIBRARY AND INFORMATION SCIENCE

### *Schedule of [1P1] Isolates*

| | |
|---|---|
| 1 | Library |
| | *Tel 1 (A2) into (A1) begins* |
| 2 | International organization |
| 3 | Foreign organization |
| 4 | Regional organization |
| 5 | Club |
| 6 | Charitable institution |
| 7 | Cultural institution |
| 8 | Trust |
| 91 | Endowment |
| 92 | Trade association |
| 93 | Trade union |
| 95 | Public |
| 96 | Community |

| | |
|---|---|
| 97 | National *To be divided by (SD) Illustrative* |
| 97(L) | National Medical Library |
| A | Academic |
| | *Tel 2 (A3) into (A2) begins* |
| B | School |
| B1 | Primary |
| B2 | Secondary |
| B21 | Higher secondary |
| C | College |
| C1 | Junior |
| C2 | Degree |
| C3 | Post-graduate |
| D | University |
| D2 | Affiliating |
| D3 | Deemed universities |
| D4 | Open |
| | *Tel 2 (A3) into (A2) ends* |
| F | Special |
| | *Tele 3 (A3) into (A2) begins* |
| G | One person library |
| H | Hybrid |
| J | Digital |
| J1 | Virtual |
| K | Research *To be divided by (SD) Illustrative* |
| K (G11) | Cell science research library |
| N | Subject library |
| | *To be divided by (SD)* *Illustrative* |
| N (4,211) | Newspaper |
| N (4,4) | Broadcasting centre |
| N (8) | Management |
| N (F) | Technology |

| | |
|---|---|
| N (J) | Agriculture |
| N (K) | Wildlife |
| N (L) | Medical |
| N (Q) | Religion |
| N (Q1) | Temple |
| N (Q2) | Church |
| N (Q3) | Mosque |
| N (W,2) | Government department |
| N (W,21) | Defence |
| N (W,211) | Army |
| N (W,212) | Navy |
| N (W,213) | Airforce |
| N (X5) | Commercial |
| N (X8) | Insurance |
| N (XX) | Industrial |
| N (Z) | Law |
| P | Other *To be by divided by (Sp1) to [1P1] Illustrative* |
| P-Ze | Mobile |
| R | Contact Divisions by (GD) For contact library of a Country in any other country, add successively after the number for the parent country the digit "-" (Hyphen) and the number for the geographical area of location. *Illustrative* |
| R56-44 | British Council Library in India |

*Tel 3 (A3) into (A2) ends*

| | |
|---|---|
| S | Information centre *To be divided by (SD)* |
| S1 | Information analysis centre *To be divided by (SD)* |

| | |
|---|---|
| T | Translation centre |
| U | Referral centre |
| | *To be divided by (SD)* |
| V | Information system |
| | *To be divided by (SD)* |
| | *Tel 1 (A2) into (A1) ends* |
| | **(Sp1) to [1P1]** |
| | *By service* |
| a | Free |
| b | Fee based |
| c | Reference |
| d | Lending |
| e | mobile |
| | *By approach* |
| f | Automated |
| f1 | Computerized |
| f11 | Networked |
| | *By accessibility* |
| j | 24 hour open |
| k | Closed access |
| m | Partially open access |
| n | Open access |
| | *By size* |
| p | Small (up to 20000 volumes) |
| q | Medium (above 20000 to 1,00,000 volumes) |
| r | Large (above 1,00,000 volumes) |
| | *By status* |
| s | Central |
| t | Branch |
| u | Departmental |
| | *To be divided by (SD) Illustrative* |

u(2) Library science

*By service area*

1 International
2 National
3 Regional
4 State
5 Divisional
6 District
7 City
91 Metropolitan
92 Urban
93 Rural

*By organizing authority*

A Private
B Government
B1 Central
B2 State
B4 District
B5 Corporation
B6 Municipality
B7 Local

*By specialization*

C *By Information source*

*To be divided by (Sp1) to [1P2]* *Illustrative.*

CB Periodical

D *By user*

*To be divided by (Sp1) to [1P2]* *Illustrative*

D9e Prisoner
D9zq Blind

*By purpose*

E Service

F Informational

G Recreational

H Depository

J Profit making

*By system of organization*

K Centralized

L Decentralized

M Cooperative

Q *By name* *To be got by (AD) Illustrative*

QA Andhra University

QU University of South Africa

***Schedule of [1P2] Isolates***

a Personnel

*Tel 1 (A2) into (A1) begins*

b Paraprofessional

c Professional

*Tel 2 (A3) into (A2) begins*

d Librarian

e Bibliographer

e1 Webliographer

f Classifier

g Cataloguer

h ILL personnel

j Reference

k Information

k1 Indexer

k2 Abstractor

k3 Translator

k4 Information broker

*Tel 2 (A3) into (A2) ends*

r Non professional

*Tel 1 (A2) into (A1) ends*

| | |
|---|---|
| x | Finance |
| x1 | Grants |
| x2 | Donations |
| x3 | Fee |
| x4 | Fine |
| 1 | Building |
| 11 | Location |
| 12 | Physical layout |
| 13 | Modular |
| 14 | Space |
| 2 | Lighting |
| 3 | Heating |
| 4 | Ventilation |
| 5 | Furniture |
| 5a | Wood |
| 5b | Metal |
| 5c | Plastic |
| 5e | Shelf |
| 5e1 | Book |
| 5e2 | Periodical |
| 5e3 | Rolling |
| 5e4 | Compact |
| 5g | Stand |
| 5g1 | Display |
| 5g2 | Newspaper |
| 5g3 | Cassette |
| 5g4 | CD |
| 5h | Map cases |
| 5k | Table *To be divided by sections* |

| | *Illustrative* |
|---|---|
| 5kL | Computer |
| 5kN | Reading room |
| 5m | Chair |
| 5n | Book trolley |
| 5p | Ladder |
| 5q | Catalogue cabinet |
| 5q1 | Card drawer |
| 5r | Vertical file |
| 5s | Tray |
| 5s1 | Catalogue card |
| 5s2 | Charging |
| 5t | Book supporter |
| 7*Z | Library technology |
| 7 | Information technology |
| 71 | Audio-visual |
| 711 | Audio cassette |
| 712 | Video cassette |
| 72 | Reprographic |
| 721 | Photocopying |
| 722 | Microforming |
| 725 | Microform reader |
| 73 | Computer |
| 731 | Hardware |
| 732 | Software |
| 74 | Storage |
| 74a | Magnetic tape |
| 74b | Magnetic disk |
| 74c | Floppy disk |
| 74d | CD-ROM |
| 74e | CD-DA |

74f CD-I
74g CD-R
74h CD-RW
74j CD-XA
74k DVD
75 Printer
76 Scanner
77 Network
A Information source
A1 Data
A2 Information
A3 Knowledge
A4 Intellectual property
B User
B1 Student
C Section

*Tel 3 (A2) into (A1) begins*

D Acquisition
D1 Selection
D2 Ordering
D3 Accessioning
E Technical processing
E1 Classification
E2 Cataloguing
E3 Physical processing
G Circulation
H Reference
J Periodical
K Information
K1 Indexing
K2 Abstracting

| | |
|---|---|
| K3 | Translation |
| K4 | Reprography |
| L | Computer |
| M | Stack room |
| N | Reading room |
| P | Research Cubicles |
| Q | Exhibition |
| R | Preservation |
| S | Binding |
| T | Administration |
| U | Accounts |
| V | Correspondence |
| W | Store |
| X | Other *To be divided by (Sp1) to [1P2] Illustrative* |
| X41 | Audio-visual section |

*Tel 3 (A2) into (A1) ends*

**(Sp1) to [1P2]**

*By age*

| | |
|---|---|
| a | Retrospective |
| b | Current |
| c | Pre-print |
| d | Advance copy |

*By area*

| | |
|---|---|
| e | Remote |
| f | Rural |
| g | village |
| h | Urban |
| j | Town |
| k | City |
| m | Metropolitan |
| n | International |

| | |
|---|---|
| p | National |
| q | State |
| r | Local |
| s | Inland |
| s1 | In-house |
| t | Foreign |
| | *By access* |
| u | Free |
| v | Fee-based |
| x | Online |
| y | Internet |
| y1 | Web site |
| y11 | Web page |
| y12 | Home page |
| y2 | Discussion group |
| | *By mode of procurement* |
| zA | Purchase |
| zB | Exchange |
| zC | Gift |
| zD | Legal deposit |
| | *By limit to circulation* |
| zE | In-print |
| zF | Out of print |
| zG | Rare |
| zH | Grey |
| zJ | Unpublished |
| zK | Copyright |
| zL | Reserved |
| zM | Reading-room |
| zN | Private circulation |
| zP | Classified |

| | *By type of binding* |
|---|---|
| zQ | Hand-bound |
| zR | Loose leaf |
| zS | Machine bound |
| zT | Hard cover |
| zU | Paperback |
| zV | Leather |
| zV1 | Half leather |
| zW | Plastic |
| zX | Cloth |
| zX1 | Half cloth |
| zY | Spiral |
| zYa | Clip |
| | *By size* |
| 0a | Pamphlet (less than 2 cm thick) |
| 0b | Undersize (less than 3cm height) |
| 0c | Oversize (over 30 cm height) |
| 0d | Giant (over 45 cm height) |
| | *By material written upon* |
| 0e | Stone |
| 0f | Metal |
| 0g | Clay |
| 0h | Wood |
| 0j | Bark |
| 0k | Papyrus |
| 0m | leaf |
| 0n | Palm leaf |
| 0p | Cloth |
| 0q | Skin |
| 0q1 | Vellum |
| 0r | Paper |

| | |
|---|---|
| 0r1 | Handmade |
| 0r2 | Newsprint |
| 0r3 | Bond |
| 0r4 | Ledger |
| 0r5 | Drawing |
| 0r6 | Photographic |
| 0r7 | Offset |
| 0r8 | India |
| 0r91 | Oxford |
| 0r92 | Chinese |
| 0r93 | Calendered |
| 0r94 | Art |
| 0s | Plastic |
| 0t | Glass |
| | *By agency of production* |
| 01 | Private |
| 02 | Corporate |
| 021 | Government |
| 022 | Institution |
| 0221 | Research |
| 0222 | Conference |
| 0223 | University |
| 0224 | Commercial |
| 03 | *By edition* |
| 03a | Revised |
| 03b | Reprint |
| 03c | Authorized |
| 03d | Pirated |
| 03e | Prescribed |
| 03f | Banned |
| 03g | Limited |

| | |
|---|---|
| 03h | Cheap |
| 03j | Library |
| 03k | Deluxe |
| 03m | Illustrated |
| 03n | Abridged |
| 03p | Special |
| 03u | Other *To be divide by (ND) Illustrative* |
| 03u1 | First |
| 0A | *By script* |
| | *To be divided by language Illustrative* |
| 0A1 | Indo-European |
| 0A2 | Semitic |
| 0A3 | Dravidian |
| | *By other script* |
| 0B | Shorthand |
| 0C | Braille |
| 0D | *By mode of exposition* |
| | *To be divided by language Illustrative* |
| 0D111 | English |
| 0D122 | French |
| 0D155 | Marathi |
| 0D157 | Bengali |
| | *By other modes* |
| 0E | Graph |
| 0F | Map |
| 0G | Chart |
| 0H | Plan |
| 0J | Picture |
| 0K | Cartoon |
| 0L | Comic |
| 0M | Globe |

| | |
|---|---|
| | *By status in family* |
| 1 | Unmarried |
| 2 | Married |
| 5 | Parent |
| | *By race* |
| 6 | Tribe |
| 7 | Ethnic |
| | *By social status* |
| 9a | Awarded |
| 9b | Minority |
| 9c | Majority |
| 9d | Delinquent |
| 9e | Prisoner |
| | *By union status* |
| 9f | Non unionized |
| 9g | Unionized |
| | *By nature of appointment* |
| 9h | Temporary |
| 9j | Permanent |
| 9k | Part-time |
| 9m | Full time |
| 9n | Trainee |
| 9p | Junior |
| 9q | Senior |
| 9r | Assistant |
| 9s | Deputy |
| 9t | Chief |
| | *By membership status* |
| 9v | Non-registered |
| 9w | Registered |
| 9x | *By occupation* |

| | | |
|---|---|---|
| 9x1 | Generalist | |
| 9x2 | Specialist | |
| 9x3 | Other | *To be divided by (SD)* |
| 9x3(A*Z) | Scientist | *Illustrative* |
| 9x3(T) | Teacher | |
| | *By quality of mental appeal* | |
| 9za | Intellectual | |
| 9zb | Emotional | |
| 9zc | Creative | |
| 9zd | Reluctant | |
| | *By value* | |
| 9zf | Spiritual | |
| 9zg | Moral | |
| 9zh | Social | |
| 9zj | Political | |
| 9zk | Inspiration | |
| 9zm | Information | |
| | *By physical abnormality* | |
| 9zp | Patient | |
| 9zq | Blind | |
| | *By sex* | |
| 9zr | Female | |
| 9zs | Male | |
| | *By standard* | |
| 91 | Children | |
| 92 | School | |
| 921 | Pre-school | |
| 922 | Elementary | |
| 923 | Secondary | |
| 93 | Adolescent | |
| 94 | Adult | |

| | |
|---|---|
| 95 | Illiterate |
| 96 | Neo-literate |
| 97 | Literate |
| 98 | Pre-university |
| 991 | Undergraduate |
| 992 | Graduate |
| 993 | Post-graduate |
| 994 | Post-master (M.Phil.) |
| 995 | Doctoral |
| 996 | Elementary |
| 997 | Advanced |
| 998 | Research |
| 9991 | Treatise |
| 9992 | Ephemera |
| 9993 | Popular |
| 9994 | Classic |
| 9995 | Archive |
| | *By dependent work* |
| 9A | Adaptation |
| 9B | Abridgement |
| 9B1 | Abstract |
| 9B11 | Author |
| 9B12 | Auto |
| 9B13 | Graphic |
| 9B14 | Indicative |
| 9B15 | Informative |
| 9B16 | Slanted |
| 9B2 | Synopsis |
| 9B3 | Summary |
| 9B4 | Digest |
| 9C | Survey |

| | |
|---|---|
| 9C1 | Review |
| 9C2 | Trend report |
| 9D | Commentary |
| 9E | Selection |
| 9G | Supplement |
| 9H | Index |
| 9J | Translation |
| | *To be divided by language* |
| 9K | Versification |
| 9L | Dramatization |
| 9M | Novelisation |
| 9N | Musical works |
| 9P | Prompt book |
| *By kind* | |
| 9R*Z | Macro-document |
| 9R | Book |
| | *Tel 1 (A2) into (A1) begins* |
| 9S | Single volume |
| 9T | Multi volume |
| 9U | Simple |
| 9V | Composite |
| 9V1 | Symposium |
| 9V2 | Festschrift |
| 9W | Lecture |
| 9W1 | Inaugural |
| 9W2 | Broadcast |
| 9Za | Discussion |
| 9Zb | Debate |
| 9Zc | Interview |
| 9Zd | Narration |
| 9Ze | Letter |

| | |
|---|---|
| 9Zg | Textbook |
| 9Zg1 | Prescribed |
| 9Zh | Do it yourself |
| 9Zj | Public relation material |
| 9Zj1 | Circular |
| 9Zj2 | Brochure |
| 9Zj3 | News release |
| 9Zk | Code |
| 9Zm | Practice |
| A | Reference |
| Ab | Dictionary |
| Ab1 | Concordance |
| Ab2 | Glossary |
| Ac | Encyclopaedia |
| Ad | Yearbook |
| Ae | Statistics |
| Af | Formula |
| Ag | Almanac |
| Ah | Directory |
| Aj | Biography |
| Aj1 | Bio-bibliography |
| Ak | Bibliography |
| Ak1 | Historical |
| Ak2 | Analytical |
| Ak3 | Systematic |
| Ak4 | Trade |
| Ak41 | Catalogue |
| Ak411 | Exhibition |
| Am | Gazetteer |
| An | Atlas |
| Ap | Guidebook |

B Periodical

B1 Learned

B2 Popular

B3 House

B4 Indexing

B5 Abstracting

B6 Reviewing

B7 Newspaper

B8 Proceeding

BA Article

C Trade literature

D Thesis

E Report

E1 Administrative

E2 Technical

F Prospectus

G Examination paper

H Short communication

J Standard

J1 Specification

K Patent

*Tel 1 (A2) into (A1) ends*

L *By subject*

*To be divided by (SD) Illustrative*

L(2) Library science

*By mode of production*

M Manuscript

N Typed

P Printed

Q Reprograph

Q1 Photocopied

| | | |
|---|---|---|
| R | Non-book material | |
| R1 | Transparency | |
| R2 | Slide | |
| R3 | Microform | |
| R31 | Microfilm | |
| R32 | Microcard | |
| R33 | Microfiche | |
| R331 | Altrafiche | |
| R34 | Aperture card | |
| R35 | Computer Output Microform | |
| R4 | Digital | |
| R41 | Audio visual | |
| R411 | Audio | |
| R4111 | Audio cassette | |
| R412 | Video cassette | |
| R42 | Database | |
| R421 | CD-ROM | |
| R422 | Multimedia | |
| R423 | Bibliographic | |
| R424 | Full text | |
| R425 | Numeric | |
| R426 | Image | |
| W | *By name* | *To be got by (AD). Illustrative* |
| WC | CDS/ISIS | |
| WI | INFLIBNET | |
| WIN | InMagic | |
| WL | LIBSYS | |
| WM | MINISIS | |
| WR | RRRLF | |
| WS | SOUL | |
| WW | WINISIS | |

**(Sp2) to [1P2]**

| | |
|---|---|
| A* | *By name. To be got by (AD) Illustrative* |
| A | Abuse-L |
| G | Guardian (The) |
| L | LISA |
| P | POPLINE |
| T | TEXINCON |
| | ***Schedule of [1MP1] Isolates*** |
| a | Standard |
| b | Availability |
| | Accessibility |
| d | Function |
| e | Role |
| f | Qualification |
| g | Knowledge |
| h | Skill |
| j | Competency |
| k | Creativity |
| m | Compatibility |
| n | Commitment |
| p | Accountability |
| q | Efficiency |
| r | Performance |
| s | Status |
| t | Obsolescence |
| u | Deterioration |
| za | Opinion |
| zb | Satisfaction |
| zc | Job satisfaction |
| zd | Job dissatisfaction |
| ze | Absenteeism |

| | |
|---|---|
| zf | Turnover |
| zg | Anxiety |
| zh | Attitude |
| zj | Information seeking behaviour |
| zk | Reading habit |
| zm | Need |
| zn | Expectation |
| zp | Demand |
| zq | Facility |
| zr | Working condition |
| zs | Salary |
| zt | Fee |
| zu | Cost |
| zv | Discount |
| zw | Use |
| zx | Loss |
| zy | Damage |
| 01 | Resource sharing |
| 011 | Cooperation |
| 012 | Consortium |
| 02 | Legislation |
| 03 | Copyright |
| 04 | Intellectual Property Right |
| 05 | Public Lending Right |
| 2 | Collection development |
| | *Tel 1 (A2) into (A1) begins* |
| 21 | Selection |
| 23 | Selection tools |
| 231 | Reader's request |
| 232 | Expert's suggestions |
| 233 | Approval method |

| | |
|---|---|
| 234 | Other |
| | *To be divided by (Sp1) to [1P2] Illustrative* |
| 234y | Internet |
| 234A95 | Bibliography |
| 3 | Acquisition |
| 3a | Ordering |
| 3a1 | Blanket ordering |
| 3b | Purchase |
| 3c | Exchange |
| 3d | Membership of Institute |
| 3e | Gift |
| 3f | Legal deposit |
| 3g | Subscribing |
| 3h | De-subscribing |
| 3j | Renewal |
| 4 | Accessioning |
| 4a | Accession register |
| 42 | Holdings |
| 43 | Physical processing |
| 431 | Stamping |
| 432 | Labeling |
| 433 | Book pocketing |
| 47 | Recording of periodical |
| 471*Z | By method |
| 471 | Register |
| 472 | Three card |
| 473 | Kardex |
| | *Tel 1 (A2) into (A1) ends* |
| 5*Z | Technical processing |
| | *Tel 2 (A2) into (A1) begins* |
| 5 | Classification |

| | | |
|---|---|---|
| 51*Z | By kind | |
| 51 | Enumerative | |
| 511 | Almost enumerative | |
| 53 | Analytico-synthetic | |
| 55 | Faceted | |
| 551 | Almost faceted | |
| 57 | Freely faceted | |
| 58 | Depth | |
| 5A | Classification schemes | *To be divided by (CD)* |
| | *Illustrative* | |
| 5M76 | Dewey decimal classification | |
| 5N01 | Library of Congress classification | |
| 5N05 | Universal decimal classification | |
| 5N06 | Subject classification | |
| 5N33 | Colon classification | |
| 5N35 | Bibliographic classification | |
| 5N36 | International classification | |
| 5U | Reclassification | |
| 6 | Cataloguing | |
| 6a | Limited cataloguing | |
| 6a1 | Simplified | |
| 6a2 | Selective | |
| 6b | Depth cataloguing | |
| 6c | Catalogue | |
| 6c1*Z | By physical forms | |
| 6c1 | Book | |
| 6c2 | Sheaf | |
| 6c3 | Card | |
| 6c4 | OPAC | |
| 6j*z | By kind of catalogue | |
| 6j | Author | |

| | |
|---|---|
| 6k | Title |
| 6m | Subject |
| 6n | Dictionary |
| 6p | Alphabetico-classed |
| 6q | Classified |
| 6r | Catalogue with annotation |
| 6s | Catalogue with abstract |
| 6u | Union catalogue |
| 6v | Shelf list |
| 6w | Re-cataloguing |
| 6x | Alphabetization |
| 6x1 | Letter by letter |
| 6x2 | Word by word |
| 6A | Catalogue code *To be divided by (CD) Illustrative* |
| 6M36 | British Museum Library Code |
| 6M76 | Cutter's Dictionary Catalogue Code |
| 6M99 | Prussian Instruction |
| 6N08 | Anglo-American Code |
| 6N34 | Classified Catalogue Code |
| 6N67 | AACR |
| 6N78 | AACRII |
| 6N88 | AACRII Revised |
| 6N98 | Manual for Archival Description |
| 6T | Bibliographic description |
| 6TA*Z | Bibliographic description standards |
| 6TA | ISBD *To be divided by (AD). Illustrative* |
| 6TG | ISBD(G) |
| 6TN | ISBD (Non book material) |
| 6U | Bibliographic exchange format |
| 6U1 | MARC |
| 6U11 | UNIMARC |

| | |
|---|---|
| 6U12 | MARC 21 |
| 6U2 | CCF |
| 6V | Metadata |
| 6V1 | Metatags |
| 6W | Retrospective conversion |
| | *Tel 2 (A2) into (A1) ends* |
| 7 | Service |
| Tel 3 | (A2) into (A1) begins |
| 8 | Circulation |
| 8a | Library rule |
| 8b | Circulation system |
| 8b1 | Ledger |
| 8b2 | Browne |
| 8b3 | Newark |
| 8c | Registration of membership |
| 8d | Issuing |
| 8e | Return |
| 8f | Overdue |
| 8g | Recovery |
| 8h | Renewal |
| 8j | Reservation |
| 8k | Routing |
| 8m | ILL |
| 8n | Document delivery |
| 8v | Theft |
| 9a | Reference |
| 9a1 | Interview |
| 9a11 | Question |
| 9a111 | Why |
| 9a2 | Ready reference service |
| 9a3 | Long range reference service |

| | |
|---|---|
| 9a4 | Readers advisory |
| 9b | User education |
| 9b1 | Orientation |
| 9c | Referral |
| 9d | Consultancy |
| 9f | Information service |
| 9g | Information storage and retrieval |
| 9g1 | Query formulation |
| 9g2 | Access |
| 9g3 | Search |
| 9g4 | Information retrieval |
| 9g41 | Recall |
| 9g42 | Precision |
| 9g5 | Information extraction |
| 9s | Bibliographic service |
| 9t | Bibliographic control |
| 9u | Literature search |
| 9A | Indexing |
| 9A1 | Indexing language |
| 9A11 | Natural |
| 9A12 | Controlled |
| 9B | Vocabulary control |
| 9B1 | Authority control |
| 9B2 | List of subject heading |
| 9B21 | Library of Congress list of subject heading |
| 9B22 | Sear's list of subject heading |
| 9B3 | Thesaurus |
| | *To be divided by (SD) Illustrative* |
| 9B3(2) | Thesaurus of Library and Information Science |
| 9B31*Z | By language |
| 9B31 | Monolingual |

| | |
|---|---|
| 9B32 | Bilingual |
| 9B33 | Multilingual |
| 9B34*Z | By arrangement |
| 9B34 | Alphabtic |
| 9B35 | Thesaurofacet |
| 9B36 | Graphic |
| 9C | By indexing system |
| 9C1 | Pre coordinate |
| 9C11 | Chain |
| 9C12 | POPSI |
| 9C13 | SLIC |
| 9C14 | PRECIS |
| 9C2 | Post coordinate |
| 9C21 | Batten |
| 9C22 | Uniterm |
| 9C3 | Keyword indexing |
| 9C31 | KWIC |
| 9C32 | KWOC |
| 9C33 | KWAC |
| 9C4 | Citation indexing |
| 9C41 | Citation |
| 9D | CAS |
| 9D1 | List of addition |
| 9D2 | Contents page |
| 9D3 | Research in progress |
| 9D4 | Clipping |
| 9D5 | Routing of periodical |
| 9D6 | SDI |
| 9D7 | Display of new arrivals |
| 9E | Condensation |
| 9E1 | Abstracting |

| | |
|---|---|
| 9E2 | Consolidation |
| 9E3 | Reviewing |
| 9E4 | Evaluation |
| 9F | Reprographic |
| 9F1 | Photocopying |
| 9F2 | Microforming |
| 9F3 | Printout |
| 9G | Translation |
| 9G1 | Teletranslation |

*Tel 3 (A2) into (A1) ends*

| | |
|---|---|
| 9H | Maintenance |
| 9H1 | Shelving |
| 9H2 | Shelf arrangement |
| 9H21 | Broken order |
| 9H22 | Compact |
| 9H8 | Stock verification |
| 9H81 | Stock rectification |
| 9J | Binding |
| 9M | Weeding |

**(Sp1) to [1MP1]**

**By cause**

| | |
|---|---|
| a | Lack of library awareness |
| b | Misinformation |
| d | Natural disaster |
| d1 | Water |
| d2 | Fire |
| e | Library technology |
| f | Biological |
| f1 | Insect |
| f2 | Cold |
| g | Language |

| | |
|---|---|
| h | Style |
| j | Contents |
| k | Depression |
| m | Duplication |
| n | Human beings |
| p | personnel |
| q | Mutilation |
| r | Non circulation |
| s | Adverse condition |
| w | Obsolescence |
| | *By information storage and retrieval properties* |
| zA*Z | Planes of work |
| zA*ZZ | Idea plane |
| zA | Class |
| zA1 | Main |
| | *To be divided by notations from respective classification scheme Illustrative* |
| zA1C | Physics |
| zA1L | Medical science |
| zA2 | By formation mode. |
| | *To be got by (AD) Illustrative* |
| zA2D | Distilled |
| zA2F | Fused |
| zA3 | Partial comprehension |
| zA4 | Basic class |
| zA5 | Specials |
| zA6 | Systems |
| zA7 | Compound class |
| zB | Isolate |
| zB1 | Common isolate |
| zB11 | Anteriorising |

| | |
|---|---|
| zB12 | Common matter property isolate |
| zB13 | Common energy isolate |
| zB14 | Language |
| zB15 | Time |
| zB16 | Space |
| zB2 | Special isolate |
| zB21 | Energy |
| zB22 | Matter |
| zB221 | Matter material |
| zB222 | Matter property |
| zB223 | Matter method |
| zB23 | Personality |
| zE | Facet |
| zE1 | Time |
| zE2 | Space |
| zE3 | Energy |
| zE4 | Matter |
| zE5 | Personality |
| zH | Phase relation |
| zH1*Z | By kind of relation |
| zH1 | General |
| zH2 | Bias |
| zH3 | Comparison |
| zH4 | Difference |
| zH5 | Application |
| zH6 | Influence |
| zH92*Z | By level of relation |
| zH92 | Inter subject |
| zH93 | Intra-facet |
| zH94 | Intra-array |
| zK | Device |

| | |
|---|---|
| zK3 | Chronological |
| zK4 | Geographical |
| zK5 | Subject |
| zK6 | Enumerative |
| zK7 | Alphabetical |
| zM*Z | Verbal plane |
| zM | Terminology |
| zR*Z | Notational plane |
| zR | Notational system |
| zRa | Pure |
| zRb | Mixed |
| zR1 | Notational digit |
| zR11 | Substantive |
| zR12 | Empty |
| zR13 | Emptying |
| zR14 | Empty-emptying |
| zR15 | Indicator |
| zT | Call number |
| zT1 | Class number |
| zT2 | Book number |
| zT21*Z | Facets of book number |
| zT21 | Language |
| zT22 | Form |
| zT23 | Year |
| zT24 | Accession part of book number |
| zT25 | Volume number |
| zT26 | Supplement number |
| zT27 | Copy number |
| zT28 | Criticism number |
| zT291 | Accession part of criticism number |
| zT3 | Collection number |

| | |
|---|---|
| zU | Mnemonic |
| zU1 | Seminal |
| zU2 | Systematic |
| zU3 | Scheduled |
| zU4 | Verbal |
| zV | Form class |
| zW | Index to the schedule |
| zW1 | Relative |
| zW2 | Specific |
| 1*Z | By bibliographic description |
| 1 | Author |
| 11 | Personal |
| 12 | Corporate |
| 121 | Government |
| 122 | Institution |
| 123 | Conference |
| 13 | Single |
| 14 | Shared |
| 16 | Collaborator |
| 161 | Editor |
| 162 | Compiler |
| 163 | Translator |
| 164 | Commentator |
| 165 | Illustrator |
| 166 | Assistant |
| 2 | Title |
| 21 | Short |
| 22 | Half |
| 23 | Alternative |
| 24 | Running |
| 25 | Fanciful |

| | |
|---|---|
| 26 | Uniformed |
| 3 | Edition |
| | *To be divided by (ND) Read as integers Illustrative* |
| 321 | 21st edition |
| 3A | Abridged *To be divided by (ND) Read as integers Illustrative* |
| 3A13 | 13th Abridged edition |
| 4 | Series |
| 41 | Single |
| 42 | Multiple |
| 5 | Imprint |
| 51 | Place |
| 52 | Publisher |
| 53 | Year |
| 6 | Collation |
| 61 | Pagination |
| 62 | Accompanying material |
| | *To be divided by (Sp1) to [1P2] Illustrative* |
| 620G | Chart |
| 63 | Size |
| 7 | Standard number |
| 71 | ISBN |
| 72 | ISSN |
| 7A | Accession number |
| 8 | Entry |
| 81 | Main |
| 82 | Added |
| 821 | Author |
| 822 | Title |
| 823 | Subject |

| | |
|---|---|
| 824 | Cross reference |
| 8241 | See |
| 8242 | See also |
| 825 | Analytical |
| 8251 | Author analytical |
| 8252 | Title analytical |
| 8253 | Subject analytical |
| 91 | Areas |
| 911 | Heading |
| 912 | Tracing |
| 913 | Other |
| | *To be divided by (Sp1) to [1MP1] i.e. Information storage and retrieval properties Illustrative* |
| 9132 | Title area |
| *By type* | |
| A | Subject |
| B | Information |
| C | Textual |
| D | Bibliographic |
| E | Retrieval |
| F | Technical |
| G | Electronic |
| H | Computerized |
| J | Offline |
| K | Online |
| L | Internet based |
| L1 | Web based |
| M | HTML |
| N | Adhesive |
| P | Cloth |

Q Leather
R Behavioural
S Academic
T Drinking water
U Reading room
V Commercial
W Organizational
X Value added
Y Saleable
Za Cooperative
Zb Centralized
Ze Self charged
Zf Traditional
Zg Backlog

*By purpose*

Z1 Research
Z2 Information source

*To be divided by (Sp1) to [1P2]*

*Illustrative*

Z202 Corporate
ZA *By name To be got by (AD)*

*Illustrative*

ZAB Blaizline

**(Sp2) to [1MP1]**

A* By name To be got by (AD) Illustrative
C CIP
CO Conspectus
R Remploy

**Schedule of [1MP2] Isolates**

1 Philosophy
2 Theory

| | |
|---|---|
| 3 | Principle |
| 4 | Policy |
| 5 | Strategy |
| 6 | Proposal |
| 7 | Programme |
| A | Standard |
| C | Guideline |
| D | Provision |
| E | Role |
| F | Quality |
| G | Efficiency |
| H | Performance |
| J | Status |
| K | Complexity |
| M | Opinion |
| N | Attitude |
| P | Need |
| Q | Fee |
| R | Fine |
| S | Cost |
| T | Discount |
| U | Form |
| V | Use |
| W | Holdings |
| X | Notification |
| Y | Renewal |
| Z1 | Search |

**(Sp1) to [1MP2]**

*By type*

| | |
|---|---|
| a | Web based |
| c | Request |

| | |
|---|---|
| d | Aesthetic |
| g | Core |
| j | Financial |
| | *By agency* |
| 1 | Personnel |
| 11 | Librarian |
| 111 | Senior |
| 2 | User |
| | *To be divided by (Sp1) to [1P2]* |
| | *Illustrative* |
| 29x3(T) | Teacher |
| A*Z | *By name To be got by (AD)* *Illustrative* |
| A | ALA |
| I | ISO |
| N | Net Book Agreement |
| Z | Z39.50 |

**Schedule of [1E] Isolates**

| | |
|---|---|
| a | Application |
| b | Creation |
| c | Production |
| d | Generation |
| e | Charging |
| f | Identification |
| g | Effect |
| h | Impact |
| j | Change |
| k | Construction |
| m | Automation |
| m1 | Computerization |
| m11 | Networking |
| q | Problem |

| | |
|---|---|
| r | Research |
| r1 | User study |
| r2 | Use study |
| r3 | Feasibility study |
| v | Analysis |
| w | Evaluation |
| x | Measuring |
| y | Designing |
| y1 | Redesigning |
| 1 | Preservation |
| 2 | Development |
| 3 | Conservation |
| 4 | Improvement |
| 5 | Prevention |
| 6 | Protection |
| 7 | Communicate |
| 8 | Management |
| 81 | Committee |
| 82 | Planning |
| 83 | Organization |
| 84 | Standardization |
| 8B | Job analysis |
| 8C | Job design |
| 8D | Vacancy |
| 8D1 | Recruitment |
| 8D11 | Interview |
| 8D12 | Selection |
| 8D13 | Appointment |
| 8D2 | Training |
| 8E | Retention |
| 8L | Leading |

| | |
|---|---|
| 8M | Motivation |
| 8N | Monitoring |
| 8P | Controlling |
| 8R | Budgeting |
| 8R1 | PPBS |
| 8R2 | ZBB |
| 8S | Misappropriation |
| 8T | Accounting |
| 8U | Auditing |
| 8V | Marketing |
| 8V1 | Market segmentation |
| 8V2 | Marketing mix |
| 8V21 | Planning |
| 8V22 | Pricing |
| 8V23 | Promotion |
| 8V231 | Public relation |
| 8V232 | Publicity |
| 8V24 | Distribution |
| 91 | Outsourcing |
| 92 | Privatization |
| 93 | Insuring |

**(Sp1) to [1E]**

*By tools*

| | |
|---|---|
| a*Z | *By common matter property associated tools / criteria* |
| a | Standard |
| b | Availability |
| c | Guideline |
| e | Policy |
| f | Strategy |
| g | Proposal |
| h | Compatibility |

| | |
|---|---|
| j | Recall |
| k | Precision |
| m | Waiting time |
| n | Delivery time |
| p | Fill rate |
| r | Definitiveness of answer |
| s | Subject coverage |
| t | Title coverage |
| u | Ease of use |
| v | Report generation capacity |
| w | Images |
| x | Search interface |
| za*Z | *By library associated tools* |
| za | Newspaper |
| zb | Title page |
| zb1 | Physical layout |
| zc | Classification |
| zd | PMEST |
| ze | Catalogue |
| zf | Union catalogue |
| zg | MARC |
| zg1 | UNIMARC |
| zh | Thesaurus |
| zj | N-gram |
| zk | Book register |
| zm | Library handbook |
| z2 | Marketing |
| z5 | Internal audit |
| z6 | System analysis |
| z7 | Management By Objectives |
| z8 | Decision Support System |

| | |
|---|---|
| z91 | PERT |
| z92 | CPM |
| z93 | Operation research |
| z931 | Game theory |
| z932 | Queuing theory |
| z94 | TQM |
| z95 | ISO 9000 |
| z96 | Cost |
| z961 | Cost effectiveness |
| zA*Z | *By Information Technology associated tools* |
| zA | Information technology |
| zD | Audio-visual |
| zD1 | Audio cassette |
| zD2 | Video cassette |
| zG | Computer |
| zH | CD-ROM |
| zJ | Multimedia |
| zK | Barcode |
| zL*Z | Programming language *To be got by (AD) Illustrative* |
| zLC | Clipper |
| zLH | HTML |
| zLJ | Jawa |
| zM*Z | Software *To be got by (AD) Illustrative* |
| zMC | CDS/ISIS |
| zMD | dBbase IV |
| zMI | InMagic |
| zML | LIBRATAS |
| zMLI | LIBSYS |
| zMM | MINISIS |
| zMO | OmniPage Pro |

| | |
|---|---|
| zMS | SOUL |
| zMW | WINISIS |
| zN | Artificial intelligence |
| zP | Knowledge based system |
| zQ | Expert system |
| zR | Natural Language Processing |
| zS | Geographic Information System |
| zT | Network |
| zU | WAN |
| zV | Internet |
| zW | WWW |
| zW1 | Web site |
| zW11 | Web page |
| zW12 | Home page |
| zX | E-mail |
| zY | LAN |
| | *By influencing factor* |
| 2 | Information source |
| 4 | Subject heading |
| 5 | Chain indexing |
| 7 | Electronic publishing |
| 8 | Epistemology |
| 9a | Multidisciplinarity |
| 9d | Higher salary |
| 9e | Promotion |
| 9f | Medical facility |
| 9g | Retirement benefit |
| 9j | Private sector |
| 9k | Public sector |
| | *By method* |
| 9A | Adequate light |

| | |
|---|---|
| 9B | Right temperature |
| 9C | Proper housing |
| 9D | Automatic |
| 9E | Digitization |
| 9F | Photocopying |
| 9G | Microfilming |
| 9H | Fumigation |
| 9J | De-acidification |
| 9J1 | Aqueous |
| 9J2 | Mass |
| 9K | Display of new arrivals |
| 9L | Extension activities |
| 9M | Exhibition |
| 9N | Library week |
| 9Q | Lecture |
| 9R | Story telling |
| 9S | Reading aloud |
| 9T | Interview with author |
| 9X*Z | By specific method |
| | *To be got by (AD) Illustrative* |
| 9XA | Attribution Theory |
| 9XK | Kantor method |
| | *By type* |
| A | Quantitative |
| B | Statistical |
| C | Technological |
| D | Verbal |
| E | Non verbal |
| F | Political |
| H | Organizational |
| J | Qualitative |

| | |
|---|---|
| K | Operational |
| L | Participative |
| M | Strategic |
| P | In-service |
| Q | Financial |
| R | Lack of user participation |
| S | Lack of confirmed prices |
| T | Delay in supply |
| U | Loss in transit |
| V | Social |
| W | Cooperative |

**(Sp2) to [1E]**

*By type*

| | |
|---|---|
| 1 | Textbook |
| 2 | Digital |
| 5*Z | *By version To be got by (AD) Illustrative* |
| 5A | Arabized |
| 5I | IDA |
| A*Z | *By name To be got by (AD) Illustrative* |
| A | ACRL |
| N | NUCSSI |

**Schedule of [2E] Isolates**

**Same as schedule of [1E]**

**(Sp1) to [2E]**

*By tool*

*By library associated tool*

**Same as (Sp1) to [1E]**

*By management associated tools*

**Same as (Sp1) to [1E]**

*By information technology associated tools*

**Same as (Sp1) to [1E]**

A*Z *By psychology associated tools*

A Humour

R*Z *By method To be got by (AD)* *Illustrative*

RC Conjoint analysis

RCO Contingent valuation

*By type*

S Security

# 5

# THESAURUS CONSTRUCTION METHODOLOGY

## 5.0 INTRODUCTION

Thesaurus construction is a time consuming and complex job. For constructing a thesaurus one must follow a systematic procedure. This chapter explains the methodology adopted in constructing the present thesaurus of LIS terms.

## 5.1 SUBJECT FIELD COVERED

As stated in the first chapter the present thesaurus covers the library and information science core subject field. As such it lists terms related with types of libraries and the basic aspects of librarianship such as personnel, library technology, furniture, building, information sources and users. It also lists terms related with various activities, services and programmes of libraries. Terms related with the managerial aspect of librarianship, such as evaluation, marketing, costing, budgeting etc. are also listed. The thesaurus however, does not include terms related with bibliometrics. This is because the thesaurus is based on a newly constructed depth classification schedule. The schedule does not list any isolates related with this subject. The reasons for excluding this subject from the classification schedule is explained in the first chapter.

## 5.2 METHODOLOGY ADOPTED

A thesaurus can be constructed by adopting the *a priori* or the posteriori method (Unesco, 1981g). Each of these methods has it's own merits and demerits. A blending of both these methods is adopted to construct the present thesaurus, so as to avail the advantages of both the methods.

### 5.2.1 Procedure adopted for preparing the alphabetical thesaurus

The entries in the alphabetical part of the thesaurus were prepared directly on the computer, using the Microsoft Word programme. The thesaural terms required were taken from the cards of micro documents arranged in classified order. Taking a card at a time, terms were input to the thesaurus file in the Microsoft Word. The faceted structure of the classification schedule helped to establish thesaural relationships. For example, the isolates forming chain division represented hierarchical relationship and the isolates across facets represented associative relationship. At the time of establishing the thesaural relationships itself the additional information, such as synonyms, scope notes was added. The procedure adopted for constructing the present thesaurus is described in section 5.3 to 5.11.

## 5.3 LANGUAGE OF THE THESAURUS

This is a monolingual thesaurus. It lists LIS terms in English language only.

## 5.4 STANDARD FOLLOWED

As reviewed in third chapter various standards are available for thesaurus construction. Unesco's *Guidelines for the establishment and development of monolingual thesauri* is one of these. As can be noticed from the name it is developed by an international organization. Secondly it forms the basis for many national standards on thesaurus construction. Even the ISO standard for thesaurus construction too is based on the *Guidelines*. So the *Guidelines* was selected for constructing the present thesaurus. Rules from the second edition of the *Guidelines* were adopted in constructing this thesaurus (Unesco, 1981). Few cases where the *Guidelines* failed to provide guidance were resolved with the help of ANSI/NISO Z39.19 standard (National, 1994).

## 5.5 SOURCES FOR THESAURAL TERMS

The thesaurus contains descriptor (preferred terms) and non-descriptor (non-preferred terms) terms. The newly constructed depth classification schedule formed the basic source for descriptor terms. Subject terms going with following three different components in the depth classification schedule formed the descriptors.

### 5.5.1 The isolate terms alone

Examples of this category are: ACADEMIC LIBRARIES,
CIRCULATION,
MANAGEMENT, etc.

### 5.5.2 The speciator terms alone

The speciator terms from (Sp1) under the (QI) 'by information storage and retrieval properties' of [1MP1] facet independently qualified as descriptors. Similarly, speciator terms from (Sp1) under the (QI) 'by tools', 'by influencing factor' and 'by method' of [1E] and [2E] facet qualified as independent descriptors, e.g. SYSTEM ANALYSIS, DIGITIZATION, etc.

### 5.5.3 The combination of speciators with isolates

The (Sp1) 'Junior' combined with the (1P2) isolate 'Cataloguer' formed the descriptor 'JUNIOR CATALOGUERS'.

The non-descriptor terms were gathered from the micro documents and other sources like glossaries (Prytherch, 1990) and encyclopaedias. These were added to the computer file at appropriate places while typing the descriptors.

## 5.6 GRAMMATICAL FORM OF TERMS USED

Adopting the *Guidelines* the following forms of terms have been preferred.

### 5.6.1 Noun forms

e.g. CATALOGUES, PERIODICALS.

### 5.6.2 Adjectival phrases

e.g. AGRICULTURAL LIBRARIES.

### 5.6.3 Verbs

Use of verbs is mostly avoided. However, when the literary warrant demanded, they were used, e.g. CATALOGUING, ACCESSIONING.

### 5.6.4 Initial articles

No suggestion is made in the *Guidelines* for initial articles. The ANSI / NISO Z39.19 Standard however, recommends keeping the articles along with the term but enter the term in the inverted order, e.g. The Guardian was written as 'GUARDIAN, THE'.

### 5.6.5 Singular and plural forms

Nouns that represent concrete entities are divided by the *Guidelines* into two categories.

#### *5.6.5.1 Count nouns*

These are the nouns which are subject to the question 'how many'. As recommended by the *Guidelines* the names of countable objects have been expressed in plural form, e.g. USERS, TEXTBOOKS.

#### *5.6.5.2 Non count nouns*

These are the nouns, which are subject to the question 'how much'. As per the *Guidelines* these were listed in singular form. e.g. CIRCULATION, COOPERATION.

*5.6.5.3 Abstract concepts*

The *Guidelines* recommends that the terms representing abstract concepts should be in singular form, so they were used in singular form. These concepts are further categorised as:

i) Abstract entities and phenomena, e.g. KNOWLEDGE, ABSENTEEISM.

ii) Properties: e.g. COMPLEXITY, COMPATIBILITY.

iii) Activities: e.g. MARKETING, INDEXING.

iv) Discipline: e.g. LIBRARY SCIENCE, VETERINARY SCIENCE.

The *Guidelines* also recommends that when an abstract concept is regarded as a class with more than one member the term representing the class should be expressed in plural, so such terms were listed in plural, e.g. HUMANITIES.

**5.6.6 Spellings**

The *Guidelines* recommends to use the most widely accepted spellings. So in this thesaurus mostly the British spellings were used, e.g. CATALOGUE (not catalog). However, looking at the increasing use of words with 'z' instead of 's', the thesaurus uses the 'z' form of words, e.g. organization (not organisation).

**5.6.7 Acronyms**

As recommended by the *Guidelines* widely used acronyms (such as CAS, SDI) were preferred. Reciprocal references were made from full form of the term to its acronym.

**5.6.8 Parenthetical qualifiers**

The qualifiers to ambiguous descriptors, particularly, homographs have been included in parenthesis. They were given next to the descriptor term, e.g.

PROMOTION (MARKETING)

PROMOTION (SERVICE ADVANCEMENT)

The parenthetical qualifiers, however were not provided for those descriptors whose meaning is expressed by the broader terms listed below the concerned descriptor, e.g.

TEXINCON

BT TEXTILE'S BIBLIOGRAPHIC DATABASE.

In this case the descriptor 'TEXINCON', needs no parenthetical qualifier.

### 5.6.9 Apostrophes

In order to show the possessiveness apostrophes are required. The *Guidelines* has not recommended any rules for this. However the ANSI / NISO Z39.19 Standard recommends the use of apostrophes. This thesaurus has used apostrophes.

### 5.6.10 Hyphen

There are no rules given in the *Guidelines* for the use of hyphens. The ANSI / NISO Standard recommends the use of hyphens, if dropping them would result in ambiguity. So whenever needed the hyphen was retained, e.g. N-GRAM, DE-ACIDIFICATION.

### 5.6.11 Capitalization

The usual conventions of capitalization have been followed, as there are no rules for this in the *Guidelines*.

## 5.7 PROPER NAMES OF INSTITUTIONS

As recommended by the *Guidelines* they were used to the minimum extent and were in the most favoured form, e.g. ACRL, ISO.

## 5.8 SCOPE NOTES AND DEFINITIONS

In order to specify exact meaning of preferred term, scope notes and definitions are required in the thesaurus. So they were added whenever needed e.g.

OVERSIZED INFORMATION SOURCES

SN *30 to 40 cm in height*

## 5.9 COMPOUND TERMS

Ideally any concept should be represented by using single term. That is why the *Guidelines* as well as almost all the manuals on the thesaurus construction recommend factoring of terms. The *Guidelines*, however, mentions that factoring is not mandatory (Unesco, 1981h). In spite of such a suggestion for representing a subject with single term, the nature of subjects discussed in the documents does not always allow doing so. Complex subjects need to be expressed by combinations of two or more terms. The terms formed by combining two or more terms are called compound terms. Compound terms increase specificity and ultimately enhance performance of ISRS. Considering this aspect, the *Guidelines* prescribed the use of compound terms in thesauri. So in the present thesaurus terms in compound forms were listed.

The classification schedule used as a basic source for thesaural terms, was developed by applying the concept of speciator. The speciators were combined with the isolates to form compound terms. Illustrative examples from each facet are:

A) The (Sp1) 'Automated' was combined with the [1P1] isolate 'University library' to form the compound term 'AUTOMATED UNIVERSITY LIBRARY'.

B) The (Sp1) 'Rural' was compounded with the [1P2] isolate 'User' to form the compound term 'RURAL USERS'.

C) The compound term 'COMPUTERIZED SDI' was formed by combining the (Sp1) 'Computerized' with the [1MP1] isolate 'SDI'.

D) The (Sp1) 'ISO' was compounded with the [1MP2] isolate 'Standard' to form the compound term 'ISO STANDARDS'.

E) The compound term 'QUANTITATIVE EVALUATION' was formed by combining the (Sp1) 'Quantitative' with the

[1E] isolate 'Evaluation'.

F) The (Sp1) 'Security' was combined with [2E] isolate 'Problems' to form the compound term 'SECURITY PROBLEMS'.

In addition to these, compound terms were also formed by combining two speciators with each other, for example, RARE BOOK WEBSITES. This was done considering the literary warrant. These terms were combined because factoring them may lead to loss of meaning.

Compound terms were also formed (though very few) by combining the two isolates across facets, e.g. the [1P2] isolate 'Personnel' was combined with the [1E] isolate 'Management' to form the compound term 'PERSONNEL MANAGEMENT'. Such combinations were formed only for those terms warranted by the literature.

Combinations of terms have been formed primarily for those terms which, occurred in the analyzed micro documents, i.e. based on literary warrant. Some compound terms were also formed on the empirical basis. For forming such compound terms help of Harrod's Glossary was taken.

### 5.9.1 Citation order of words in compound terms

The *Guidelines* recommends the use of direct form, so while preparing compound terms the direct form was preferred to the indirect form, e.g. COOPERATIVE CATALOGUING *not* CATALOGUING, COOPERATIVE.

## 5.10 THESAURAL RELATIONSHIPS

Methods used for establishing the three types of thesaural relationships are:

### 5.10.1 The equivalence relationship

The data required for establishing the equivalence relationships was collected during the analysis of micro documents. Additional data required for this purpose was gathered from glossaries and encyclopaedias. This relationship has been shown in the thesaurus through the usual convention of USE as a prefix to the preferred term and UF (USE FOR) as a prefix to the non-preferred term. Reciprocal entries have been made from preferred to non-preferred term and vice-versa. The equivalence relationship existed between the terms of various categories such as:

*5.10.1.1 Synonyms*

The synonymous terms were identified during the analysis of assorted micro documents and by using the Harrod's glossary of LIS terms (Prytherch, 1990). The preferred term was selected as descriptor under which the non-preferred term was shown as UF (stood for 'Use for'). Reciprocal entry was made under the non-preferred term directing the user towards the preferred term through the convention of 'USE', indicating the preference, e.g.

LIST OF ADDITIONS

UF Accession lists

Accession lists

USE LIST OF ADDITIONS

***5.10.1.2 Terms of different linguistic origin***

Different linguistics origins may have different names for the same concept, e.g. periodicals are also referred to as serials. Relations between such variations have been established giving reference from preferred to non-preferred term and vice-versa, e.g.

PERIODICALS

UF Serials

Serials

USE PERIODICALS

#### *5.10.1.3 Acronyms*

The *Guidelines* does not give clear guidance about forming equivalence relationship between the acronym and its full form. As given in the *Guidelines*, the well-known acronyms were used as preferred terms and cross-reference was given to its full form, e.g.

KWIC
  UF Key-Words-In-Context

Key-Words-In-Context
  USE KWIC

### 5.10.2 The hierarchical relationship

Hierarchical relationship shows levels of super-ordination and sub-ordination. The hierarchical relationship has been shown by using the BT (Broader Term) and NT (Narrower Term) convention. In this thesaurus the hierarchical relationship was established between two different components of the schedule i.e.

A) Relationship between isolates forming chain division.

B) Relationship between an isolate and the compound term prepared by combining the speciator with the isolate.

The *Guidelines* identified four categories of hierarchical relationship, i.e.

#### *5.10.2.1 Generic relationship*

The generic relationship exists between a class or category and its member or species. In the present thesaurus this type of relationship was established between isolates forming chain in [1P1], [1P2], [1MP1] and [1E] isolates. Example of generic relationship is-

UNIVERSITY LIBRARIES
  BT ACADEMIC LIBRARIES

ACADEMIC LIBRARIES

NT UNIVERSITY LIBRARIES

The generic relationship also existed between the [1P1], [1P2], [1MP1] and [1MP2] isolates and their speciators. This is because the speciators of these facets represent the types of the concept represented by their isolates and so they form hierarchical relations.

However, the (Sp1) under the (QI) 'by cause' of the [1MP1] facet do not represent generic relationship because they are not types of their isolate terms. On the contrary these speciators in the context of their respective isolates indicate cause and effect type of relation, as such they generate associative relationship. Similarly, all the speciator of [1E] and [2E] facet do not generate generic relationship. It is only the speciators under the (QI) 'by type' of the [1E] and [2E] facet generate generic relationship.

### *5.10.2.2 Whole-part relationship*

This relationship existed mostly between isolates forming chain division, e.g.

ACQUISITION

BT COLLECTION DEVELOPMENT

COLLECTION DEVELOPMENT

NT ACQUISITION

### *5.10.2.3 Instance relationship*

Instance relationship exists between general category represented by a common noun and its instance represented by a proper noun. This relationship mostly existed between the speciator kind 2 and the compound term formed by combining the isolate term and the speciator of kind 1, e.g.

LISA

BT ABSTRACTING PERIODICALS

ABSTRACTING PERIODICALS

NT LISA

No instance relationship was established for the type of libraries and their proper names. As the number of proper names of libraries to be listed was too large and their recall value is beyond doubt.

### 5.10.3 The associative relationship

Terms forming part of associative relationship are referred to as Related Terms (RT).

Using the faceted structure of the depth classification schedule the associative relationship was formed for various components, such as:

#### *5.10.3.1 Isolates across facets*

Associative relationship was established between isolates across facets. For example, in the subject 'circulation in academic libraries', the function 'circulation' belongs to [1MP1] facet, whereas the type of libraries i.e. the 'academic libraries' belongs to [1P1] facet. As the two isolates belong to different facets the associative relationship between them was established, i. e.

ACADEMIC LIBRARIES

RT CIRCULATION

The associative relationship too is reciprocal, so a reciprocal entry was prepared under the another related term i.e.

CIRCULATION

RT ACADEMIC LIBRARIES

Some times a document has isolates coming from the more than two facets also. In such cases the associative relationship was established between all of them, giving reciprocal reference from each other, e.g.

The subject, 'designing [1E] standards [1MP1] for academic libraries [1P1]', derives associative relationship such as:

ACADEMIC LIBRARIES

RT DESIGNING

STANDARDS

DESIGNING

RT ACADEMIC LIBRARIES

STANDARDS

STANDARDS

RT ACADEMIC LIBRARIES

DESIGNING

*5.10.3.2 Speciators under the (QI) 'by cause' to [1MP1] isolates*

The speciator to [1MP1] under the (QI) 'by cause' represented associative relationship. This is because these speciators fulfill the criteria of 'cause – effect' recommended by the *Guidelines* for establishing associative relationship.

***5.10.3.3 Speciators under the (QI) 'by tools' to [1E] and [2E] isolates***

It has been noticed that the speciators to [1P1], [1P2], [1MP1] and [1MP2] (except the speciators under the (QI) 'by cause') represent a type, part or a class. However this is not true of all the speciators to [1E] and [2E]. All the speciators to these facets do not represent types, parts or class of isolates. So all of them do not form part of the associative relationship. As such a different treatment is given to them while establishing thesaural relationship for terms prepared by combining these speciators. Illustrations of these treatments are:

Speciators under the (QI) 'by tool', 'by influencing factor' and 'by methods'. have been shown as RT to the respective isolates in [1E] and [2E] facet. That is because they fit in the 'operation and instrument' and other criteria suggested by the *Guidelines* for forming associative relationship, e.g. the speciator 'fill rate' forms RT to the descriptor 'evaluation'. This was done for two reasons. (a) the speciator 'fill rate' does not represent type of evaluation, and (b) it fits in the type of associative relation named 'an operation or process and its agent or instrument', given in the *Guidelines*.

#### *5.10.3.4 Terms within facet*

It is usually noticed that most of the terms indented as isolate terms in a faceted systematic display form hierarchical relationship. However as warned by Aitchison, Gilchrist and Bawden (2000f) it is not true for all terms of such a category. They may even lead to associative relationship. So associative relationship was also established between terms which, were indented under a term in the same facet, e.g.

CATALOGUE CODES
    RT CATALOGUING
CATALOGUING
    RT CATALOGUE CODES

## 5.11 DISPLAY

### 5.11.1 Parts of the thesaurus

The thesaurus has been displayed in two parts i.e.

a) The systematic part: it is a faceted depth classification schedule, given in chapter four.

b) The alphabetical part: this displays the thesaural entries in alphabetical format showing the equivalence, hierarchical and the associative relationships of the descriptors. However, there were some descriptors without any relationships. Such descriptors are called 'single descriptors'. No descriptors in the thesaurus accompanied class numbers. That is because the newly constructed depth classification schedule has been designed by using the concept of speciators. A speciator may go with one or more than one isolate. As such it becomes impossible to imagine and identify all possible combinations of the speciators and the isolates.

An index to the depth classification schedule is prepared. It lists all the isolates and their speciators. This index is an alternative mechanism to link the alphabetical thesaurus to the systematic part.

e.g. the descriptor 'catalogue' in the thesaurus will take the searcher to the following entry in the index of the classification schedule.

Catalogue [1MP1] 6c; (Sp1) to [1E] ze; (Sp1) to [2E], ze

From this entry the user can reach to respective concept in the depth classification schedule.

Apart from this function the index helps to find concepts from the depth classification schedule, when the schedule alone is to be used.

### 5.11.2 Reference structure

The sequence of various types of terms in the thesaurus is as:

PREFERRED TERM

| | |
|---|---|
| *SN* | *Scope note* |
| UF | Refers to equivalent non-preferred terms |
| BT | Reference to broader terms |
| NT | Reference to narrower terms |
| RT | Reference to related terms |

Non-preferred term

USE PREFERRED TERM

Example:

PERIODICALS

UF Journals

Serials

BT INFORMATION SOURCES

NT ABSTRACTING PERIODICALS

RT ACADEMIC LIBRARIES

When there were more than one terms under a specific relationship they were arranged alphabetically.

### 5.11.3 Alphabetization

The word by word method was used for arranging the thesaural entries.

### 5.11.4 Typography

In order to enable easy identification of information in the thesaurus, each item in the reference structure was presented by using different typography, e.g.

a) All the preferred descriptors and BT, NT, and RT references were typed in uppercase letters.

b) The non-descriptors were typed in lower case letters.

c) The associated terms (i.e. related terms) not encountered in the assorted micro documents and identified on the *a priori* basis were typed in italics.

d) Scope notes (SN) were typed in lower-case italics.

## 5.12 TESTING OF THE THESAURUS

The present thesaurus was tested by preparing subject headings for 590 assorted micro documents. The derivation of subject headings was easy and satisfactory. The subject headings derived were expressive enough to disclose the subject of the micro documents.

The next chapter presents the thesaurus of LIS terms.

# 6

# THESAURUS OF LIBRARY AND INFORMATION SCIENCE TERMS

AACR

UF Anglo-American Cataloguing Rules

BT CATALOGUE CODES

RT *CLASSIFIED CATALOGUE CODE*

AACRII

UF Anglo-American Cataloguing Rules II

BT CATALOGUE CODES

NT CORPORATE INFORMATION SOURCES IN AACR II

AACR II REV

UF Anglo-American Cataloguing Rules II Revised

BT CATALOGUE CODES

Abridged DDC

USE ABRIDGED DEWEY DECIMAL CLASSIFICATION

ABRIDGED DEWEY DECIMAL CLASSIFICATION

UF Abridged DDC

BT DEWEY DECIMAL CLASSIFICATION

ABRIDGED EDITION

BT EDITION (BIBLIOGRAPHIC DESCRIPTION)
EDITIONS (INFORMATION SOURCES)

ABRIDGEMENTS

BT INFORMATION SOURCES
NT ABSTRACTS
DIGESTS
SUMMARIES
SYNOPSIS

ABSENTEEISM

RT COLD
DEPRESSION
PERSONNEL

ABSTRACTING PERIODICALS

BT PERIODICALS
NT LISA
RT *INDEXING PERIODICALS*

ABSTRACTING SECTION

BT INFORMATION SECTION

ABSTRACTING SERVICES

BT CONDENSATION SERVICES
NT COMPUTERIZED ABSTRACTING SERVICE
RT *ABSTRACTS*
TECHNOLOGICAL LIBRARIES

ABSTRACTORS

BT INFORMATION PERSONNEL

ABSTRACTS

BT ABRIDGEMENTS
NT AUTHOR ABSTRACTS
AUTO ABSTRACTS
GRAPHIC ABSTRACTS
INDICATIVE ABSTRACTS
INFORMATIVE ABSTRACTS
SLANTED ABSTRACTS

RT *ABSTRACTING SERVICES*
*INDEXES*

ABUSE-L

SN *A discussion group on Internet.*
BT DISCUSSION GROUPS

ACADEMIC LIBRARIES

BT LIBRARIES
NT BRANCH ACADEMIC LIBRARIES
COLLEGE LIBRARIES
NETWORKED ACADEMIC LIBRARIES
SCHOOL LIBRARIES
UNIVERSITY LIBRARIES
RT ACCESSIBILITY
APPLICATION
ARTISTS STUDENTS
ATTRIBUTION THEORY
AVAILABILITY
CATALOGUERS.
CHANGE
CHARGING (LEVYING MONETARY CHARGES)
CIRCULATION
COLLECTION DEVELOPMENT
COMMITTEES
COMPUTERIZATION
CONJOINT ANALYSIS
CONSORTIUM
CONTINGENT VALUATION
COST.
COST-EFFECTIVENESS.
CREATIVITY.
DAMAGE
DEFINITIVENESS OF ANSWERS
DEMANDS
DESIGNING
EVALUATION

FEASIBILITY STUDY
FILL RATE
FINANCE
FINE
HOLDINGS
HUMOUR
ILL
IMPACT
IMPROVEMENT
INFORMATION SOURCES
INSURING
JOB SATISFACTION
KANTOR METHOD
LIBRARIANS
LIBRARY SCIENCE INFORMATION SOURCES
LOSS
MARKETING
MEASURING
NETWORKS
OPAC
OPERATIONAL MANAGEMENT
ORGANIZATIONAL CHANGE
OUTSOURCING
PARAPROFESSIONAL PERSONNEL
PERFORMANCE
PERIODICALS
PERSONNEL
PHOTOCOPYING SERVICES
PRESCRIBED TEXTBOOKS
PREVENTION
PROBLEMS
PROTECTION
QUALIFICATIONS
RARE BOOKS
READING ROOM INFORMATION SOURCES

REDESIGNING
REFERENCE PERSONNEL
REFERENCE SERVICE
REMOTE USERS
RESOURCE SHARING
ROLE
SERVICES
SKILLS
STANDARDS (EVALUATION CRITERIA)
STANDARDS (INFORMATION SOURCES)
STRATEGIC PLANNING
SUBJECT COMPETENCIES
TEXTBOOKS
TEXTBOOK'S AVAILABILITY
THEFT
USE
WAITING TIME
WEB BASED SERVICES
WORKING CONDITION

ACADEMIC STATUS
UF Faculty status
BT STATUS
RT LIBRARIANS

ACCESS
BT INFORMATION STORAGE AND RETRIEVAL
RT FREE INTERNET INFORMATION SOURCES
FULL TEXT PERIODICALS DATABASE
HOLDINGS

ACCESSIBILITY
RT ACADEMIC LIBRARIES
PRESCRIBED TEXTBOOKS

Accessions lists
USE LISTS OF ADDITIONS

ACCESSION NUMBER
BT BIBLIOGRAPHIC DESCRIPTION

ACCESSION PART OF
BOOK NUMBERS
BT BOOK NUMBERS

ACCESSION PART OF
CRITICISM NUMBER
BT BOOK NUMBERS

ACCESSION REGISTER
RT *ACCESSIONING*

ACCESSIONING
RT *ACCESSION REGISTER*

ACCESSIONING SECTION
BT ACQUISITION SECTION

ACCOMPANYING MATERIAL
BT COLLATION

ACCOUNTABILITY
RT LIBRARIANS
MISINFORMATION

ACCOUNTING
BT MANAGEMENT
RT *AUDITING*
PERIODICALS SECTION
CENTRAL TECHNOLOGICAL LIBRARIES

ACCOUNTS SECTION
BT SECTIONS

ACQUISITION
BT COLLECTION DEVELOPMENT
NT COOPERATIVE ACQUISITION
DE-SUBSCRIBING
EXCHANGE
GIFTS
LEGAL DEPOSITS
MEMBERSHIP OF INSTITUTIONS
PURCHASE
ORDERING
RENEWAL(SUBSCRIPTION)
SUBSCRIBING

RT APPLICATION
DIGITAL INFORMATION SOURCES
DISCOUNT
FOREIGN INFORMATION SOURCES
LIBSYS
MANAGEMENT LIBRARIES
PERIODICALS
STANDARDIZATION
TQM
UNIVERSITY LIBRARIES

ACQUISITION SECTION
BT SECTIONS
NT ACCESSIONING SECTION
ORDERING SECTION
SELECTION (INFORMATION SOURCES) SECTION
RT EVALUATION

ACRL STANDARDS
UF Association of College and Research Libraries Standards
BT STANDARDS (EVALUATION CRITERIA)
RT EVALUATION
BRANCH ACADEMIC LIBRARIES

ADAPTATIONS
BT INFORMATION SOURCES

ADDED ENTRIES
BT ENTRIES
NT ANALYTICAL ENTRIES
AUTHOR ADDED ENTRIES
CROSS REFERENCE ENTRIES
SUBJECT ADDED ENTRIES
TITLE ADDED ENTRIES
RT *MAIN ENTRY*

ADEQUATE LIGHT
RT CONSERVATION
INFORMATION SOURCES

ADHESIVE BINDING

BT BINDING

NT REMPLOY ADHESIVE BINDING

ADMINISTRATION SECTION

BT SECTIONS

ADMINISTRATIVE REPORTS

BT REPORTS

ADOLESCENT STUDENTS

BT STUDENTS

RT BOOK REGISTERS

DEVELOPMENT

READING HABIT

SCHOOL LIBRARIES

ADOLESCENT USERS

BT USERS

ADULT USERS

BT USERS

RT SERVICES

UNIVERSITY LIBRARIES

ADVANCE COPIES

BT INFORMATION SOURCES

ADVANCED INFORMATION SOURCES

SN *Higher level information sources*

BT INFORMATION SOURCES

ADVERSE CONDITION

RT JOB DISSATISFACTION

PERSONNEL

AERONAUTICAL RESEARCH LIBRARIES

BT RESEARCH LIBRARIES

RT APPLICATION

ISO 9000

AESTHETIC OF NOTIFICATION

BT NOTIFICATION

RT SCIENCE INFORMATION CENTRE

SDI

AFFILIATING UNIVERSITY LIBRARIES

BT UNIVERSITY LIBRARIES

AGRICULTURAL BIBLIOGRAPHIES

BT BIBLIOGRAPHIES

AGRICULTURAL INFORMATION SYSTEM

BT INFORMATION SYSTEMS

NT AGRICULTURAL RESEARCH INFORMATION SYSTEM

*AGRIS*

RT SERVICES

AGRICULTURAL LIBRARIES

BT SPECIAL LIBRARIES

RT DEVELOPMENT

NETWORKING

AGRICULTURAL RESEARCH INFORMATION SYSTEM

UF ARIS

BT AGRICULTURAL INFORMATION SYSTEM

INFORMATION SYSTEM

AGRICULTURAL UNIVERSITY LIBRARIES

BT UNIVERSITY LIBRARIES

RT APPLICATION

CD-ROM DATABASES

NETWORKS

RESOURCE SHARING

USE

AGRIS

UF International Information System for Agricultural Sciences and Technology

BT AGRICULTURAL INFORMATION SYSTEM

AI

USE ARTIFICIAL INTELLIGENCE

AIRFORCE LIBRARIES
BT DEFENCE LIBRARIES

ALA GUIDELINES
UF American Library Association Guidelines
BT GUIDELINES
RT FICTIONS (INFORMATION SOURCES) INDEXING

ALMANACS
BT REFERENCE SOURCES
RT *YEARBOOKS*

ALMOST ENUMERATIVE CLASSIFICATION SCHEMES
BT CLASSIFICATION SCHEMES (SPECIES)

ALMOST FACETED CLASSIFICATION SCHEMES
BT CLASSIFICATION SCHEMES (SPECIES)

ALPHABETICAL DEVICE
BT DEVICES

ALPHABETICAL THESAURI
BT THESAURI

ALPHABETICO CLASSED CATALOGUES
BT CATALOGUES

ALPHABETIZATION
BT CATALOGUING
NT LETTER BY LETTER ALPHABETIZATION
WORD BY WORD ALPHABETIZATION

ALTERNATIVE TITLE
BT TITLE

ALTRAFICHE
BT MICROFICHE

American Library Association Guidelines
USE ALA GUIDELINES

ANALYSIS
NT STATISTICAL ANALYSIS
ANALYTICAL BIBLIOGRAPHIES
BT BIBLIOGRAPHIES
ANALYTICAL ENTRIES
BT ADDED ENTRIES
NT AUTHOR ANALYTICAL ENTRIES
SUBJECT ANALYTICAL ENTRIES
TITLE ANALYTICAL ENTRIES
ANALYTICO-SYNTHETIC CLASSIFICATION SCHEMES
BT CLASSIFICATION SCHEMES (SPECIES)
Anglo-American Cataloguing Rules
USE AACR
Anglo-American Cataloguing Rules II
USE AACR II
Anglo-American Cataloguing Rules II Revised
USE AACR II REV
ANGLO AMERICAN CODE
BT CATALOGUE CODES
ANTERIORISING COMMON ISOLATES
BT COMMON ISOLATES
ANXIETY
RT LACK OF LIBRARY AWARENESS
LIBRARY TECHNOLOGY
PERSONNEL
USERS
APERTURE CARD

BT MICROFORMS

APPLICATION

RT ACADEMIC LIBRARIES
ACQUISITION
AERONAUTICAL RESEARCH LIBRARIES
AGRICULTURAL UNIVERSITY LIBRARIES
ARABIZED CDS/ISIS
ARABIZED MINISIS
ARTIFICIAL INTELLIGENCE
AUDIO CASSETTES
AUDIO INFORMATION SOURCES
BARCODES
BIBLIOGRAPHIC DATABASES
BIBLIOGRAPHIC DESCRIPTION
BRANCH PUBLIC LIBRARIES
CATALOGUING
CDS/ISIS
CIRCULATION
CLASSIFICATION
CLIPPER
COLLEGE LIBRARIES
COMMERCIAL LIBRARIES
COMPUTERS
CONJOINT ANALYSIS
CONSORTIUM
CONTINGENT VALUATION
CONTROL
CREATION
DBASE IV
DECISION SUPPORT SYSTEM
DESIGNING
DIGITAL LIBRARIES
DOCUMENT DELIVERY SERVICES
E-MAIL
EVALUATION

EXHIBITIONS
EXPERT SYSTEM
FORMS
GEOGRAPHICAL INFORMATION SYSTEMS
HTML
HUMOUR
IDA VERSION
IDENTIFICATION
ILL
IMPROVEMENT
INDEXING
INDUSTRIAL LIBRARIES
INFORMATION SEEKING BEHAVIOUR
INFORMATION STORAGE RETRIEVAL
INFORMATION TECHNOLOGY
INTERNET
ISO 9000
KNOWLEDGE BASED SYSTEM
LAN
LIBRARY HANDBOOKS
LIBRATAS
LIBSYS
LOCAL NEWSPAPERS
MANAGEMENT
MANAGEMENT BY OBJECTIVES
MANAGEMENT LIBRARIES
MANAGEMENT PRINCIPLES
MARKETING
MONITORING
MULTIMEDIA
MULTIMEDIA E-MAIL
NATURAL LANGUAGE PROCESSING
NETWORKED ACADEMIC LIBRARIES
NETWORKS
N-GRAM

NUCSSI
OMNIPAGE-PRO
ONLINE DATABASES
ONLINE INFORMATION RETRIEVAL
OPAC
PERT
PHYSICAL LAYOUT OF TITLE PAGE
PMEST
PROBLEMS
PUBLIC LIBRARIES
QUERY FORMULATION
QUEUING THEORY
RARE BOOKS
RARE BOOKS BIBLIOGRAPHIC DATABASE
RECALL
REFERENCE SERVICE
REMOTE USERS
REQUEST FORMS
RESOURCE SHARING
RETROSPECTIVE CONVERSION
SEARCH
SECURITY PROBLEMS
SERVICES
SPECIAL LIBRARIES
STOCK VERIFICATION
TECHNICAL PROCESSING
TEXTUAL INFORMATION RETRIEVAL
THESAURI CONSTRUCTION
TQM
UNIMARC
UNIVERSITY LIBRARIES
USE STUDY
USER EDUCATION
WEB BASED FORMS
WORKING CONDITION
WWW

APPLICATION PHASE RELATIONS
BT PHASE RELATIONS

APPOINTMENT
BT RECRUITMENT

APPROVAL METHOD
BT SELECTION TOOLS

AQUEOUS DE-ACIDIFICATION
BT DE-ACIDIFICATION
RT MANUSCRIPTS
PRESERVATION

ARABIZED CDS/ISIS
BT CDS/ISIS
RT APPLICATION
UNIVERSITY LIBRARIES

ARABIZED MINISIS
BT MINISIS
RT APPLICATION
UNIVERSITY LIBRARIES

ARCHIVES
BT INFORMATION SOURCES

AREAS (CATALOGUE ENTRIES)
NT HEADING AREA
TRACING AREA
RT *ENTRIES*

ARIS
USE AGRICULTURAL RESEARCH INFORMATION SYSTEM

ARMY LIBRARIES
BT DEFENCE LIBRARIES

ART PAPER INFORMATION SOURCES
BT PAPER BASED INFORMATION

SOURCES

ARTICLES

BT PERIODICALS

ARTIFICIAL INTELLIGENCE

UF AI

RT APPLICATION

ONLINE INFORMATION

RETRIEVAL

ARTIST STUDENTS

BT STUDENTS

RT ACADEMIC LIBRARIES

Assessment

USE EVALUATION

ASSISTANT LIBRARIANS

BT LIBRARIANS

ASSISTANTS (AUTHORS)

BT COLLABORATORS

Association of College and Research Libraries Standards

USE ACRL STANDARDS

ATLASES

BT REFERENCE SOURCES

ATTITUDE

NT LIBRARIAN'S ATTITUDE

RT IMPACT

ATTRIBUTION THEORY

RT ACADEMIC LIBRARIES

MEASURING

PERFORMANCE

AUDIO CASSETTES

BT DIGITAL INFORMATION SOURCES

AUDIO VISUAL TECHNOLOGY

RT APPLICATION

PUBLIC LIBRARIES

USER EDUCATION

AUDIO INFORMATION SOURCES

BT AUDIO VISUAL INFORMATION SOURCES

NT AUDIO CASSETTES

RT APPLICATION
CLASSIFICATION
PMEST

AUDIO LIBRARIES

SN *Libraries of audio information sources*

BT SPECIAL LIBRARIES

RT LIBRARIANS
ROLE
USE

AUDIO VISUAL INFORMATION SOURCES

BT DIGITAL INFORMATION SOURCES

NT VIDEO CASSETTES

RT CATALOGUING

AUDIO VISUAL TECHNOLOGY

BT INFORMATION TECHNOLOGY

NT AUDIO CASSETTES
VIDEO CASSETTES

AUDITING

BT MANAGEMENT

RT *ACCOUNTING*
CENTRAL TECHNOLOGICAL LIBRARIES
PERIODICAL SECTION

AUTHOR ABSTRACTS

BT ABSTRACTS

AUTHOR ADDED ENTRIES

BT ADDED ENTRIES

AUTHOR ANALYTICAL ENTRIES

BT ANALYTICAL ENTRIES

AUTHOR CATALOGUES
BT CATALOGUES
RT *SUBJECT CATALOGUES*
*TITLE CATALOGUES*

AUTHORIZED EDITIONS
BT EDITIONS

AUTHORITY CONTROL
RT *VOCABULARY CONTROL*

AUTHORS
BT BIBLIOGRAPHIC DESCRIPTION
NT COLLABORATORS
CORPORATE AUTHORS
PERSONAL AUTHORS
SHARED AUTHORSHIP
SINGLE AUTHOR

AUTO ABSTRACTS
BT ABSTRACTS

AUTOMATED LIBRARIES
BT SPECIAL LIBRARIES
NT COMPUTERIZED LIBRARIES
NETWORKED LIBRARIES
RT ROLE
SHELF LIST

AUTOMATED UNIVERSITY LIBRARIES
BT UNIVERSITY LIBRARIES
RT OPAC
USE

AUTOMATIC
RT IDENTIFICATION

AUTOMATION
NT COMPUTERIZATION
RT MANAGEMENT
PUBLIC LIBRARIES

AUTOMOBILES BIBLIOGRAPHIC

DATABASES

BT BIBLIOGRAPHIC DATABASES

AVAILABILITY

NT TEXTBOOK'S AVAILABILITY

RT ACADEMIC LIBRARIES

CD-ROM DATABASES

EVALUATION

KANTOR METHOD

MEASURING

PRESCRIBED TEXTBOOKS

SCHOOL LIBRARIES

USE

AWARDED FARMERS

BT USERS

RT INFORMATION SEEKING BEHAVIOR

BACKLOG CATALOGUING

BT CATALOGUING

RT MANAGEMENT

UNIVERSITY LIBRARIES

BANNED EDITIONS

BT EDITIONS

BARCODES

BT INFORMATION TECHNOLOGY

RT APPLICATION

CIRCULATION

SECURITY PROBLEMS

STOCK VERIFICATION

BARK INFORMATION SOURCES

SN *Information sources written on barks*

BT INFORMATION SOURCES

BASIC CLASS

BT CLASS

BATTEN SYSTEM

BT POST COORDINATE INDEXING SYSTEMS

BEHAVIORAL PERFORMANCE
BT PERFORMANCE
RT GUIDELINE
INFORMATION PERSONNEL
REFERENCE PERSONNEL

BENGALI INFORMATION SOURCES
BT INFORMATION SOURCES
SCIENCE INFORMATION SOURCES

BIAS PHASE RELATIONS
BT PHASE RELATIONS

BIBLIOGRAPHERS
BT PROFESSIONAL PERSONNEL
NT WEBLIOGRAPHERS

BIBLIOGRAPHIC CLASSIFICATION (BLISS)
BT CLASSIFICATION SCHEMES (EXAMPLES)

BIBLIOGRAPHIC CONTROL
RT DALIT LITERATURE
PAMPHLETS

BIBLIOGRAPHIC DATABASES
BT DATABASES
NT AUTOMOBILE'S BIBLIOGRAPHIC DATABASES
CD-ROM BIBLIOGRAPHIC DATABASES
IN-HOUSE BIBLIOGRAPHIC DATABASES
RARE BOOKS BIBLIOGRAPHIC DATABASES
TEXTILES BIBLIOGRAPHIC DATABASES
RT APPLICATION
CDS/ISIS
CREATION
MANAGEMENT
OMNIPAGE PRO
UNIMARC

BIBLIOGRAPHIC DESCRIPTION
NT ACCESSION NUMBER

AUTHORS
BIBLIOGRAPHIC DESCRIPTION STANDARDS
COLLATION
EDITION
IMPRINT
SERIES
STANDARD NUMBERS
TITLE
RT APPLICATION
*CATALOGUING*
IDENTIFICATION
PHYSICAL LAYOUT OF TITLE PAGE

BIBLIOGRAPHIC DESCRIPTION STANDARDS
BT BIBLIOGRAPHIC DESCRIPTION
NT ISBD(A)
ISBD(CF)
ISBD(CM)
ISBD(CP)
ISBD(ER)
ISBD(G)
ISBD(M)
ISBD(NBM)
ISBD(PM)
ISBD(S)

BIBLIOGRAPHIC EXCHANGE FORMATS
NT CCF
MARC
RT *CATALOGUING*

BIBLIOGRAPHIC INFORMATION RETRIEVAL
BT INFORMATION RETRIEVAL

Bibliographic instructions
USE USER EDUCATION

BIBLIOGRAPHIC SERVICES

BT SERVICES
NT ONLINE BIBLIOGRAPHIC SERVICES
RT PRICING
TECHNOLOGICAL LIBRARIES

BIBLIOGRAPHIES
BT REFERENCE SOURCES
SELECTION TOOLS
NT AGRICULTURAL BIBLIOGRAPHIES
ANALYTICAL BIBLIOGRAPHIES
CURRENT BIBLIOGRAPHIES
HISTORICAL BIBLIOGRAPHIES
LOCAL BIBLIOGRAPHIES
NATIONAL BIBLIOGRAPHIES
RETROSPECTIVE BIBLIOGRAPHIES
STATE BIBLIOGRAPHIES
SYSTEMATIC BIBLIOGRAPHIES
TRADE BIBLIOGRAPHIES

BILINGUAL THESAURI
BT THESAURI

BINDING
NT ADHESIVE BINDING
CLOTH BINDING
LEATHER BINDING
RT ISO STANDARDS

BINDING SECTION
BT SECTIONS

BIO-BIBLIOGRAPHIES
BT BIOGRAPHIES

BIOGRAPHIES
BT REFERENCE SOURCES
NT BIO-BIBLIOGRAPHIES

BIOLOGICAL CAUSES
NT COLD (CAUSAL FACTORS)
INSECTS (CAUSAL FACTORS)
RT DETERIORATION

PRINTED INFORMATION SOURCES

BLANKET ORDERING
BT ORDERING
RT QUANTITATIVE EVALUATION

BLAIZLINE
BT OPAC
RT EVALUATION
NATIONAL LIBRARIES

BLIND USERS
BT USERS

BLIND USER'S LIBRARIES
BT SPECIAL LIBRARIES

BOND PAPER INFORMATION SOURCES
BT PAPER BASED INFORMATION SOURCES

BOOK FORM CATALOGUES
BT CATALOGUES

BOOK NUMBERS
BT CALL NUMBERS
COLON CLASSIFICATION
NT ACCESSION PART OF BOOK NUMBERS
ACCESSION PART OF CRITICISM NUMBERS
COPY NUMBERS
CRITICISM NUMBERS
FORM OF PUBLICATION
LANGUAGE PART OF BOOK NUMBERS
SUPPLEMENT NUMBERS
VOLUME NUMBERS
YEAR OF PUBLICATION

BOOK POCKETING
BT PHYSICAL PROCESSING

BOOK REGISTERS
SN *Registers used for recording the circulation data*

RT ADOLESCENT STUDENTS
DEVELOPMENT
READING HABIT
RELUCTANT STUDENTS
SCHOOL LIBRARIES

Book selection
USE SELECTION (INFORMATION SOURCES)

Book selection section
USE SELECTION (INFORMATION SOURCES) SECTION

BOOK SHELVES
BT SHELVES

BOOK SUPPORTERS
BT FURNITURE

BOOK TROLLEYS
BT FURNITURE

BOOKS
BT INFORMATION SOURCES
RT USE

BRAILLE INFORMATION SOURCES
BT INFORMATION SOURCES

BRAILLE LIBRARIES
BT SPECIAL LIBRARIES
RT LIBRARIANS
ROLE
USE

BRANCH ACADEMIC LIBRARIES
BT ACADEMIC LIBRARIES
RT ACRL STANDARDS
COMPACT SHELVING
EVALUATION

BRANCH LIBRARIES
BT LIBRARIES

RT *CENTRAL LIBRARIES*

BRANCH NATIONAL LIBRARIES
BT NATIONAL LIBRARIES
RT GOVERNMENT INFORMATION SOURCES
USE

BRANCH PUBLIC LIBRARIES
BT PUBLIC LIBRARIES
RT APPLICATION
GEOGRAPHICAL INFORMATION SYSTEM
USE STUDY

BRITISH MUSEUM CATALOGUE CODE
BT CATALOGUE CODES

BROADCAST LECTURES
BT LECTURES (PRINTED)

BROADCASTING CENTRE LIBRARIES
BT SPECIAL LIBRARIES
RT EVALUATION
SERVICES

BROCHURES
BT PUBLIC RELATION MATERIALS

BROKEN ORDER
BT SHELF ARRANGEMENT

BROWNE CHARGING SYSTEM
BT CIRCULATION SYSTEMS

BUDGETING
BT MANAGEMENT
NT PPBS
ZBB

BUILDINGS
NT LOCATION OF BUILDINGS
MODULAR BUILDINGS
PHYSICAL LAYOUT OF BUILDINGS

SPACE
RT PLANNING
UNIVERSITY LIBRARIES

BUSINESS DIRECTORIES
BT DIRECTORIES

CALENDAR PAPER INFORMATION SOURCES
SN *Information sources produced on calendar paper*
BT PAPER BASED INFORMATION SOURCES

CALL NUMBERS
BT CLASSIFICATION
NT BOOK NUMBERS
CLASS NUMBERS
COLLECTION NUMBERS

CARD CATALOGUES
BT CATALOGUES

CARTOONS
BT INFORMATION SOURCES

CAS
UF Current Awareness Services
BT SERVICES
NT CLIPPING SERVICES
CONTENTS PAGE SERVICES
DISPLAY OF NEW ARRIVALS
LISTS OF ADDITIONS
RESEARCH IN PROGRESS
ROUTING OF PERIODICALS
SDI

CASSETTE STANDS
BT STANDS (FURNITURE)

CATALOGUE CABINETS
BT FURNITURE
NT CATALOGUE CARD DRAWERS

CATALOGUE CARD DRAWERS

BT CATALOGUE CABINETS

CATALOGUE CARD TRAYS

BT TRAYS

CATALOGUE CODES

NT AACR
AACRII
AACR II REV
ANGLO-AMERICAN CODE
BRITISH MUSEUM CATALOGUE CODE
CLASSIFIED CATALOGUE CODE
CUTTER'S DICTIONARY CATALOGUE CODE
MANUAL FOR ARCHIVAL DESCRIPTION
PRUSSIAN INSTRUCTIONS

RT *CATALOGUING*
DIGITAL INFORMATION SOURCES

CATALOGUES

NT ALPHABETICO-CLASSED CATALOGUES
AUTHOR CATALOGUES
BOOK FORM CATALOGUES
CARD CATALOGUES
CATALOGUES WITH ABSTRACTS
CATALOGUES WITH ANNOTATIONS
CLASSIFIED CATALOGUE
DICTIONARY CATALOGUES
ENTRIES
OPAC
SHEAF FORM CATALOGUES
SHELF LISTS
SUBJECT CATALOGUES
TITLE CATALOGUES
TRADITIONAL CATALOGUES
UNION CATALOGUES

RT *CATALOGUING*

UNIVERSITY LIBRARIES
USE STUDY
USER EDUCATION

CATALOGUES WITH ABSTRACTS
BT CATALOGUES

CATALOGUES WITH ANNOTATIONS
BT CATALOGUES

CATALOGUERS
BT PROFESSIONAL PERSONNEL
NT JUNIOR CATALOGUERS
RT ACADEMIC LIBRARIES
SKILLS

CATALOGUING
BT TECHNICAL PROCESSING
NT ALPHABETIZATION
BACKLOG CATALOGUING
CENTRALIZED CATALOGUING
COOPERATIVE CATALOGUING
DEPTH CATALOGUING
LIMITED CATALOGUING
RE-CATALOGUING
RETROSPECTIVE CONVERSION
RT APPLICATION
AUDIO VISUAL INFORMATION SOURCES
*BIBLIOGRAPHIC DESCRIPTION*
*BIBLIOGRAPHIC EXCHANGE FORMATS*
*CATALOGUE CODES*
*CATALOGUES*
*CLASSIFICATION*
DIGITAL PERIODICALS
GLOBES
*INDEXING*
INTERNET

INTERNET INFORMATION SOURCES
MAPS
METADATA
OUTSOURCING
RARE BOOKS

CATALOGUING IN PUBLICATION
UF CIP
BT CENTRALIZED CATALOGUING

CATALOGUING SECTION
BT TECHNICAL PROCESSING SECTIONS
RT VACANCIES

CCF
UF Common Communication Format
BT BIBLIOGRAPHIC EXCHANGE FORMAT
RT *MARC*
*UNIMARC*

CD-DA
UF Compact Disk-Digital Audio
BT STORAGE TECHNOLOGY

CD-I
UF Compact Disk-Interactive
BT STORAGE TECHNOLOGY

CD-R
UF Compact Disk-Recordable
BT STORAGE TECHNOLOGY

CD-ROM
UF Compact Disk Read Only Memory
BT STORAGE TECHNOLOGY
RT COLLECTION DEVELOPMENT
IMPACT
SELECTION (INFORMATION SOURCES)

CD-ROM BIBLIOGRAPHIC DATABASES
BT BIBLIOGRAPHIC DATABASES

NT POPLINE
RT INFORMATION SEEKING BEHAVIOR
USERS

CD-ROM DATABASES
UF Offline databases
BT DATABASES
RT AGRICULTURAL UNIVERSITY LIBRARIES
AVAILABILITY
COST
ONLINE DATABASES
OPEN ACCESS PUBLIC LIBRARIES
PUBLIC LIBRARIES
SCHOOL LIBRARIES
SEARCH
SELECTION (INFORMATION SOURCES)
SOCIAL SCIENCE INFORMATION CENTRES
TECHNOLOGICAL LIBRARIES
USE

CD-ROM ENCYCLOPAEDIAS
BT ENCYCLOPAEDIAS

CD-RW
UF Compact Disk-Rewritable
BT STORAGE TECHNOLOGY

CD STANDS
BT STANDS (FURNITURE)

CDS/ISIS
BT SOFTWARES
NT ARABIZED CDS/ISIS
RT APPLICATION
BIBLIOGRAPHIC DATABASES
CREATION
RETROSPECTIVE CONVERSION
UNIVERSITY LIBRARIES

CD-XA
UF Compact Disk Extended Architecture

BT STORAGE TECHNOLOGY

CELL SCIENCE RESEARCH LIBRARIES

BT RESEARCH LIBRARIES

RT DATABASES

OFFLINE SEARCH

ONLINE SEARCH

CENTRAL GOVERNMENT LIBRARIES

BT GOVERNMENT LIBRARIES

CENTRAL LIBRARIES

UF Main libraries

BT LIBRARIES

RT *BRANCH LIBRARIES*

CENTRAL LIBRARIES OF UNIVERSITIES

BT UNIVERSITY LIBRARIES

RT USER EDUCATION

CENTRAL TECHNOLOGICAL LIBRARIES

BT TECHNOLOGICAL LIBRARIES

RT ACCOUNTING

AUDITING

PERIODICAL SECTION

CENTRAL UNIVERSITY LIBRARIES

BT UNIVERSITY LIBRARIES

CENTRALIZED CATALOGUING

BT CATALOGUING

NT CATALOGUING IN PUBLICATION

RT *COOPERATIVE CATALOGUING*

CENTRALIZED ILL

BT ILL

RT MEDICAL LIBRARIES

CENTRALIZED LIBRARIES

BT LIBRARIES

RT *DECENTRALIZED LIBRARIES*

CENTRALIZED UNIVERSITY LIBRARIES

BT UNIVERSITY LIBRARIES

RT COLLECTION DEVELOPMENT POLICY

CHAIN INDEXING

BT PRE-COORDINATE INDEXING SYSTEMS

RT IMPACT

LISA

CHAIRS

BT FURNITURE

CHANGE

NT ORGANIZATIONAL CHANGE

TECHNOLOGICAL CHANGE

RT ACADEMIC LIBRARIES

MANAGEMENT

Charging (circulation)

USE ISSUING

CHARGING (LEVYING MONETARY CHARGES)

RT ACADEMIC LIBRARIES

DAMAGE

DOCUMENT DELIVERY SERVICES

FEE

FINE

ILL

INFORMATION SOURCES

LOSS

PRINTOUT SERVICES

SERVICES

UNIVERSITY LIBRARIES

CHARGING TRAYS

BT TRAYS

CHARITABLE INSTITUTION'S

LIBRARIES
BT LIBRARIES

CHARTS
BT INFORMATION SOURCES

CHEAP EDITIONS
BT EDITIONS

CHEMICAL DATABASES
BT DATABASES
RT ONLINE INFORMATION RETRIEVAL
SCIENCE INFORMATION CENTRE

CHEMICAL PATENTS
BT PATENTS

CHIEF LIBRARIANS
BT LIBRARIANS
RT COMMERCIAL LIBRARIES
SKILLS

CHILDREN INFORMATION SOURCES
BT INFORMATION SOURCES
RT CIRCULATION
SCHOOL LIBRARIES

CHILDREN LIBRARIES
BT SPECIAL LIBRARIES

CHILDREN USERS
BT USERS
RT DEVELOPMENT
INTERVIEW WITH AUTHOR
READING ALOUD
READING HABIT

CHINESE PAPER INFORMATION SOURCES
BT PAPER BASED INFORMATION SOURCES

CHRONOLOGICAL DEVICE
BT DEVICES

CIP
USE CATALOGUING IN PUBLICATION

CIRCULARS

BT PUBLIC RELATION MATERIALS

CIRCULATION

BT SERVICES

NT CIRCULATION SYSTEMS

ISSUING

OVERDUE

RECOVERY OF INFORMATION SOURCES (ISSUED)

REGISTRATION OF MEMBERSHIP

RENEWAL (ISSUED INFORMATION SOURCES)

RESERVATION

RETURN OF INFORMATION SOURCES

ROUTING OF PERIODICALS

RT ACADEMIC LIBRARIES

APPLICATION

BARCODES

CHILDREN INFORMATION SOURCES

CLIPPER

*LIBRARY RULES*

LIBRARY SCIENCE INFORMATION SOURCES

PERIODICALS

SCHOOL LIBRARIES

SECURITY PROBLEMS

CIRCULATION SECTION

BT SECTIONS

CIRCULATION SYSTEMS

BT CIRCULATION

NT BROWNE CHARGING SYSTEM

LEDGER SYSTEM

NEWARK CHARGING SYSTEM

CITATION INDEXING

BT INDEXING SYSTEMS

RT *CITATIONS*

CITATIONS

RT *CITATION INDEXING*

CITY LIBRARIES

BT LIBRARIES

CLASS

UF Subject

BT IDEA PLANE

NT BASIC CLASS

COMPOUND CLASS

DISTILLED CLASS

FUSED CLASS

MAIN CLASS

PARTIAL COMPREHENSION CLASS

SPECIALS

SYSTEMS

CLASS NUMBERS

BT CALL NUMBERS

CLASSICS

BT INFORMATION SOURCES

CLASSIFICATION

BT TECHNICAL PROCESSING

NT CALL NUMBERS

CLASSIFICATION SCHEMES (EXAMPLES)

CLASSIFICATION SCHEMES (SPECIES)

PLANES OF WORK

RECLASSIFICATION

RT APPLICATION

AUDIO INFORMATION SOURCES

*CATALOGUING*

COMPUTERS

*INDEXING*

ONLINE DATABASES

OPAC

RESEARCH

SEARCH

STANDARDS (INFORMATION SOURCES)

THEORIES OF CLASSIFICATION

CLASSIFICATION SCHEMES (EXAMPLES)
BT CLASSIFICATION
NT BIBLIOGRAPHIC CLASSIFICATION (BLISS)
COLON CLASSIFICATION
DEWEY DECIMAL CLASSIFICATION
INTERNATIONAL CLASSIFICATION
LIBRARY OF CONGRESS CLASSIFICATION
SUBJECT CLASSIFICATION (BROWN)
UNIVERSAL DECIMAL CLASSIFICATION
RT IMPACT
MULTIDISCIPLINARITY

CLASSIFICATION SCHEMES (SPECIES)
BT CLASSIFICATION
NT ALMOST ENUMERATIVE CLASSIFICATION SCHEMES
ALMOST FACETED CLASSIFICATION SCHEMES
ANALYTICO-SYNTHETIC CLASSIFICATION SCHEMES
DEPTH CLASSIFICATION SCHEME
ENUMERATIVE CLASSIFICATION SCHEMES
FACETED CLASSIFICATION SCHEMES
FREELY FACETED CLASSIFICATION SCHEMES

CLASSIFICATION SECTION
BT TECHNICAL PROCESSING SECTION

CLASSIFIED CATALOGUE CODE
BT CATALOGUE CODES
RT *AACR*

CLASSIFIED CATALOGUES

BT CATALOGUES
RT *DICTIONARY CATALOGUES*

CLASSIFIED (SECRET) INFORMATION SOURCES
BT INFORMATION SOURCES
RT DEFENCE LIBRARIES MANAGEMENT

CLASSIFIERS
BT PROFESSIONAL PERSONNEL

CLAY INFORMATION SOURCES
SN *Information written on clay tablets*
BT INFORMATION SOURCES

CLIP BOUND INFORMATION SOURCES
BT INFORMATION SOURCES

CLIPPER
BT PROGRAMMING LANGUAGES
RT APPLICATION
CIRCULATION

CLIPPING SERVICES
BT CAS
RT NEWSPAPER LIBRARIES
WILDLIFE INSTITUTION'S LIBRARIES

CLOSED ACCESS LIBRARIES
BT LIBRARIES
RT OPEN ACCESS LIBRARIES

CLOTH BINDING
BT BINDING

CLOTH BOUND INFORMATION SOURCES
BT INFORMATION SOURCES
NT HALF CLOTH BOUND INFORMATION SOURCES

CLOTH INFORMATION
SOURCES
SN *Information written on cloth*
BT INFORMATION SOURCES

CLUB'S LIBRARIES
BT LIBRARIES

CODE BOOKS
BT INFORMATION SOURCES

COLD(CAUSAL FACTOR)
SN *Illness causing catarrh and sneezing*
BT BIOLOGICAL CAUSES
RT ABSENTEEISM
PERSONNEL

COLLABORATORS
BT AUTHORS
NT ASSISTANTS (AUTHORS)
COMMENTATORS
COMPILERS
EDITORS
ILLUSTRATORS
TRANSLATORS

COLLATION
BT BIBLIOGRAPHIC DESCRIPTION
NT ACCOMPANYING MATERIAL
PAGINATION
SIZE (INFORMATION SOURCES)

Collection
USE HOLDINGS

COLLECTION NUMBERS
BT CALL NUMBERS
COLON CLASSIFICATION

COLLECTION DEVELOPMENT
NT ACQUISITION
COOPERATIVE COLLECTION
DEVELOPMENT
SELECTION

WEEDING
RT ACADEMIC LIBRARIES
CD-ROM
CENTRALIZED UNIVERSITY LIBRARIES
COLLEGE LIBRARIES
DECENTRALIZED UNIVERSITY LIBRARIES
DIGITAL INFORMATION SOURCES
DIGITAL LIBRARIES
ELECTRONIC PUBLISHING
FINANCIAL PROBLEMS
HYBRID LIBRARIES
IMPACT
INTERNET
PHILOSOPHY
POLICY
PROBLEM OF DELAYED SUPPLY
PROBLEM OF LACK OF CONFIRMED PRICES
PROBLEM OF LACK OF USER PARTICIPATION
PROBLEM OF LOSS IN TRANSIT
PROBLEMS
SPECIAL LIBRARIES
STANDARDS (INFORMATION SOURCES)
STATISTICAL INFORMATION SOURCES
UNIVERSITY LIBRARIES

COLLEGE LIBRARIES
BT ACADEMIC LIBRARIES
NT DEGREE COLLEGE LIBRARIES
EDUCATION COLLEGE LIBRARIES
ENGINEERING COLLEGE LIBRARIES
JUNIOR COLLEGE LIBRARIES
POSTGRADUATE COLLEGE LIBRARIES
SMALL COLLEGE LIBRARIES
RT APPLICATION
COLLECTION DEVELOPMENT

COMPUTERS
EVALUATION
JOB SATISFACTION
LIBRARIANS
LIBRATAS
ORIENTATION
PROGRAMMES
SERVICES
STANDARDS (EVALUATION CRITERIA)
STOCK VERIFICATION

COLON CLASSIFICATION
BT CLASSIFICATION SCHEMES (EXAMPLES)
NT BOOK NUMBERS
COLLECTION NUMBER
MAIN CLASS
RT *FREELY FACETED CLASSIFICATION SCHEMES*

COM
USE COMPUTER OUTPUT MICROFORM

COMICS
BT INFORMATION SOURCES

COMMENTARIES
BT INFORMATION SOURCES

COMMENTATORS
BT COLLABORATORS

COMMERCIAL DOCUMENT DELIVERY SERVICES
BT DOCUMENT DELIVERY SERVICES
RT COST
ILL

COMMERCIAL INSTITUTION'S PUBLICATIONS
BT INSTITUTIONAL INFORMATION SOURCES

COMMERCIAL LIBRARIES
BT SPECIAL LIBRARIES
RT APPLICATION

CHIEF LIBRARIANS
INFORMATION TECHNOLOGY
SKILLS

COMMITMENT
NT ORGANIZATIONAL COMMITMENT

COMMITTEES
BT MANAGEMENT
RT ACADEMIC LIBRARIES
UNIVERSITY LIBRARIES

Common auxiliaries
USE COMMON ISOLATES

Common Communication Format
USE CCF

COMMON ENERGY ISOLATES
BT COMMON ISOLATES

COMMON ISOLATES
UF Common auxiliaries
Standard subdivisions
BT ISOLATES
NT ANTERIORISING COMMON ISOLATES
COMMON ENERGY ISOLATES
COMMON MATTER PROPERTY ISOLATES
LANGUAGE ISOLATES
SPACE ISOLATES
TIME ISOLATES
RT *SPECIAL ISOLATES*

COMMON MATTER PROPERTY ISOLATES
BT COMMON ISOLATES

COMMUNICATION
NT NON-VERBAL COMMUNICATION
VERBAL COMMUNICATION

COMMUNITY LIBRARIES
BT LIBRARIES

Compact Disk-Digital Audio
USE CD-DA

Compact Disk-Extended
Architecture
USE CD-XA

Compact Disk-Interactive
USE CD-I

Compact Disk Read Only
Memory
USE CD-ROM

Compact Disk -Recordable
USE CD-R

Compact Disk-Rewritable
USE CD-RW

COMPACT SHELVES
BT SHELVES

COMPACT SHELVING
BT SHELF ARRANGEMENT
RT BRANCH ACADEMIC LIBRARIES

COMPARISON PHASE
RELATIONS
BT PHASE RELATIONS

COMPATIBILITY
RT EVALUATION
SOFTWARES

COMPETENCIES
NT SUBJECT COMPETENCIES

COMPILERS
BT COLLABORATORS

COMPLEXITY
RT LIBRARY OF CONGRESS LIST
OF SUBJECT HEADINGS

COMPOSIT BOOKS
BT INFORMATION SOURCES
NT FESTSCHRIFTS
SYMPOSIUMS
RT *SIMPLE BOOKS*

COMPOUND CLASS

BT CLASS

COMPUTER OUTPUT MICROFORMS

UF COM

BT MICROFORMS

COMPUTER SECTION

BT SECTIONS

COMPUTER TABLES

SN *Tables used for keeping computers*

BT TABLES

COMPUTERIZATION

BT AUTOMATION

NT NETWORKING

RT ACADEMIC LIBRARIES

FEASIBILITY STUDY

IMPACT

PARAPROFESSIONAL PERSONNEL

UNIVERSITY LIBRARIES

COMPUTERISED ABSTRACTING SERVICE

BT ABSTRACTING SERVICE

COMPUTERISED DOCUMENT DELIVERY SERVICES

BT DOCUMENT DELIVERY SERVICES

COMPUTERISED ILL

BT ILL

COMPUTERISED LIBRARIES

BT AUTOMATED LIBRARIES

COMPUTERISED POPSI

BT POPSI

COMPUTERISED SDI

BT SDI

RT DEVELOPMENT

QUANTITATIVE EVALUATION

SCIENCE INFORMATION CENTRE

TECHNOLOGICAL LIBRARIES

COMPUTERISED SIMPLIFIED CATALOGUING
BT SIMPLIFIED CATALOGUING

COMPUTERS
BT INFORMATION TECHNOLOGY
NT HARDWARE
SOFTWARES
RT APPLICATION
CLASSIFICATION
COLLEGE LIBRARIES
DIGITAL LIBRARIES
IMPACT
INDEXING
INFORMATION SEEKING BEHAVIOR
INFORMATION STORAGE AND RETRIEVAL
LIBRARIAN'S ATTITUDE
MONITORING
QUERY FORMULATION
REMOTE USERS
STOCK VERIFICATION
TRAINING

CONCORDANCES
BT DICTIONARIES

CONDENSATION SERVICES
BT SERVICES
NT ABSTRACTING SERVICES
CONSOLIDATION SERVICES
EVALUATION SERVICES
REVIEWING SERVICES

CONFERENCE (AUTHOR)
BT CORPORATE AUTHORS

CONFERENCE PUBLICATIONS
BT INSTITUTIONAL INFORMATION SOURCES

CONJOINT ANALYSIS
RT ACADEMIC LIBRARIES
APPLICATION

EVALUATION
REFERENCE SERVICE
CONSERVATION
RT ADEQUATE LIGHT
DAMAGE
INFORMATION SOURCES
PRESERVATION
PRINTED INFORMATION SOURCES
PROPER HOUSING
RIGHT TEMPERATURE
WATER (CAUSE OF DISASTER)

CONSOLIDATION SERVICES
BT CONDENSATION SERVICES

CONSORTIUM
BT RESOURCE SHARING
RT ACADEMIC LIBRARIES
APPLICATION

CONSPECTUS
BT COOPERATIVE COLLECTION DEVELOPMENT

CONSULTANCY SERVICES
BT SERVICES
NT ONLINE CONSULTANCY SERVICES

CONTACT LIBRARIES
SN *Libraries of one country functioning in another country such as British Council libraries in India*
BT LIBRARIES
NT NETWORKED CONTACT LIBRARIES

CONTENTS
SN *Information contained in information sources*
RT INFORMATION SOURCES
OBSOLESCENCE

CONTENTS PAGE SERVICE
BT CAS

CONTINGENT VALUATION
RT ACADEMIC LIBRARIES
APPLICATION
EVALUATION
REFERENCE SERVICE

CONTROL
BT MANAGEMENT
RT APPLICATION
FINANCE
INTERNAL AUDIT
MISAPPROPRIATION
PMEST
PROBLEMS
PUBLIC LIBRARIES
RECALL
THESAURI

CONTROLLED LANGUAGE
BT INDEXING LANGUAGES
RT *NATURAL LANGUAGE*
*VOCABULARY CONTROL*

COOPERATION
BT RESOURCE SHARING

COOPERATIVE ACQUISITION
BT ACQUISITION
RT UNIVERSITY LIBRARIES

COOPERATIVE CATALOGUING
BT CATALOGUING
RT *CENTRALIZED CATALOGUING*
NATIONAL LIBRARIES
UNIVERSITY LIBRARIES

COOPERATIVE COLLECTION DEVELOPMENT
BT COLLECTION DEVELOPMENT
NT CONSPECTUS

COOPERATIVE INDEXING
BT INDEXING

RT NEWSPAPERS

COOPERATIVE LIBRARIES

BT LIBRARIES

COOPERATIVE PRESERVATION

BT PRESERVATION

COPY NUMBERS

BT BOOK NUMBERS

COPYRIGHT

RT DATABASES

DIGITAL INFORMATION SOURCES

DOCUMENT DELIVERY SERVICES

USE

COPYRIGHTED INFORMATION SOURCES

BT INFORMATION SOURCES

CORE HOLDINGS

BT HOLDINGS

RT IDENTIFICATION

RETROSPECTIVE CONVERSION

CORPORATE AUTHORS

BT AUTHORS

NT CONFERENCE

GOVERNMENT

INSTITUTIONS

RT *PERSONAL AUTHORS*

CORPORATE INFORMATION SOURCES

UF Corporate publications

BT INFORMATION SOURCES

NT GOVERNMENT INFORMATION SOURCES

INSTITUTIONAL INFORMATION SOURCES

CORPORATE INFORMATION SOURCES IN AACR II

BT AACR II

Corporate publications

USE CORPORATE INFORMATION SOURCES

CORPORATION LIBRARIES
BT GOVERNMENT LIBRARIES

CORRESPONDENCE SECTION
BT SECTIONS

COST
UF Price
RT ACADEMIC LIBRARIES
CD-ROM DATABASES
COMMERCIAL DOCUMENT DELIVERY SERVICES
DIGITAL PERIODICALS
ELECTRONIC DOCUMENT DELIVERY SERVICES
EVALUATION
FRENCH TEXTBOOKS
HOLDINGS
HUMANITIES TEXTBOOKS
ILL
NATIONAL LIBRARIES
ONLINE INFORMATION RETRIEVAL
PERIODICALS
REFERENCE SERVICE
SEARCH
SOCIAL SCIENCE INFORMATION CENTRES

COST-EFFECTIVENESS
RT ACADEMIC LIBRARIES
EVALUATION
RESOURCE SHARING

Costing
USE PRICING

COUNCILLORS
BT USERS
RT INFORMATION NEEDS

CPM
UF Critical Path Method
RT *PERT*

CREATION
RT APPLICATION
BIBLIOGRAPHIC DATABASES
CDS/ISIS
INFORMATION TECHNOLOGY
IN-HOUSE BIBLIOGRAPHIC DATABASES
OMNIPAGE PRO
PROBLEMS
RARE BOOKS BIBLIOGRAPHIC DATABASES
TEXINCON (BIBLIOGRAPHIC DATABASE)
UNIMARC

CREATIVE INFORMATION SOURCES
BT INFORMATION SOURCES

CREATIVITY
RT ACADEMIC LIBRARIES
LIBRARIANS

Critical Path Method
USE CPM

CRITICISM NUMBERS
BT BOOK NUMBERS

CROSS REFERENCE ENTRIES
BT ADDED ENTRIES
NT SEE ALSO ENTRIES
SEE ENTRIES

CULTURAL INSTITUTION'S LIBRARIES
BT LIBRARIES

Current Awareness Service
USE CAS

CURRENT BIBLIOGRAPHIES
BT BIBLIOGRAPHIES

CURRENT INFORMATION SOURCES
BT INFORMATION SOURCES

CUTTER'S DICTIONARY

CATALOGUE CODE
UF Dictionary catalogue code
BT CATALOGUE CODES

DALIT LITERATURE
BT INFORMATION SOURCES
RT BIBLIOGRAPHIC CONTROL

DAMAGE
RT ACADEMIC LIBRARIES
CHARGING (LEVYING MONETARY CHARGES)
CONSERVATION
FINE
INFORMATION SOURCES
PRINTED INFORMATION SOURCES
WATER (CAUSAL FACTOR)

DATA
BT INFORMATION SOURCES

Databanks
USE NUMERIC DATABASES

DATABASES
BT DIGITAL INFORMATION SOURCES
NT BIBLIOGRAPHIC DATABASES
CD-ROM DATABASES
CHEMICAL DATABASES
FULL TEXT DATABASES
IMAGE DATABASES
INDIGENOUS DATABASES
MULTIMEDIA DATABASES
NUMERIC DATABASES
ONLINE DATABASES
RT CELL SCIENCE RESEARCH LIBRARIES
COPYRIGHT
EVALUATION
OFFLINE SEARCH
ONLINE SEARCH
USE

dBASE IV

BT SOFTWARES
RT APPLICATION
INDEXING
LOCAL NEWSPAPERS

DDC

USE DEWEY DECIMAL CLASSIFICATION

DE-ACIDIFICATION

SN *The process which rises the pH value for paper documents to a minimum of 7.0 to assist in their preservation.*
NT AQUEOUS DE-ACIDIFICATION
MASS DE-ACIDIFICATION

DEBATES

SN *Information sources containing debates*
BT INFORMATION SOURCES

DECENTRALIZED LIBRARIES

BT LIBRARIES
RT *CENTRALIZED LIBRARIES*

DECENTRALIZED UNIVERSITY LIBRARIES

BT UNIVERSITY LIBRARIES
RT COLLECTION DEVELOPMENT POLICY

DECISION SUPPORT SYSTEM

UF DSS
RT APPLICATION

DEEMED UNIVERSITY LIBRARIES

BT UNIVERSITY LIBRARIES

DEFENCE INFORMATION CENTRES

BT INFORMATION CENTRES
RT SERVICES

DEFENCE LIBRARIES

BT SPECIAL LIBRARIES
NT AIRFORCE LIBRARIES
ARMY LIBRARIES
NAVY LIBRARIES
RT CLASSIFIED (SECRET) INFORMATION SOURCES
MANAGEMENT

DEFENCE RESEARCH LIBRARIES
BT RESEARCH LIBRARIES
RT NETWORKING

DEFINITIVENESS OF ANSWERS
RT ACADEMIC LIBRARIES
EVALUATION
REFERENCE SERVICE

DEGREE COLLEGE LIBRARIES
BT COLLEGE LIBRARIES
RT READING HABIT
TEACHERS

DELINQUENT USERS
BT USERS
RT UNIVERSITY LIBRARIES

DELIVERY TIME
RT ELECTRONIC DOCUMENT DELIVERY SERVICES
EVALUATION
NATIONAL LIBRARIES

DELUXE EDITIONS
BT EDITIONS

DEMANDS
RT ACADEMIC LIBRARIES
PRESCRIBED TEXTBOOKS

DEPARTMENTAL LIBRARIES
BT LIBRARIES

DEPOSITORY LIBRARIES
BT LIBRARIES

DEPRESSION
RT ABSENTEEISM
PERSONNEL

DEPTH CATALOGUING
BT CATALOGUING

DEPTH CLASSIFICATION SCHEMES
BT CLASSIFICATION SCHEMES (SPECIES)

DEPUTY LIBRARIANS
BT LIBRARIANS

Descriptors
USE SUBJECT HEADINGS

De-selection
USE DE-SUBSCRIBING

DESIGNING
NT REDESIGNING
RT ACADEMIC LIBRARIES
APPLICATION
FORMS
HTML
ILL
PROGRAMMES
REQUEST FORMS
STANDARDS (EVALUATION CRITERIA)
USER EDUCATION
WEB BASED FORMS

DE-SUBSCRIBING
UF De-selection
BT ACQUISITION
RT PERIODICALS
RENEWAL (SUBSCRIPTION)
UNIVERSITY LIBRARIES

DETERIORATION
RT BIOLOGICAL CAUSES
NATURAL DISASTER
PRINTED INFORMATION SOURCES

DEVELOPMENT

RT ADOLESCENT STUDENTS
AGRICULTURAL LIBRARIES
BOOK REGISTERS
CHILDREN USERS
COMPUTERIZED SDI
DIGITAL LIBRARIES
GUIDELINES
INTERVIEW WITH AUTHOR
PROBLEMS
READING ALOUD
READING HABIT
RELUCTANT STUDENTS
SCHOOL LIBRARIES
SERVICES
STRATEGY
TECHNOLOGICAL LIBRARIES
UNIVERSITY LIBRARIES

DEVICES

BT IDEA PLANE
NT ALPHABETICAL DEVICE
CHRONOLOGICAL DEVICE
ENUMERATIVE DEVICE
GEOGRAPHICAL DEVICE
SUBJECT DEVICE

DEWEY DECIMAL CLASSIFICATION

UF DDC
BT CLASSIFICATION SCHEMES (EXAMPLES)
NT ABRIDGED DEWEY DECIMAL CLASSIFICATION
MAIN CLASS
RT *RELATIVE INDEX*
*UNIVERSAL DECIMAL CLASSIFICATION*

DICTIONARIES

BT REFERENCE SOURCES
NT CONCORDANCES

GLOSSARIES

Dictionary catalogue code

USE CUTTER'S DICTIONARY CATALOGUE CODE

DICTIONARY CATALOGUES

BT CATALOGUES

RT *CLASSIFIED CATALOGUES*

DIFFERENCE PHASE RELATIONS

BT PHASE RELATIONS

DIGESTS (INFORMATION SOURCES)

BT ABRIDGEMENTS

DIGITAL BOOKS

UF E-books

Electronic books

Soft books

BT DIGITAL INFORMATION SOURCES

DIGITAL INFORMATION SOURCES

UF Electronic information sources

BT INFORMATION SOURCES

NON-BOOK MATERIALS

NT AUDIO INFORMATION SOURCES

AUDIO VISUAL INFORMATION SOURCES

DATABASES

DIGITAL BOOKS

DIGITAL PERIODICALS

RT ACQUISITION

CATALOGUE CODES

COLLECTION DEVELOPMENT

COPYRIGHT

DOCUMENT DELIVERY SERVICES

IMPACT

LIBRARIANS

METADATA

POLICY

RESEARCH
USERS

DIGITAL LIBRARIES
UF Electronic libraries
BT SPECIAL LIBRARIES
NT VIRTUAL LIBRARIES
RT APPLICATION
COLLECTION DEVELOPMENT
COMPUTERS
DEVELOPMENT
DOCUMENT DELIVERY SERVICES
EVALUATION
GUIDELINES
HOLDINGS
INFORMATION SEEKING BEHAVIOR
KNOWLEDGE (QUALITIES OF PERSONNEL)
MONITORING
ONLINE REFERENCE SERVICE
PERSONNEL
POLICY
PROBLEMS
PROFESSIONAL PERSONNEL
REMOTE USERS
SERVICES
SKILLS
USER STUDY

DIGITAL PERIODICALS
UF E-journals
Electronic journals
BT DIGITAL INFORMATION SOURCES
PERIODICALS
RT CATALOGUING
COST
HOLDINGS
MANAGEMENT

Digital Video Disk

USE DVD

DIGITISATION

RT EXAMINATION PAPERS
INFORMATION SOURCES
PRESERVATION
UNIVERSITY LIBRARIES

Direct ILL

USE SELF-CHARGED ILL

DIRECTORIES

BT REFERENCE SOURCES
NT BUSINESS DIRECTORIES

Discharging

USE RETURN OF INFORMATION SOURCES

DISCOUNT

NT NET BOOK AGREEMENT
RT ACQUISITION
PERIODICALS

DISCUSSION GROUPS

BT INTERNET INFORMATION SOURCES
NT ABUSE-L

DISCUSSIONS

SN *Information sources containing discussions*
BT INFORMATION SOURCES

DISPLAY OF NEW ARRIVALS

BT CAS
RT PUBLICITY

DISPLAY STANDS

BT STANDS (FURNITURE)

Dissertations

USE THESIS

DISTILLED CLASS

BT CLASS

DISTRIBUTION

BT MARKETING MIX

DISTRICT GOVERNMENT (ZHILA

PARISHAD) LIBRARIES
BT GOVERNMENT LIBRARIES

DISTRICT LIBRARIES
BT LIBRARIES

DIVISIONAL LIBRARIES
BT LIBRARIES

DO IT YOURSELF
BT INFORMATION SOURCES

DOCTORAL STUDENTS
BT STUDENTS

DOCUMENT DELIVERY SERVICES
UF Document supply services
BT SERVICES
NT COMMERCIAL DOCUMENT DELIVERY SERVICES
COMPUTERIZED DOCUMENT DELIVERY SERVICES
ELECTRONIC DOCUMENT DELIVERY SERVICES
ONLINE DOCUMENT DELIVERY SERVICES
RT APPLICATION
CHARGING (LEVYING MONETARY CHARGES)
COPYRIGHT
DIGITAL INFORMATION SOURCES
DIGITAL LIBRARIES
FEE
INFORMATION TECHNOLOGY
INTERNET
PROBLEMS
REMOTE USERS
RESEARCH
SCIENCE INFORMATION CENTRES
SDI
UNIVERSITY LIBRARIES

Document supply services

USE DOCUMENT DELIVERY SERVICES

Documentation services

USE INFORMATION SERVICES

Documents

USE INFORMATION SOURCES

DONATIONS

BT FINANCE

DRAMATIZATIONS

SN *A dramatized version*

BT INFORMATION SOURCES

DRAWING PAPER INFORMATION SOURCES

SN *Information source produced on drawing paper*

BT PAPER BASED INFORMATION SOURCES

DRINKING WATER FACILITY

BT FACILITIES

RT POSTGRADUATE STUDENTS
UNIVERSITY LIBRARIES

DSS

USE DECISION SUPPORT SYSTEM

DUPLICATION

RT INFORMATION SOURCES
WEEDING

DUTIES

USE FUNCTIONS

DVD

UF Digital Video Disk

BT STORAGE TECHNOLOGY

EASE OF USE

RT EVALUATION
SOFTWARES

E-Books

USE DIGITAL BOOKS

ECONOMIC HISTORY
BT INFORMATION SOURCES
NT REVIEW

EDITION (BIBLIOGRAPHIC DESCRIPTION)
SN *A description in an entry*
BT BIBLIOGRAPHIC DESCRIPTION
NT ABRIDGED EDITIONS

EDITIONS (INFORMATION SOURCES)
NT ABRIDGED EDITIONS
AUTHORIZED EDITIONS
BANNED EDITIONS
CHEAP EDITIONS
DELUXE EDITIONS
ILLUSTRATED EDITIONS
LIBRARY EDITIONS
LIMITED EDITIONS
PIRATED EDITIONS
PRESCRIBED EDITIONS
REPRINT EDITIONS
REVISED EDITIONS
SPECIAL EDITIONS

EDITORS
BT COLLABORATORS

EDUCATION COLLEGE LIBRARIES
BT COLLEGE LIBRARIES
RT SELECTION (INFORMATION SOURCES)

EFFECT
RT GOVERNMENT LIBRARIES
INFORMATION TECHNOLOGY
ORGANIZATION
OUTSOURCING
UNDER GRADUATE STUDENTS
UNIVERSITY LIBRARIES

USER EDUCATION

EFFICIENCY

E-journals

USE DIGITAL PERIODICALS

Electronic books

USE DIGITAL BOOKS

ELECTRONIC DOCUMENT DELIVERY SERVICES

BT DOCUMENT DELIVERY SERVICES

RT COST

DELIVERY TIME

EVALUATION

NATIONAL LIBRARIES

PUBLIC LIBRARIES

SUBJECT COVERAGE

Electronic information sources

USE DIGITAL INFORMATION SOURCES

Electronic journals

USE DIGITAL PERIODICALS

Electronic libraries

USE DIGITAL LIBRARIES

Electronic mail

USE E-MAIL

ELECTRONIC PUBLISHING

RT COLLECTION DEVELOPMENT

IMPACT

ELEMENTARY INFORMATION SOURCES

BT INFORMATION SOURCES

ELEMENTARY SCHOOL STUDENTS

BT SCHOOL STUDENTS

E-MAIL

UF Electronic mail

BT INTERNET

NT MULTIMEDIA E-MAIL

RT APPLICATION
NETWORKED ACADEMIC LIBRARIES

EMOTIONAL INFORMATION SOURCES
BT INFORMATION SOURCES

EMPTY DIGITS
BT NOTATIONAL DIGITS

EMPTY EMPTYING DIGITS
BT NOTATIONAL DIGITS

EMPTYING DIGITS
BT NOTATIONAL DIGITS

ENCYCLOPAEDIAS
BT REFERENCE SOURCES
NT CD-ROM ENCYCLOPAEDIAS

ENDOWMENT'S LIBRARIES
BT LIBRARIES

ENERGY FACET
BT FACETS
RT *PMEST*

ENERGY ISOLATES
BT SPECIAL ISOLATES

ENGINEERING COLLEGE LIBRARIES
BT COLLEGE LIBRARIES
RT SERVICES

ENTRIES
BT CATALOGUES
NT ADDED ENTRIES
MAIN ENTRY
RT *AREAS (CATALOGUE ENTRIES)*

ENUMERATIVE CLASSIFICATION SCHEMES
BT CLASSIFICATION SCHEMES (SPECIES)
RT *FACETED CLASSIFICATION SCHEMES*

*LIBRARY OF CONGRESS CLASSIFICATION SCHEME*

ENUMERATIVE DEVICE
BT DEVICES

ENVIRONMENTAL SCIENCE INFORMATION SYSTEM
BT INFORMATION SYSTEMS
RT SERVICES

EPHEMERA
BT INFORMATION SOURCES

EPISTEMOLOGY
RT IMPACT

ETHNIC USERS
BT USERS
RT PUBLIC LIBRARIES
SERVICES

EVALUATION
UF Assessment
NT QUALITATIVE EVALUATION
QUANTITATIVE EVALUATION
RT ACADEMIC LIBRARIES
ACQUISITION SECTION
ACRL STANDARDS
APPLICATION
AVAILABILITY
BLAIZLINE
BRANCH ACADEMIC LIBRARIES
BROADCASTING CENTRE LIBRARIES
COLLEGE LIBRARIES
COMPATIBILITY
CONJOINT ANALYSIS
CONTINGENT VALUATION
COST
COST-EFFECTIVENESS
DATABASES
DEFINITIVENESS OF ANSWERS

DELIVERY TIME
DIGITAL LIBRARIES
EASE OF USE
ELECTRONIC DOCUMENT
DELIVERY SERVICES
FILL RATE
FINANCE
FULL TEXT PERIODICALS DATABASES
GOVERNMENT PRIMARY
SCHOOL LIBRARIES
GUIDELINES
HOLDINGS
HTML METATAGS
IMAGES
INFORMATION NEEDS
INFORMATION STORAGE AND RETRIEVAL
INFORMATION TECHNOLOGY
INMAGIC
JOURNALISTS
MUNICIPALITY LIBRARIES
NATIONAL LIBRARIES
OPAC
ORIENTATION
PERFORMANCE
PRECISION
PROGRAMMES
RARE BOOKS WEBSITES
RECALL
REFERENCE SERVICE
REPORT GENERATION CAPACITY
RESEARCH
RESOURCE SHARING
SEARCH INTERFACE
SERVICES
SOFTWARES
STANDARDS (EVALUATION CRITERIA)

SUBJECT COVERAGE
TEXTBOOK'S AVAILABILITY
TITLE COVERAGE
UNIVERSITY LIBRARIES
WAITING TIME
WINISIS

EVALUATION SERVICES
BT CONSOLIDATION SERVICES

EXAMINATION PAPERS
BT INFORMATION SOURCES
RT DIGITISATION
PRESERVATION
UNIVERSITY LIBRARIES

EXCHANGE
BT ACQUISITION

EXCHANGED INFORMATION SOURCES
BT INFORMATION SOURCES

EXHIBITION CATALOGUES
BT TRADE CATALOGUES

EXHIBITION SECTION
BT SECTIONS

EXHIBITIONS
BT EXTENSION ACTIVITIES
RT APPLICATION
PUBLICITY
UNIVERSITY LIBRARIES
USER EDUCATION

EXPECTATIONS
RT REMOTE USERS

EXPERT SYSTEM
RT APPLICATION

EXPERT'S SUGGESTIONS
BT SELECTION TOOLS

EXTENSION ACTIVITIES
NT EXHIBITIONS

INTERVIEW WITH AUTHORS
LECTURES (TALKS)
LIBRARY WEEKS
READING ALOUD
STORY TELLING
RT PUBLICITY

FACETED CLASSIFICATION SCHEMES
BT CLASSIFICATION SCHEMES (SPECIES)
RT ENUMERATIVE CLASSIFICATION SCHEMES

FACETS
BT IDEA PLANE
NT ENERGY FACET
MATTER FACET
PERSONALITY FACET
SPACE FACET
TIME FACET

FACILITIES
NT DRINKING WATER FACILITY
READING ROOM FACILITY

Faculty status
USE ACADEMIC STATUS

FANCIFUL TITLE
BT TITLE

FEASIBILITY STUDY
BT RESEARCH
RT ACADEMIC LIBRARIES
COMPUTERIZATION

FEE
BT FINANCE
RT CHARGING (LEVYING MONETARY CHARGES)
DOCUMENT DELIVERY SERVICES
ILL
SERVICES

UNIVERSITY LIBRARIES

FEE-BASED INFORMATION SOURCES
BT INFORMATION SOURCES

FEE-BASED LIBRARIES
BT LIBRARIES

FEE-BASED PUBLIC LIBRARIES
BT PUBLIC LIBRARIES
RT OPINION
USERS

FEMALE STUDENTS
BT STUDENTS
RT INFORMATION SEEKING BEHAVIOR
UNIVERSITY LIBRARIES

FEMALE USERS
BT USERS

FESTSCHRIFTS
BT COMPOSITE BOOKS

FICTION THESAURI
SN *Thesauri of terms related with the literary form, fiction*
BT THESAURI
RT THESAURI CONSTRUCTION

FICTIONS (INFORMATION SOURCES)
BT LITERARY INFORMATION SOURCES
RT ALA GUIDELINES
INDEXING

FILL RATE
SN *Number of items provides / queries satisfied*
RT ACADEMIC LIBRARIES
EVALUATION
ILL
MEASURING
NETWORKED ACADEMIC LIBRARIES

PERFORMANCE
REFERENCE SERVICE

FINANCE
NT DONATIONS
FEE
FINE
GRANTS
RT ACADEMIC LIBRARIES
CONTROL
EVALUATION
GENERATION (FINANCE)
INTERNAL AUDIT
MARKETING
MISAPPROPRIATION
PUBLIC LIBRARIES
RESEARCH
RRRLF
SCIENCE AND TECHNOLOGY LIBRARIES
TECHNOLOGICAL LIBRARIES
UNIVERSITY LIBRARIES

FINANCIAL IMPACT
BT IMPACT
RT INFORMATION SOURCES
PUBLIC LIBRARIES
USE

FINANCIAL PROBLEMS
BT PROBLEMS
RT COLLECTION DEVELOPMENT
UNIVERSITY LIBRARIES

FINANCIAL PROVISION
RT LEGISLATION
PUBLIC LIBRARIES

FINE
BT FINANCE
RT ACADEMIC LIBRARIES

CHARGING (LEVYING MONETARY CHARGES)
DAMAGE
INFORMATION SOURCES
LOSS

FIRE (CAUSAL FACTOR)
BT NATURAL DISASTER

FLOPPY DISKS
BT STORAGE TECHNOLOGY

FOREIGN INFORMATION SOURCES
BT INFORMATION SOURCES
RT ACQUISITION

FOREIGN ORGANIZATION'S LIBRARIES
BT LIBRARIES

FOREIGN PERIODICALS
BT PERIODICALS

FORM CLASSES

FORM OF PUBLICATION
BT BOOK NUMBERS

FORMS
NT REQUEST FORMS
WEB BASED FORMS
RT APPLICATION
DESIGNING
HTML
ILL

FORMULA BOOKS
BT REFERENCE SOURCES

FREE INFORMATION SOURCES
UF Gratis information sources
BT INFORMATION SOURCES

FREE INTERNET INFORMATION SOURCES
BT INTERNET INFORMATION

SOURCES
RT ACCESS

FREE LIBRARIES
BT LIBRARIES

FREELY FACETED CLASSIFICATION SCHEMES
BT CLASSIFICATION SCHEMES (SPECIES)
RT *COLON CLASSIFICATION*

FRENCH INFORMATION SOURCES
BT INFORMATION SOURCES

FRENCH TEXTBOOKS
BT TEXTBOOKS
RT COST

FULL TEXT DATABASES
BT DATABASES
NT FULL TEXT PERIODICALS DATABASES

FULL TEXT PERIODICALS DATABASES
BT FULL TEXT DATABASES
RT ACCESS
EVALUATION
TITLE COVERAGE

FULL TIME PERSONNEL
BT PERSONNEL

FUMIGATION
RT INFORMATION SOURCES
PRESERVATION
PRINTED INFORMATION SOURCES
UNIVERSITY LIBRARIES

FUNCTIONS
UF Duties
RT IMPACT
INFORMATION TECHNOLOGY

NON-PROFESSIONAL PERSONNEL
PROFESSIONAL PERSONNEL
PERSONNEL

Fundamental categories
USE PMEST

FURNITURE
NT BOOK SUPPORTER
BOOK TROLLEYS
CATALOGUE CABINETS
CHAIRS
LADDERS
MAP CASES
METAL FURNITURE
PLASTIC FURNITURE
SHELVES
STANDS
TABLES
TRAYS
VERTICAL FILES
WOODEN FURNITURE

FUSED CLASS
BT CLASS

GAME THEORY
BT OPERATIONS RESEARCH

GAZETTED OFFICERS
BT USERS
RT GOVERNMENT DEPARTMENT LIBRARIES

GAZETTEERS
BT REFERENCE SOURCES

GENERAL PHASE RELATIONS
BT PHASE RELATIONS

GENERAL USERS
BT USERS

GENERATION (FINANCE)

RT FINANCE
MARKETING
SCIENCE AND TECHNOLOGY LIBRARIES
TECHNOLOGICAL LIBRARIES

GEOGRAPHICAL DEVICE
BT DEVICES

GEOGRAPHICAL INFORMATION SYSTEM
UF GIS
RT APPLICATION
BRANCH PUBLIC LIBRARIES
USE STUDY

GIANT INFORMATION SOURCES
SN *Over 45 cm height*
BT INFORMATION SOURCES

GIFTED INFORMATION SOURCES
BT INFORMATION SOURCES

GIFTS
BT ACQUISITION
RT POLICY

GIS
USE GEOGRAPHICAL INFORMATION SYSTEM

GLASS INFORMATION SOURCES
SN *Information printed on glass material*
BT INFORMATION SOURCES

GLOBES
BT INFORMATION SOURCES
RT CATALOGUING

GLOSSARIES
BT DICTIONARIES

GOLF INFORMATION SOURCES
BT INFORMATION SOURCES
RT SELECTION (INFORMATION SOURCES)

GOVERNMENT (AUTHORS)
BT CORPORATE AUTHORS

GOVERNMENT DEPARTMENT LIBRARIES
BT LIBRARIES
RT GAZETTED OFFICERS

GOVERNMENT INFORMATION SOURCES
UF Government publications
BT CORPORATE INFORMATION SOURCES
RT BRANCH NATIONAL LIBRARIES
USE

GOVERNMENT LIBRARIES
BT LIBRARIES
NT CENTRAL GOVERNMENT LIBRARIES
CORPORATION LIBRARIES
DISTRICT GOVERNMENT (ZHILA PARISHAD) LIBRARIES
LOCAL GOVERNMENT LIBRARIES
MUNICIPALITY LIBRARIES
STATE GOVERNMENT LIBRARIES
RT EFFECT
OUTSOURCING

GOVERNMENT PRIMARY SCHOOL LIBRARIES
BT PRIMARY SCHOOL LIBRARIES
RT EVALUATION

Government publications
USE GOVERNMENT INFORMATION SOURCES

GOVERNMENT SCHOOL LIBRARIES
BT SCHOOL LIBRARIES
RT HIGHER SALARY
MEDICAL FACILITIES
MOTIVATION
PERSONNEL

PROMOTION (SERVICE ADVANCEMENT)
RETIREMENT BENEFITS

GRANTS
BT FINANCE

GRAPHIC ABSTRACTS
BT ABSTRACTS

GRAPHIC THESAURI
BT THESAURI

GRAPHS
BT INFORMATION SOURCES

Gratis information sources
USE FREE INFORMATION SOURCES

GREY LITERATURE
BT INFORMATION SOURCES

GUARDIAN, THE
BT NEWSPAPERS
RT INDEXING

GUIDEBOOKS
BT REFERENCE SOURCES

GUIDELINES
NT ALA GUIDELINES
RT BEHAVIORAL PERFORMANCE
DEVELOPMENT
DIGITAL LIBRARIES
EVALUATION
INFORMATION PERSONNEL
INFORMATION SOURCES
INFORMATION TECHNOLOGY
REFERENCE PERSONNEL
SOFTWARES
WEEDING

HALF-CLOTH BOUND INFORMATION SOURCES
BT CLOTH BOUND INFORMATION SOURCES

HALF-LEATHER BOUND

INFORMATION SOURCES

BT LEATHER BOUND INFORMATION SOURCES

HALF TITLE

BT TITLE

HAND-BOUND INFORMATION SOURCES

BT INFORMATION SOURCES

HAND-MADE PAPER INFORMATION SOURCES

SN *Information printed on handmade paper*

BT PAPER BASED INFORMATION SOURCES

HARDCOVER BOUND INFORMATION SOURCES

BT INFORMATION SOURCES

HARDWARE

BT COMPUTERS

HEADING AREA

BT AREAS

HEATING

HIGHER SALARY

RT GOVERNMENT SCHOOL LIBRARIES
MOTIVATION
PERSONNEL
PRIVATE SCHOOL LIBRARIES

HIGHER SECONDARY SCHOOL LIBRARIES

BT SECONDARY SCHOOL LIBRARIES

RT READING HABIT
STATUS
STUDENTS

HISTORICAL BIBLIOGRAPHIES

BT BIBLIOGRAPHIES

HOLDINGS

UF Collection

NT CORE HOLDINGS

RT ACADEMIC LIBRARIES

ACCESS
COST
DIGITAL LIBRARIES
DIGITAL PERIODICALS
EVALUATION
INSURING
PROTECTION

HOMEPAGES
BT WEBSITES
RT PUBLICITY
UNIVERSITY LIBRARIES

HOME PERIODICALS
UF In-house journals
In-house periodicals
BT PERIODICALS

HTML
BT PROGRAMMING LANGUAGES
RT APPLICATION
DESIGNING
FORMS
ILL
REQUEST FORMS
WEB BASED FORMS

HTML METATAGS
BT METATAGS
RT EVALUATION

HUMAN BEINGS (CAUSAL FACTOR)

HUMANITIES INFORMATION CENTRES
BT INFORMATION CENTRES
RT PLANNING

HUMANITIES INFORMATION SOURCES
BT INFORMATION SOURCES

HUMANITIES TEXTBOOKS

BT. TEXTBOOKS
RT COST

HUMANITIES THESAURI
BT THESAURI
RT NEEDS

HUMOUR
RT ACADEMIC LIBRARIES
APPLICATION
IMPROVEMENT
WORKING CONDITION

HYBRID LIBRARIES
BT SPECIAL LIBRARIES
RT COLLECTION DEVELOPMENT
JOB DESIGN
PERSONNEL
QUALIFICATIONS
TECHNICAL PROCESSING

IDA VERSION
BT JAVA
RT APPLICATION
RETROSPECTIVE CONVERSION

IDEA PLANE
BT PLANES OF WORK
NT CLASS (SUBJECTS)
DEVICES
FACETS
ISOLATES
PHASE RELATIONS

IDENTIFICATION
RT APPLICATION
AUTOMATIC
BIBLIOGRAPHIC DESCRIPTION
CORE HOLDINGS
PHYSICAL LAYOUT OF TITLE PAGE
RETROSPECTIVE CONVERSION

ILL

UF Interlending

Inter library loan

BT SERVICES

NT CENTRALIZED ILL

COMPUTERIZED ILL

SELF-CHARGED ILL

WEB BASED ILL

RT ACADEMIC LIBRARIES

APPLICATION

CHARGING (LEVYING MONETARY CHARGES)

COMMERCIAL DOCUMENT DELIVERY SERVICES

COST

DESIGNING

FEE

FILL RATE

FORMS

HTML

MEASURING

NETWORKED ACADEMIC LIBRARIES

NUCSSI

PERFORMANCE

PRICING

REQUEST FORMS

RESEARCH LIBRARIES

STANDARDIZATION

UNIVERSITY LIBRARIES

WEB BASED FORMS

ILL PERSONNEL

BT PROFESSIONAL PERSONNEL

RT TRAINING

ILLITERATE USERS

BT USERS

ILLUSTRATED EDITIONS

BT EDITIONS

ILLUSTRATORS

BT COLLABORATORS

IMAGE DATABASES

BT DATABASES

IMAGES

RT EVALUATION
RARE BOOKS WEBSITES
UNIVERSITY LIBRARIES

IMPACT

NT FINANCIAL IMPACT
POLITICAL IMPACT
SOCIAL IMPACT

RT ACADEMIC LIBRARIES
ATTITUDE
CD-ROM
CHAIN INDEXING
CLASSIFICATION SCHEMES (EXAMPLES)
COLLECTION DEVELOPMENT
COMPUTERIZATION
COMPUTERS
DIGITAL INFORMATION SOURCES
ELECTRONIC PUBLISHING
EPISTEMOLOGY
FUNCTIONS
INFORMATION TECHNOLOGY
IN-SERVICE TRAINING
INTERNET
LAN
LIBRARIANS
LIBRARIAN'S ATTITUDE
LISA
MEDIUM SIZED LIBRARIES
MULTIDISCIPLINARITY
MULTIMEDIA

ORGANIZATION
PARAPROFESSIONAL PERSONNEL
PERSONNEL
REFERENCE PERSONNEL
SCHOOL LIBRARIES
SERVICES
SUBJECT HEADINGS
TECHNOLOGICAL UNIVERSITY LIBRARIES
THESIS
TRAINING
USE
USERS
VALUE ADDED INFORMATION SERVICES

IMPRINT
BT BIBLIOGRAPHIC DESCRIPTION
NT PLACE OF PUBLICATION
PUBLISHER
YEAR OF PUBLICATION

IMPROVEMENT
RT ACADEMIC LIBRARIES
APPLICATION
HUMOUR
PROPOSALS
SCHOOL LIBRARIES
SERVICES
WORKING CONDITION

INAUGURAL LECTURES
SN *Information sources containing inaugural lectures*
BT LECTURES

INDEX TO THE CLASSIFICATION SCHEDULE
NT RELATIVE INDEX
SPECIFIC INDEX

INDEXERS

BT INFORMATION PERSONNEL

INDEXES

BT INFORMATION SOURCES

NT ONLINE INDEXES

PRINTED INDEXES

RT *ABSTRACTS*

INDEXING

NT COOPERATIVE INDEXING

RT ALA GUIDELINES

APPLICATION

*CATALOGUING*

*CLASSIFICATION*

COMPUTERS

DBASE IV

FICTIONS (INFORMATION SOURCES)

GUARDIAN, THE

*INDEXING LANGUAGES*

INTERNET INFORMATION SOURCES

LOCAL NEWSPAPERS

THEORIES OF INDEXING

INDEXING LANGUAGES

NT CONTROLLED LANGUAGE

NATURAL LANGUAGE

RT *INDEXING*

INDEXING PERIODICALS

BT PERIODICALS

RT *ABSTRACTING PERIODICALS*

INDEXING SECTION

BT INFORMATION SECTION

INDEXING SERVICES

RT TECHNOLOGICAL LIBRARIES

INDEXING SYSTEMS

NT CITATION INDEXING

KEYWORD INDEXING

POST COORDINATE INDEXING SYSTEM

PRE-COORDINATE INDEXING SYSTEMS

INDIA PAPER INFORMATION SOURCES
BT PAPER BASED INFORMATION SOURCES

INDICATIVE ABSTRACTS
BT ABSTRACTS

INDICATOR DIGITS
BT NOTATIONAL DIGITS

INDIGENOUS DATABASES
BT DATABASES
RT SCIENCE AND TECHNOLOGY LIBRARIES
USE

INDUSTRIAL LIBRARIES
BT SPECIAL LIBRARIES
RT APPLICATION
ISO 9000

INFLIBNET
UF Information and Library Network
BT WAN

INFLUENCE PHASE RELATIONS
BT PHASE RELATIONS

INFORMATION
BT INFORMATION SOURCES
RT INFORMATION AUDIT

INFORMATION ANALYSIS CENTRES
BT INFORMATION CENTRES

Information and Library Network
USE INFLIBNET

INFORMATION AUDIT
RT INFORMATION

INFORMATION BROKERS
BT INFORMATION PERSONNEL

RT ONLINE CONSULTANCY SERVICES

INFORMATION CENTRES

NT DEFENCE INFORMATION CENTRES

HUMANITIES INFORMATION CENTRES

INFORMATION ANALYSIS CENTRES

LAW INFORMATION CENTRES

SCIENCE INFORMATION CENTRES

SOCIAL SCIENCE INFORMATION CENTRES

TECHNOLOGICAL INFORMATION CENTRES

RT SERVICES

INFORMATION DEMANDS

RT MEASURING

USERS

INFORMATION EXTRACTION

BT INFORMATION STORAGE AND RETRIEVAL

INFORMATION NEEDS

BT NEEDS

RT COUNCILLORS

EVALUATION

JOURNALISTS

PARENTS

REMOTE USERS

RURAL USERS

UNIVERSITY LIBRARIES

INFORMATION PERSONNEL

BT PROFESSIONAL PERSONNEL

NT ABSTRACTORS

INDEXERS

INFORMATION BROKERS

TRANSLATORS

RT BEHAVIORAL PERFORMANCE

GUIDELINES

INFORMATION RETRIEVAL

BT INFORMATION STORAGE AND RETRIEVAL

NT BIBLIOGRAPHIC INFORMATION RETRIEVAL

OFFLINE INFORMATION RETRIEVAL

ONLINE INFORMATION RETRIEVAL
TEXTUAL INFORMATION RETRIEVAL
RT INTERNET
RESEARCH
USERS
Z39.50
STANDARDS

INFORMATION SECTION
BT SECTIONS
NT ABSTRACTING SECTION
INDEXING SECTION
REPROGRAPHY SECTION
TRANSLATION SECTION

INFORMATION SEEKING BEHAVIOR
RT APPLICATION
AWARDED FARMERS
CD-ROM BIBLIOGRAPHIC DATABASES
COMPUTERS
DIGITAL LIBRARIES
FEMALE STUDENTS
INTERNET USERS
LITERARY WRITERS
MONITORING
PHYSICAL SCIENTISTS
POPLINE
POSTGRADUATE STUDENTS
REMOTE USERS
SOCIAL SCIENTISTS
UNIVERSITY LIBRARIES
USERS

INFORMATION SERVICES
UF Documentation services
BT SERVICES
NT VALUE ADDED INFORMATION SERVICES

INFORMATION SOURCES

UF Documents

Publications

NT ABRIDGEMENTS

ADAPTATIONS

ADVANCE COPIES

ADVANCED INFORMATION SOURCES

ARCHIVES

BARK INFORMATION SOURCES

BENGALI INFORMATION SOURCES

BOOKS

BRAILLE INFORMATION SOURCES

CARTOONS

CHARTS

CHILDREN INFORMATION SOURCES

CLASSICS

CLASSIFIED (SECRET) INFORMATION SOURCES

CLAY INFORMATION SOURCES

CLIP BOUND INFORMATION SOURCES

CLOTH BOUND INFORMATION SOURCES

CLOTH INFORMATION SOURCES

CODE BOOKS

COMICS

COMMENTARIES

COMPOSITE BOOKS

COPYRIGHTED INFORMATION SOURCES

CORPORATE INFORMATION SOURCES

CREATIVE INFORMATION SOURCES

CURRENT INFORMATION SOURCES

DALIT LITERATURE

DATA

DEBATES

DIGITAL INFORMATION SOURCES

DISCUSSIONS

DO IT YOURSELF
DRAMATIZATIONS
ECONOMIC HISTORY
ELEMENTARY INFORMATION SOURCES
EMOTIONAL INFORMATION SOURCES
EPHEMERA
EXAMINATION PAPERS
EXCHANGED INFORMATION SOURCES
FEE-BASED INFORMATION SOURCES
FOREIGN INFORMATION SOURCES
FREE INFORMATION SOURCES
FRENCH INFORMATION SOURCES
GIANT INFORMATION SOURCES
GIFTED INFORMATION SOURCES
GLASS INFORMATION SOURCES
GLOBES
GOLF INFORMATION SOURCES
GRAPHS
GREY LITERATURE
HAND BOUND INFORMATION SOURCES
HARDCOVER INFORMATION SOURCES
HUMANITIES INFORMATION SOURCES
INDEXES
INFORMATION
INFORMATIONAL INFORMATION SOURCES
INLAND INFORMATION SOURCES
INPRINT INFORMATION SOURCES
INSPIRATIONAL INFORMATION SOURCES
INTELLECTUAL INFORMATION SOURCES (QUALITY OF MENTAL APPEAL)
INTELLECTUAL PROPERTY
INTERNET INFORMATION SOURCES
INTERVIEWS
KNOWLEDGE (CONTENTS OF INFORMATION SOURCES)

LEAF INFORMATION SOURCES
LEATHER BOUND INFORMATION SOURCES
LECTURES
LEGAL DEPOSITED INFORMATION SOURCES
LETTERS
LIBRARY SCIENCE INFORMATION SOURCES
LITERARY INFORMATION SOURCES
LOOSE LEAF INFORMATION SOURCES
MACHINE BOUND INFORMATION SOURCES
MANUSCRIPTS
MAPS
METALLIC INFORMATION SOURCES
MORAL INFORMATION SOURCES
MULTI-VOLUME INFORMATION SOURCES
MUSIC INFORMATION SOURCES
NARRATIONS
NON-BOOK MATERIALS
NOVELISATIONS
OUT OF PRINT INFORMATION SOURCES
OVERSIZED INFORMATION SOURCES
PAMPHLETS
PAPERBACK INFORMATION SOURCES
PAPER BASED INFORMATION SOURCES
PAPYRUS INFORMATION SOURCES
PARODIES
PATENTS
PERIODICALS
PICTURES
PLANS
PLASTIC BOUND INFORMATION SOURCES
PLASTIC INFORMATION SOURCES
POLITICAL INFORMATION SOURCES
POPULAR INFORMATION SOURCES
PRACTICE BOOKS
PRE-PRINTS

PRINTED INFORMATION SOURCES
PRIVATE CIRCULATION
(INFORMATION SOURCES FOR)
PRIVATE PUBLICATIONS
PROMPT BOOKS
PROSPECTUS
PUBLIC RELATION MATERIAL
PURCHASED INFORMATION SOURCES
RARE BOOKS
READING ROOM INFORMATION SOURCES
REFERENCE SOURCES
REPORTS
REPROGRAPHED INFORMATION SOURCES
RESEARCH INFORMATION SOURCES
RESERVED INFORMATION SOURCES
RETROSPECTIVE INFORMATION SOURCES
SCIENCE INFORMATION SOURCES
SELECTIONS
SHORT COMMUNICATIONS
SHORTHAND INFORMATION SOURCES
SIMPLE BOOKS
SINGLE VOLUME INFORMATION SOURCES
SKIN INFORMATION SOURCES
SOCIAL INFORMATION SOURCES
SPIRAL BOUND INFORMATION SOURCES
SPIRITUAL INFORMATION SOURCES
STANDARDS
STONE INFORMATION SOURCES
SUPPLEMENTS
SURVEYS
TEXTBOOKS
THESIS
TRADE LITERATURE
TRANSLATIONS
TREATISE
TYPED INFORMATION SOURCES

UNDERSIZED INFORMATION SOURCES
UNPUBLISHED INFORMATION SOURCES
VELLUM INFORMATION SOURCES
VERSIFICATIONS
VETERINARY INFORMATION SOURCES
WOODEN INFORMATION SOURCES

RT ACADEMIC LIBRARIES
ADEQUATE LIGHT
CHARGING (LEVYING MONETARY CHARGES)
CONSERVATION
CONTENTS
DAMAGE
DIGITISATION
DUPLICATION
FINANCIAL IMPACT
FINE
FUMIGATION
GUIDELINES
LANGUAGE
LOSS
MEDICAL LIBRARIES
MICROFILMING (PRESERVATION METHOD)
MUTILATION
NON-CIRCULATION
OBSOLESCENCE
PHOTOCOPYING (PRESERVATION METHOD)
PRESERVATION
PROPER HOUSING
PUBLIC LIBRARIES
RIGHT TEMPERATURE
SELECTION (INFORMATION SOURCES)
STYLE (OF WRITING)
TEACHER'S ROLE
UNIVERSITY LIBRARIES

USE
WEEDING

INFORMATION STORAGE AND RETRIEVAL
UF ISR
NT ACCESS
INFORMATION EXTRACTION
INFORMATION RETRIEVAL
QUERY FORMULATION
SEARCH
RT APPLICATION
COMPUTERS
EVALUATION
PERFORMANCE
*PRECISION*
*RECALL*
*THESAURI*

INFORMATION SYSTEMS
NT AGRICULTURAL INFORMATION SYSTEM
ENVIRONMENTAL SCIENCE INFORMATION SYSTEM

INFORMATION TECHNOLOGY
UF IT
BT LIBRARY TECHNOLOGY
NT AUDIO VISUAL TECHNOLOGY
BARCODES
COMPUTERS
MULTIMEDIA
NETWORKS
PRINTERS
PROGRAMMING LANGUAGES
REPROGRAPHIC TECHNOLOGY
SCANNERS
STORAGE TECHNOLOGY
RT APPLICATION

COMMERCIAL LIBRARIES
CREATION
DOCUMENT DELIVERY SERVICES
EFFECT
EVALUATION
FUNCTIONS
GUIDELINES
IMPACT
ORGANIZATION
PERSONNEL
PROBLEMS
PUBLIC LIBRARIES
RARE BOOKS BIBLIOGRAPHIC DATABASES
REFERENCE PERSONNEL
SPECIAL LIBRARIES
UNIVERSITY LIBRARIES
USERS
VALUE ADDED INFORMATION SERVICES

INFORMATIONAL INFORMATION SOURCES
SN *Information sources having informational value*
BT INFORMATION SOURCES

INFORMATIONAL LIBRARIES
BT LIBRARIES

INFORMATIVE ABSTRACTS
BT ABSTRACTS

IN-HOUSE BIBLIOGRAPHIC DATABASES
BT BIBLIOGRAPHIC DATABASES
RT CREATION
MAINTENANCE
PROBLEMS

In-house journals
USE HOUSE PERIODICALS

In-house periodicals

USE HOUSE PERIODICALS

Initiation

USE ORIENTATION

INLAND INFORMATION SOURCES

BT INFORMATION SOURCES

InMAGIC

BT SOFTWARES

RT EVALUATION

REPORT GENERATION CAPACITY

INPRINT INFORMATION SOURCES

BT INFORMATION SOURCES

RT *OUT OF PRINT INFORMATION SOURCES*

INSECTS (CAUSAL FACTOR)

BT BIOLOGICAL CAUSES

IN-SERVICE TRAINING

BT TRAINING

RT IMPACT

LIBRARIANS

SCHOOL LIBRARIES

INSPIRATIONAL INFORMATION SOURCES

BT INFORMATION SOURCES

INSTITUTIONS (AUTHORS)

BT CORPORATE AUTHORS

INSTITUTIONAL INFORMATION SOURCES

BT CORPORATE INFORMATION SOURCES

NT COMMERCIAL INSTITUTION'S PUBLICATIONS

CONFERENCE PUBLICATIONS

RESEARCH INSTITUTION'S PUBLICATIONS

UNIVERSITY PUBLICATIONS

INSURANCE LIBRARIES

BT SPECIAL LIBRARIES

INSURING

RT ACADEMIC LIBRARIES

HOLDINGS

INTELLECTUAL (QUALITY OF MENTAL APPEAL) INFORMATION SOURCES

BT INFORMATION SOURCES

INTELLECTUAL PROPERTY

BT INFORMATION SOURCES

INTELLECTUAL PROPERTY RIGHTS

UF IPR

Interlending

USE ILL

Inter library loan

USE ILL

INTER SUBJECT PHASE RELATIONS

BT PHASE RELATIONS

INTERNAL AUDIT

RT CONTROL

FINANCE

MISAPPROPRIATION

PUBLIC LIBRARIES

INTERNATIONAL CLASSIFICATION

BT CLASSIFICATION SCHEMES (SPECIES)

International Information System for Agricultural Science and Technology

USE AGRIS

INTERNATIONAL LIBRARIES

BT LIBRARIES

International Organization for
Standardization Standards

USE ISO STANDARDS

INTERNATIONAL
ORGANIZATION'S
LIBRARIES

BT LIBRARIES

International Standard
Book Numbers

USE ISBN

International Standard
Serial Number

USE ISSN

INTERNATIONAL STUDENTS

BT STUDENTS

RT TECHNOLOGICAL UNIVERSITY
LIBRARIES

USE

INTERNATIONAL USERS

BT USERS

INTERNET

BT SELECTION TOOLS
WAN

NT E-MAIL
WWW

RT APPLICATION
CATALOGUING
COLLECTION DEVELOPMENT
DOCUMENT DELIVERY SERVICES
IMPACT
INFORMATION RETRIEVAL
RARE BOOKS
RESEARCH
RESOURCE SHARING

INTERNET BASED SERVICES
BT SERVICES
RT PUBLIC LIBRARIES

INTERNET INDUSTRIAL INFORMATION SOURCES
SN *Information sources available on the Internet on the subject industry*
BT INTERNET INFORMATION SOURCES

INTERNET INFORMATION SOURCES
BT INFORMATION SOURCES
NT FREE INTERNET INFORMATION SOURCES
DISCUSSION GROUPS
INTERNET INDUSTRIAL INFORMATION SOURCES
INTERNET MULTIMEDIA DATABASES
INTERNET PERIODICALS
INTERNET REFERENCE SOURCES
WEBSITES
RT CATALOGUING
INDEXING
PROFESSIONAL PERSONNEL
RESEARCH USE

INTERNET MULTIMEDIA DATABASES
SN *Multimedia databases available on the Internet*
BT INTERNET INFORMATION SOURCES
MULTIMEDIA DATABASES
RT PERSONNEL
ROLE
USE

INTERNET PERIODICALS
SN *Periodicals available on the Internet*
BT INTERNET INFORMATION SOURCES
PERIODICALS

NT LIBRARY SCIENCE INFORMATION SOURCES

INTERNET REFERENCE SOURCES

SN *Reference sources available on the Internet*

BT INTERNET INFORMATION SOURCES

REFERENCE SOURCES

INTERNET USERS

BT USERS

RT INFORMATION SEEKING BEHAVIOUR

INTERVIEW (PERSONNEL MANAGEMENT)

BT RECRUITMENT

INTERVIEW WITH AUTHOR

BT EXTENSION ACTIVITIES

RT CHILDREN USERS

DEVELOPMENT

READING HABIT

INTERVIEWS

SN *Information sources containing interviews*

BT INFORMATION SOURCES

INTRA-ARRAY PHASE RELATIONS

BT PHASE RELATIONS

INTRA-FACET PHASE RELATIONS

BT PHASE RELATIONS

IPR

USE INTELLECTUAL PROPERTY RIGHTS

ISBD (A)

BT BIBLIOGRAPHIC DESCRIPTION STANDARDS

ISBD (CF)

BT BIBLIOGRAPHIC DESCRIPTION STANDARDS

ISBD (CM)

BT BIBLIOGRAPHIC DESCRIPTION STANDARDS

ISBD (CP)

BT BIBLIOGRAPHIC DESCRIPTION STANDARDS

ISBD (ER)

BT BIBLIOGRAPHIC DESCRIPTION STANDARDS

ISBD(G)

BT BIBLIOGRAPHIC DESCRIPTION STANDARDS

ISBD (M)

BT BIBLIOGRAPHIC DESCRIPTION STANDARDS

ISBD (NBM)

BT BIBLIOGRAPHIC DESCRIPTION STANDARDS

ISBD (PM)

BT BIBLIOGRAPHIC DESCRIPTION STANDARDS

ISBD (S)

BT BIBLIOGRAPHIC DESCRIPTION STANDARDS

ISBN

UF International Standard Book Numbers
BT STANDARD NUMBERS
RT ISSN

ISO 9000

BT ISO STANDARDS
RT AERONAUTICAL RESEARCH LIBRARIES
APPLICATION
INDUSTRIAL LIBRARIES
SERVICES

ISO STANDARDS

UF International Organization for Standardization Standards
BT STANDARDS
NT ISO 9000
RT BINDING

ISOLATES

BT IDEA PLANE
NT COMMON ISOLATES
SPECIAL ISOLATES

ISR

USE INFORMATION STORAGE AND RETRIEVAL

ISSN
UF International Standard Serial Number
BT STANDARD NUMBERS
RT *ISBN*

ISSUING
UF Charging (circulation)
Lending
BT CIRCULATION
RT RETURN OF INFORMATION SOURCES

IT
USE INFORMATION TECHNOLOGY

JAVA
BT PROGRAMMING LANGUAGES
NT IDA VERSION

JOB ANALYSIS
BT PERSONNEL MANAGEMENT

JOB DESIGN
BT PERSONNEL MANAGEMENT
RT HYBRID LIBRARIES

JOB DISSATISFACTION
RT ADVERSE CONDITION
PERSONNEL

JOB SATISFACTION
RT ACADEMIC LIBRARIES
COLLEGE LIBRARIANS
LIBRARIANS
PERSONNEL
UNIVERSITY LIBRARIES
USERS

JOURNALISTS
BT USERS
RT EVALUATION
INFORMATION NEEDS

Journals
USE PERIODICALS

JUNIOR CATALOGUERS
BT CATALOGUERS
RT SKILLS

JUNIOR COLLEGE LIBRARIES
BT COLLEGE LIBRARIES

JUNIOR PERSONNEL
BT PERSONNEL

JUNIOR REFERENCE PERSONNEL
BT REFERENCE PERSONNEL
RT ORIENTATION
ROLE
SENIOR LIBRARIANS

KANTOR METHOD
RT ACADEMIC LIBRARIES
AVAILABILITY
MEASURING
TEXT BOOKS

KARDEX
BT RECORDING OF PERIODICALS

Keyword And Context
USE KWAC

Keyword in context
USE KWIC

KEYWORD INDEXING
BT INDEXING SYSTEMS
NT KWAC
KWIC
KWOC

Keyword out of context
USE KWOC

KNOWLEDGE
SN *Information sources containing knowledge*
BT INFORMATION SOURCES

KNOWLEDGE (QUALITIES
OF PERSONNEL)

RT DIGITAL LIBRARIES
PROFESSIONAL PERSONNEL

KNOWLEDGE BASED SYSTEM
RT APPLICATION
TECHNICAL PROCESSING

KNOWLEDGE MANAGEMENT
BT MANAGEMENT

KWAC
UF Key word and context
BT KEYWORD INDEXING

KWIC
UF Key word in context
BT KEYWORD INDEXING

KWOC
UF Key word out of context
BT KEYWORD INDEXING

LABELING
BT PHYSICAL PROCESSING

LACK OF LIBRARY AWARENESS
RT ANXIETY
USERS

LADDERS
BT FURNITURE

LAN
UF Local Area Networks
BT NETWORKS
RT APPLICATION
IMPACT
MANAGEMENT
MEDIUM SIZED LIBRARIES
RESOURCE SHARING
SERVICES
WAN

LANGUAGE (INFORMATION SOURCES)

RT INFORMATION SOURCES
OBSOLESCENCE

LANGUAGE ISOLATES
BT COMMON ISOLATES

LANGUAGE PART OF BOOK NUMBERS
BT BOOK NUMBERS

LARGE LIBRARIES
SN *Library holding more than 100000 volumes*
BT LIBRARIES

LAW INFORMATION CENTRES
BT INFORMATION CENTRES

LAW LIBRARIES
BT SPECIAL LIBRARIES
RT ONLINE DATABASES
USE

LEADING
SN *Providing leadership*
BT PERSONNEL MANAGEMENT

LEAF INFORMATION SOURCES
SN *Information written on leaves of tree*
BT INFORMATION SOURCES
NT PALM LEAF INFORMATION SOURCES

LEARNED PERIODICALS
BT PERIODICALS

LEATHER BINDING
BT BINDING

LEATHER BOUND INFORMATION SOURCES
BT INFORMATION SOURCES
NT HALF LEATHER BOUND INFORMATION SOURCES

LECTURES (PRINTED)

BT INFORMATION SOURCES

NT BROADCAST LECTURES

INAUGURAL LECTURES

LECTURES (TALKS)

BT EXTENSION ACTIVITIES

LEDGER PAPER INFORMATION SOURCES

BT PAPER BASED INFORMATION SOURCES

LEDGER SYSTEM

BT CIRCULATION SYSTEMS

LEGAL DEPOSITED INFORMATION SOURCES

BT INFORMATION SOURCES

LEGAL DEPOSITS

BT ACQUISITION

LEGISLATION

RT FINANCIAL PROVISION

PUBLIC LIBRARIES

Lending

USE ISSUING

LENDING LIBRARIES

BT LIBRARIES

LETTER BY LETTER ALPHABETIZATION

BT ALPHABETIZATION

RT WORD BY WORD ALPHABETIZATION

LETTERS

BT INFORMATION SOURCES

LIBRARIANS

BT PROFESSIONAL PERSONNEL

NT ASSISTANT LIBRARIANS

CHIEF LIBRARIANS

DEPUTY LIBRARIANS

SENIOR LIBRARIANS
RT ACADEMIC LIBRARIES
ACADEMIC STATUS
ACCOUNTABILITY
AUDIO LIBRARIES
BRAILLE LIBRARIES
COLLEGE LIBRARIES
CREATIVITY
DIGITAL INFORMATION SOURCES
IMPACT
IN-SERVICE TRAINING
JOB SATISFACTION
MISINFORMATION
QUALIFICATIONS
ROLE
SALARY
SCHOOL LIBRARIES
TRAINING
UNIVERSITY LIBRARIES
USE

LIBRARIAN'S ATTITUDE
BT ATTITUDE
RT COMPUTER
IMPACT
RESOURCE SHARING
TRAINING

LIBRARIES
NT ACADEMIC LIBRARIES
BRANCH LIBRARIES
CENTRAL LIBRARIES
CENTRALIZED LIBRARIES
CHARITABLE INSTITUTION'S LIBRARIES
CITY LIBRARIES
CLOSED ACCESS LIBRARIES
CLUB'S LIBRARIES

COMMUNITY LIBRARIES
CONTACT LIBRARIES
COOPERATIVE LIBRARIES
CULTURAL INSTITUTION'S LIBRARIES
DECENTRALIZED LIBRARIES
DEPARTMENTAL LIBRARIES
DEPOSITORY LIBRARIES
DISTRICT LIBRARIES
DIVISIONAL LIBRARIES
ENDOWMENT'S LIBRARIES
FEE BASED LIBRARIES
FOREIGN ORGANIZATION'S LIBRARIES
FREE LIBRARIES
GOVERNMENT DEPARTMENT LIBRARIES
GOVERNMENT LIBRARIES
INFORMATIONAL LIBRARIES
INTERNATIONAL LIBRARIES
INTERNATIONAL ORGANIZATION'S LIBRARIES
LARGE LIBRARIES
LENDING LIBRARIES
MEDIUM SIZED LIBRARIES
METROPOLITAN LIBRARIES
NATIONAL LIBRARIES
OPEN ACCESS LIBRARIES
PARTIALLY OPEN ACCESS LIBRARIES
PRIVATE LIBRARIES
PROFIT MAKING LIBRARIES
PUBLIC LIBRARIES
RECREATIONAL LIBRARIES
REFERENCE LIBRARIES
REGIONAL LIBRARIES
REGIONAL ORGANIZATION'S LIBRARIES
RURAL LIBRARIES
SERVICE LIBRARIES
SMALL LIBRARIES

SPECIAL LIBRARIES
STATE LIBRARIES
TRADE ASSOCIATION'S LIBRARIES
TRADE UNION'S LIBRARIES
TRUST'S LIBRARIES
URBAN LIBRARIES
RT USE

Library and Information Science Abstracts
USE LISA

LIBRARY EDITIONS
BT EDITIONS

LIBRARY HANDBOOKS
RT APPLICATION
USER EDUCATION

LIBRARY OF CONGRESS CLASSIFICATION SCHEME
BT CLASSIFICATION SCHEMES (EXAMPLES)
RT *ENUMERATIVE CLASSIFICATION SCHEMES*

LIBRARY OF CONGRESS LIST OF SUBJECT HEADINGS
BT LISTS OF SUBJECT HEADINGS
RT COMPLEXITY
*SEAR'S LIST OF SUBJECT HEADINGS*

LIBRARY RULES
RT *CIRCULATION*

LIBRARY SCIENCE INFORMATION SOURCES
BT INFORMATION SOURCES
RT ACADEMIC LIBRARIES
CIRCULATION
INTERNET PERIODICALS

Library softwares
USE SOFTWARES

LIBRARY TECHNOLOGY
NT INFORMATION TECHNOLOGY
RT ANXIETY
USERS

LIBRARY WEEKS
BT EXTENSION ACTIVITIES

LIBRATAS
BT SOFTWARES
RT APPLICATION
COLLEGE LIBRARIES
STOCK VERIFICATION

LIBSYS
BT SOFTWARES
RT ACQUISITION
APPLICATION

LIGHTING

LIMITED CATALOGUING
BT CATALOGUING
NT SELECTIVE CATALOGUING
SIMPLIFIED CATALOGUING

LIMITED EDITIONS
BT EDITIONS

LISA
UF Library and Information Science Abstracts
BT ABSTRACTING PERIODICALS
RT CHAIN INDEXING
IMPACT

LISTS OF ADDITIONS
UF Accession lists
BT CAS

LISTS OF SUBJECT HEADINGS
NT LIBRARY OF CONGRESS LIST OF SUBJECT HEADINGS
SEAR'S LIST OF SUBJECT HEADINGS
RT *VOCABULARY CONTROL*

LITERARY INFORMATION SOURCES
BT INFORMATION SOURCES
NT FICTIONS (INFORMATION SOURCES)
POEMS (INFORMATION SOURCES)

LITERARY WRITERS
BT USERS
RT INFORMATION SEEKING BEHAVIOR

LITERATE USERS
BT USERS

LITERATURE SEARCH SERVICES
BT SERVICES

Local Area Networks
USE LAN

LOCAL BIBLIOGRAPHIES
BT BIBLIOGRAPHIES

LOCAL GOVERNMENT LIBRARIES
UF Panchayat libraries
BT GOVERNMENT LIBRARIES

LOCAL NEWSPAPERS
BT NEWSPAPERS
RT APPLICATION
DBASE IV
INDEXING

LOCATION OF BUILDINGS
BT BUILDINGS

LONG RANGE REFERENCE SERVICE
BT REFERENCE SERVICE

LOOSE LEAF BOUND INFORMATION SOURCES
BT INFORMATION SOURCES

LOSS
RT ACADEMIC LIBRARIES

CHARGING (LEVYING MONETARY CHARGES)
FINE
INFORMATION SOURCES

MACHINE BOUND INFORMATION SOURCES
BT INFORMATION SOURCES

Machine Readable Catalogue
USE MARC

MAD
USE MANUAL FOR ARCHIVAL DESCRIPTION

MAGNETIC DISKS
BT STORAGE TECHNOLOGY

MAGNETIC TAPES
BT STORAGE TECHNOLOGY

Magazines
USE PERIODICALS

MAIN CLASS
BT CLASS
DEWEY DECIMAL CLASSIFICATION
COLON CLASSIFICATION

MAIN ENTRY
BT ENTRIES
RT *ADDED ENTRIES*

Main libraries
USE CENTRAL LIBRARIES

MAINTENANCE
NT SHELF ARRANGEMENT
SHELVING
RT IN-HOUSE BIBLIOGRAPHIC DATABASES
PROBLEMS

MAJORITY USERS
BT USERS

MALE USERS
BT USERS

MAN

UF Metropolitan Area Networks

BT NETWORKS

MANAGEMENT

NT ACCOUNTING

AUDITING

BUDGETING

COMMITTEES

CONTROL

KNOWLEDGE MANAGEMENT

MARKETING

MONITORING

OPERATIONAL MANAGEMENT

ORGANIZATION

PARTICIPATIVE MANAGEMENT

PERSONNEL MANAGEMENT

PLANNING

STANDARDIZATION

RT APPLICATION

AUTOMATION

BACKLOG CATALOGUING

BIBLIOGRAPHIC DATABASES

CHANGE

CLASSIFIED (SECRET) INFORMATION SOURCES

DEFENCE LIBRARIES

DIGITAL PERIODICALS

LAN

MANAGEMENT LIBRARIES

NETWORKED PUBLIC LIBRARIES

ONE PERSON LIBRARIES

SPACE

TECHNOLOGICAL CHANGE

UNIVERSITY LIBRARIES

MANAGEMENT BY OBJECTIVES

UF MBO

RT APPLICATION
UNIVERSITY LIBRARIES

MANAGEMENT LIBRARIES
BT SPECIAL LIBRARIES
RT ACQUISITION
APPLICATION
MANAGEMENT
PERIODICALS
RESOURCE SHARING
TECHNOLOGICAL CHANGE
TQM

MANAGEMENT PRINCIPLES
RT APPLICATION

MANUAL FOR ARCHIVAL DESCRIPTION
UF MAD
BT CATALOGUE CODES

MANUSCRIPTS
BT INFORMATION SOURCES
RT AQUEOUS DE-ACIDIFICATION
PRESERVATION
PROBLEMS
PURCHASE

MANUSCRIPTS VIRTUAL LIBRARIES
BT VIRTUAL LIBRARIES

MAP CASES
BT FURNITURE

MAP LIBRARIES
BT SPECIAL LIBRARIES

MAPS
BT INFORMATION SOURCES
RT CATALOGUING

MARC
UF Machine Readable Catalogue
BT BIBLIOGRAPHIC EXCHANGE FORMATS

NT MARC 21
UNIMARC
RT *CCF*

MARC 21
BT MARC

MARKET SEGMENTATION
BT MARKETING

MARKETING
BT MANAGEMENT
NT MARKET SEGMENTATION
MARKETING MIX
RT ACADEMIC LIBRARIES
APPLICATION
FINANCE
GENERATION (FINANCE)
NETWORKED CONTACT LIBRARIES
PUBLIC LIBRARIES
REMOTE USERS
SALEABLE SERVICES
SERVICES
STRATEGY
UNIVERSITY LIBRARIES
USER EDUCATION
VIRTUAL LIBRARIES

MARKETING MIX
BT MARKETING
NT DISTRIBUTION
PLANNING
PRICING
PROMOTION
RT SERVICES

MASS DE-ACIDIFICATION
BT DE-ACIDIFICATION
RT PRESERVATION
PRINTED INFORMATION SOURCES

MATTER FACET

BT FACETS
RT *PMEST*

MATTER ISOLATES
BT SPECIAL ISOLATES
NT MATTER MATERIAL ISOLATES
MATTER METHOD ISOLATES
MATTER PROPERTY ISOLATES

MATTER MATERIAL ISOLATES
BT MATTER ISOLATES

MATTER METHOD ISOLATES
BT MATTER ISOLATES

MATTER PROPERTY ISOLATES
BT MATTER ISOLATES

MBO
USE MANAGEMENT BY OBJECTIVES

MEASURING
RT ACADEMIC LIBRARIES
ATTRIBUTION THEORY
AVAILABILITY
FILL RATE
ILL
INFORMATION DEMANDS
KANTOR METHOD
NETWORKED ACADEMIC LIBRARIES
PERFORMANCE
PERIODICALS
QUALITY
RESEARCH LIBRARIES
SERVICES
TEXTBOOKS
UNIVERSITY LIBRARIES
USE
USERS

MEDICAL FACILITIES
RT GOVERNMENT SCHOOL LIBRARIES
MOTIVATION

PERSONNEL
PRIVATE SCHOOL LIBRARIES

MEDICAL LIBRARIES
BT SPECIAL LIBRARIES
RT CENTRALIZED ILL
INFORMATION SOURCES
NETWORKING
NURSES
PAMPHLETS
PERSONNEL
PHYSICIANS
REMOTE USERS
SELF-CHARGED ILL
SERVICES

MEDIUM SIZED LIBRARIES
SN *Library with 20000 to one lac holdings*
BT LIBRARIES
RT IMPACT
LAN
SERVICES

Me-mail
USE MULTIMEDIA E-MAIL

MEMBERSHIP OF INSTITUTIONS
BT ACQUISITION

METADATA
NT METATAGS
RT CATALOGUING
DIGITAL INFORMATION SOURCES
STANDARDS (EVALUATION CRITERIA)

METAL FURNITURE
BT FURNITURE

METALLIC INFORMATION SOURCES
SN *Information produced on metal material*
BT INFORMATION SOURCES

METATAGS

BT METADATA
NT HTML METATAGS

METROPOLITAN AREA NETWORKS
USE MAN

METROPOLITAN LIBRARIES
BT LIBRARIES
RT NETWORKS

MICROCARDS
BT MICROFORMS

MICROFICHE
BT MICROFORMS
NT ALTRAFICHE

MICROFILMING (PRESERVATION METHOD)
RT INFORMATION SOURCES
NEWSPAPERS
PRESERVATION
UNIVERSITY LIBRARIES

MICROFILMS
BT MICROFORMS

MICROFORM READER
BT MICROFORMING TECHNOLOGY

MICROFORMING SERVICES
BT REPROGRAPHIC SERVICES

MICROFORMING TECHNOLOGY
BT REPROGRAPHIC TECHNOLOGY
NT MICROFORM READER

MICROFORMS
BT NON-BOOK MATERIALS
NT APERTURE CARD
COMPUTER OUTPUT MICROFORM
MICROCARD
MICROFICHE
MICROFILMS

MINISIS

BT SOFTWARES
NT ARABIZED MINISIS

MINORITY PERSONNEL
BT PERSONNEL
RT RECRUITMENT
UNIVERSITY LIBRARIES

MINORITY USERS
BT USERS
RT PUBLIC LIBRARIES
SERVICES

MISAPPROPRIATION
RT FINANCE
CONTROL
INTERNAL AUDIT
PUBLIC LIBRARIES

MISINFORMATION
RT ACCOUNTABILITY
LIBRARIANS

MIXED NOTATIONS
BT NOTATIONAL SYSTEMS
RT *PURE NOTATIONS*

MNEMONICS
NT SCHEDULED MNEMONICS
SEMINAL MNEMONICS
SYSTEMATIC MNEMONICS
VERBAL MNEMONICS

MOBILE LIBRARIES
BT SPECIAL LIBRARIES

MODULAR BUILDINGS
BT BUILDINGS

MONOLINGUAL THESAURI
BT THESAURI

MONITORING
BT MANAGEMENT
RT APPLICATION

COMPUTERS
DIGITAL LIBRARIES
INFORMATION SEEKING BEHAVIOR
REMOTE USERS

MORAL INFORMATION SOURCES
SN *Information sources preaching value of morality*
BT INFORMATION SOURCES

MOTIVATION
BT PERSONNEL MANAGEMENT
RT GOVERNMENT SCHOOL LIBRARIES
HIGHER SALARY
MEDICAL FACILITIES
PERSONNEL
PRIVATE SCHOOL LIBRARIES
PROMOTION (SERVICE ADVANCEMENT)
RETIREMENT BENEFITS
UNIVERSITY LIBRARIES

MULTIDISCIPLINARITY
RT CLASSIFICATION SCHEME (EXAMPLES)
IMPACT

MULTILINGUAL THESAURI
BT THESAURI
RT THESAURI CONSTRUCTION

MULTIMEDIA
BT INFORMATION TECHNOLOGY
RT APPLICATION
IMPACT

MULTIMEDIA DATABASES
UF Multimedia information sources
BT DATABASES
NT INTERNET MULTIMEDIA DATABASES

MULTIMEDIA E-MAIL
UF Me-mail
BT E-MAIL
RT APPLICATION

Multimedia information
sources
USE MULTIMEDIA DATABASES

MULTIPLE SERIES
BT SERIES

MULTIVOLUME INFORMATION
SOURCES
BT INFORMATION SOURCES

MUNICIPALITY LIBRARIES
BT GOVERNMENT LIBRARIES
RT EVALUATION

MUSIC INFORMATION
SOURCES
BT INFORMATION SOURCES
RT NATIONAL LIBRARIES

MUTILATION
RT INFORMATION SOURCES
WEEDING

NARRATIONS
SN *Event describing information sources.*
BT INFORMATION SOURCES

NATIONAL BIBLIOGRAPHIES
BT BIBLIOGRAPHIES
RT PRODUCTION
PRIVATE SECTOR
PUBLIC SECTOR

NATIONAL LIBRARIES
BT LIBRARIES
NT BRANCH NATIONAL LIBRARIES
NATIONAL MEDICAL LIBRARIES
RT BLAIZLINE
COOPERATIVE CATALOGUING
COST
DELIVERY TIME
ELECTRONIC DOCUMENT
DELIVERY SERVICES

EVALUATION
MUSIC INFORMATION SOURCES
SUBJECT COVERAGE

NATIONAL MEDICAL LIBRARIES
BT NATIONAL LIBRARIES
RT NUMERIC DATABASES
ONLINE DATABASES

National Union Catalogue of Scientific Serials in India
USE NUCSSI

NATURAL DISASTER
NT FIRE(CAUSAL FACTOR)
WATER (CAUSAL FACTOR)
RT DETERIORATION
PRINTED INFORMATION SOURCES

NATURAL LANGUAGE
BT INDEXING LANGUAGES
RT *CONTROLLED LANGUAGE*

NATURAL LANGUAGE PROCESSING
RT APPLICATION
THESAURI CONSTRUCTION

NAVY LIBRARIES
BT DEFENCE LIBRARIES

NEEDS
NT INFORMATION NEEDS
RT HUMANITIES THESAURI
REMOTE USERS

NEO LITERATE USERS
BT USERS

NET BOOK AGREEMENT
BT DISCOUNT

NETWORKED ACADEMIC LIBRARIES
BT ACADEMIC LIBRARIES
RT APPLICATION

E-MAIL
FILL RATE
ILL
MEASURING
PERFORMANCE

NETWORKED CONTACT LIBRARIES
BT CONTACT LIBRARIES
RT MARKETING
SERVICES

NETWORKED LIBRARIES
BT AUTOMATED LIBRARIES

NETWORKED PUBLIC LIBRARIES
BT PUBLIC LIBRARIES
RT MANAGEMENT

NETWORKING
BT COMPUTERIZATION
RT AGRICULTURAL LIBRARIES
DEFENCE RESEARCH LIBRARIES
MEDICAL LIBRARIES
NEWSPAPER LIBRARIES
PUBLIC LIBRARIES

NETWORKS
BT INFORMATION TECHNOLOGY
NT LAN
MAN
WAN
RT ACADEMIC LIBRARIES
AGRICULTURAL UNIVERSITY LIBRARIES
APPLICATION
METROPOLITAN LIBRARIES
RESOURCE SHARING
RURAL LIBRARIES
USE

NEWARK CHARGING SYSTEM

BT CIRCULATION SYSTEMS

NEWSPAPER LIBRARIES

BT SPECIAL LIBRARIES

RT CLIPPING SERVICES

NETWORKING

NEWSPAPER STANDS

BT STANDS (FURNITURE)

NEWSPAPERS

UF Press

BT PERIODICALS

NT LOCAL NEWSPAPERS

GUARDIAN, THE

RT COOPERATIVE INDEXING

MICROFILMING

PRESERVATION

PUBLICITY

NEWSPRINT INFORMATION SOURCES

SN *Information sources printed on papers used for newspapers*

BT PAPER BASED INFORMATION SOURCES

NEWS RELEASE

BT PUBLIC RELATION MATERIALS

N-GRAM

SN *N-gram is a string of 'n' characters (usually adjacent) extracted from a section of a continuous text*

RT APPLICATION

TEXTUAL INFORMATION RETRIEVAL

NON-BOOK MATERIALS

BT INFORMATION SOURCES

NT DIGITAL INFORMATION SOURCES

MICROFORMS

SLIDES

TRANSPARENCIES

NON-CIRCULATION

RT INFORMATION SOURCES
WEEDING

NON-PROFESSIONAL PERSONNEL
BT PERSONNEL
RT FUNCTIONS
PROFESSIONAL PERSONNEL
SALARY

NON-REGISTERED USERS
BT USERS

NON-UNIONISED PROFESSIONAL PERSONNEL
BT PROFESSIONAL PERSONNEL
RT ORGANIZATIONAL COMMITMENT
RESEARCH LIBRARIES
UNIONISED PERSONNEL

NON-VERBAL COMMUNICATION
BT COMMUNICATION
RT REFERENCE PERSONNEL
*VERBAL COMMUNICATION*

NOTATIONAL DIGITS
BT NOTATIONAL SYSTEMS
NT EMPTY DIGITS
EMPTY EMPTYING DIGITS
EMPTYING DIGITS
INDICATOR DIGITS
SUBSTANTIVE DIGITS

NOTATIONAL PLANE
BT PLANES OF WORK
NT NOTATIONAL SYSTEMS

NOTATIONAL SYSTEMS
UF Notations
BT NOTATIONAL PLANE
NT MIXED NOTATIONS
NOTATIONAL DIGITS
PURE NOTATIONS

Notations

USE NOTATIONAL SYSTEMS

NOTIFICATION

NT AESTHETIC OF NOTIFICATION

NOVELISATIONS

SN *A novelized version*

BT INFORMATION SOURCES

NUCSSI

UF National Union Catalogue of Scientific Serials in India

BT UNION CATALOGUE

RT APPLICATION

ILL

UNIVERSITY LIBRARIES

NUMERIC DATABASES

UF Databanks

BT DATABASES

RT NATIONAL MEDICAL LIBRARIES

NURSES

BT USERS

RT MEDICAL LIBRARIES

SERVICES

OBSOLESCENCE

RT CONTENTS

INFORMATION SOURCES

LANGUAGE

STYLE (OF WRITING)

WEEDING

Offline databases

USE CD-ROM DATABASES

OFFLINE INFORMATION RETRIEVAL

BT INFORMATION RETRIEVAL

RT *ONLINE INFORMATION RETRIEVAL*

OFFLINE SEARCH

BT SEARCH

RT CELL SCIENCE RESEARCH LIBRARIES
DATABASES
*ONLINE SEARCH*

OFFSET PAPER INFORMATION SOURCES
BT PAPER BASED INFORMATION SOURCES

OMNIPAGE PRO
BT SOFTWARES
RT APPLICATION
BIBLIOGRAPHIC DATABASES
CREATION

ONE PERSON LIBRARIES
UF OPL
BT SPECIAL LIBRARIES
RT MANAGEMENT
SPACE
STRATEGIC PLANNING

ONLINE BIBLIOGRAPHIC SERVICES
BT BIBLIOGRAPHIC SERVICES
RT PRICING

ONLINE CONSULTANCY SERVICES
BT CONSULTANCY SERVICES
RT INFORMATION BROKERS

ONLINE DATABASES
BT DATABASES
RT APPLICATION
CD-ROM DATABASES
CLASSIFICATION
LAW LIBRARIES
NATIONAL MEDICAL LIBRARIES
SEARCH
USE

ONLINE DOCUMENT DELIVERY SERVICES

BT DOCUMENT DELIVERY SERVICES
RT PRICING

ONLINE INDEXES
BT INDEXES
RT PRINTED INDEXES
RETRIEVAL PERFORMANCE

ONLINE INFORMATION RETRIEVAL
BT INFORMATION RETRIEVAL
RT APPLICATION
ARTIFICIAL INTELLIGENCE
CHEMICAL DATABASES
COST
*OFFLINE INFORMATION RETRIEVAL*
SCIENCE INFORMATION CENTRES
SHIP ENGINEERING RESEARCH LIBRARIES
USER'S ATTITUDE

Online Public Access Catalogues
USE OPAC

ONLINE REFERENCE SERVICE
BT REFERENCE SERVICE
RT DIGITAL LIBRARIES
REMOTE USERS

ONLINE SEARCH
BT SEARCH
RT CELL SCIENCE RESEARCH LIBRARIES
DATABASE
*OFFLINE SEARCH*
STRATEGY

OPAC
UF Online Public Access Catalogues
BT CATALOGUES
NT BLAIZLINE
RT ACADEMIC LIBRARIES

APPLICATION
AUTOMATED UNIVERSITY LIBRARIES
CLASSIFICATION
EVALUATION
SEARCH
TRADITIONAL CATALOGUES
USE

OPEN ACCESS LIBRARIES
BT LIBRARIES
RT *CLOSED ACCESS LIBRARIES*

OPEN ACCESS PUBLIC LIBRARIES
BT PUBLIC LIBRARIES
RT CD-ROM DATABASES

OPEN UNIVERSITY LIBRARIES
BT UNIVERSITY LIBRARIES

OPERATIONAL MANAGEMENT
BT MANAGEMENT
RT ACADEMIC LIBRARIES

OPERATIONS RESEARCH
UF OR
NT GAME THEORY
QUEUING THEORY

OPINION
RT FEE BASED PUBLIC LIBRARIES
USERS

OPL
USE ONE PERSON LIBRARIES

OR
USE OPERATIONS RESEARCH

ORDERING
BT ACQUISITION
NT BLANKET ORDERING

ORDERING SECTION
BT ACQUISITION

ORGANIZATION

BT MANAGEMENT
RT EFFECT
IMPACT
INFORMATION TECHNOLOGY
UNIVERSITY LIBRARIES

ORGANIZATIONAL CHANGE
BT CHANGE
RT ACADEMIC LIBRARIES

ORGANIZATIONAL COMMITMENT
BT COMMITMENT
RT NON-UNIONISED PROFESSIONAL PERSONNEL
RESEARCH LIBRARIES
UNIONISED PROFESSIONAL PERSONNEL

ORIENTATION
UF Initiation
BT USER EDUCATION
RT COLLEGE LIBRARIES
EVALUATION
JUNIOR REFERENCE PERSONNEL
PROGRAMMES
ROLE
SENIOR LIBRARIANS

OUT OF PRINT INFORMATION SOURCES
BT INFORMATION SOURCES
RT *INPRINT INFORMATION SOURCES*

OUTSOURCING
RT ACADEMIC LIBRARIES
CATALOGUING
EFFECT
GOVERNMENT LIBRARIES
PHOTOCOPYING SERVICES
PRIVATIZATION
SERVICES

OVERDUE (ISSUED

INFORMATION
SOURCES)
BT CIRCULATION
RT STATISTICAL ANALYSIS
UNIVERSITY LIBRARIES

OVERSIZED INFORMATION SOURCES
SN *30 to 44 cm in height*
BT INFORMATION SOURCES

OXFORD PAPER INFORMATION SOURCES
BT PAPER BASED INFORMATION SOURCES

PAGINATION
BT COLLATION

PALM LEAF INFORMATION SOURCES
SN *Information written on palm leaf*
BT LEAF INFORMATION SOURCES

PAMPHLETS
SN *Less than 2 cm thick*
BT INFORMATION SOURCES
RT BIBLIOGRAPHIC CONTROL
MEDICAL LIBRARIES

Panchayat libraries
USE LOCAL GOVERNMENT LIBRARIES

PAPERBACK INFORMATION SOURCES
BT INFORMATION SOURCES
RT PURCHASE
SMALL COLLEGE LIBRARIES

PAPER BASED INFORMATION SOURCES
SN *Information written / printed on paper*
BT INFORMATION SOURCES
NT ART PAPER INFORMATION SOURCES
BOND PAPER INFORMATION SOURCES

CALENDAR PAPER INFORMATION SOURCES
CHINESE PAPER INFORMATION SOURCES
DRAWING PAPER INFORMATION SOURCES
HANDMADE PAPER INFORMATION SOURCES
INDIA PAPER INFORMATION SOURCES
LEDGER PAPER INFORMATION SOURCES
NEWSPAPER PAPER INFORMATION SOURCES
OFFSET PAPER INFORMATION SOURCES
OXFORD PAPER INFORMATION SOURCES
PHOTOGRAPHIC PAPER INFORMATION SOURCES

PAPYRUS INFORMATION SOURCES
SN *Information written on papyrus*
BT INFORMATION SOURCES

PARAPROFESSIONAL PERSONNEL
BT PERSONNEL
RT ACADEMIC LIBRARIES
COMPUTERIZATION
IMPACT
PROFESSIONAL PERSONNEL
REFERENCE SERVICE
TECHNICAL PROCESSING

PARENTS
BT USERS
RT INFORMATION NEEDS

PARODIES
BT INFORMATION SOURCES

PARTIAL COMPREHENSION CLASS
BT CLASS

PARTIALLY OPEN ACCESS

LIBRARIES

BT LIBRARIES

PARTICIPATIVE MANAGEMENT

BT MANAGEMENT

RT UNIVERSITY LIBRARIES

PART-TIME PERSONNEL

BT PERSONNEL

PATENTS

BT INFORMATION SOURCES

NT CHEMICAL PATENTS

PATIENTS

BT USERS

PERFORMANCE

NT BEHAVIORAL PERFORMANCE
RETRIEVAL PERFORMANCE

RT ACADEMIC LIBRARIES
ATTRIBUTION THEORY
EVALUATION
FILL RATE
ILL
INFORMATION STORAGE AND RETRIEVAL
MEASURING
NETWORKED ACADEMIC LIBRARIES
PRECISION
RECALL
RESEARCH LIBRARIES

PERIODICAL SECTION

BT SECTION

RT ACCOUNTING
AUDITING
CENTRAL TECHNOLOGICAL LIBRARIES

PERIODICAL SHELVES

BT SHELVES

PERIODICALS

UF Journals
Magazines

Serials

BT INFORMATION SOURCES

NT ABSTRACTING PERIODICALS
ARTICLES
DIGITAL PERIODICALS
FOREIGN PERIODICALS
INDEXING PERIODICALS
IN-HOUSE PERIODICALS
INTERNET PERIODICALS
LEARNED PERIODICALS
NEWSPAPERS
POPULAR PERIODICALS
PROCEEDINGS
REVIEWING PERIODICALS

RT ACADEMIC LIBRARIES
ACQUISITION
CIRCULATION
COST
DE-SUBSCRIBING
DISCOUNT
MANAGEMENT LIBRARIES
MEASURING
PROBLEMS
PUBLIC LIBRARIES
REMPLOY ADHESIVE BINDING
RENEWAL (SUBSCRIPTION)
RESOURCE SHARING
SELECTION (INFORMATION SOURCES)
SUBSCRIBING
UNIVERSITY LIBRARIES
USE

PERIODICAL`S LIBRARIES

BT SPECIAL LIBRARIES

PERMANENT PERSONNEL

BT PERSONNEL

PERSONAL AUTHORS

BT AUTHORS
RT *CORPORATE AUTHORS*

PERSONALITY FACET
BT FACETS
RT *PMEST*

PERSONALITY ISOLATES
BT SPECIAL ISOLATES

PERSONNEL
UF Staff
NT FULL TIME PERSONNEL
JUNIOR PERSONNEL
MINORITY PERSONNEL
NON PROFESSIONAL PERSONNEL
PARAPROFESSIONAL PERSONNEL
PART-TIME PERSONNEL
PERMANENT PERSONNEL
PROFESSIONAL PERSONNEL
SENIOR PERSONNEL
TEMPORARY PERSONNEL
TRAINEE PERSONNEL
RT ACADEMIC LIBRARIES
ABSENTEEISM
ADVERSE CONDITION
ANXIETY
COLD
DEPRESSION
DIGITAL LIBRARIES
FUNCTIONS
GOVERNMENT SCHOOL LIBRARIES
HIGHER SALARY
HYBRID LIBRARIES
IMPACT
INFORMATION TECHNOLOGY
INTERNET MULTIMEDIA DATABASES
JOB DISSATISFACTION
JOB SATISFACTION

MEDICAL FACILITIES
MEDICAL LIBRARIES
MOTIVATION
POLICY
PRIVATE SCHOOL LIBRARIES
PROMOTION (SERVICE ADVANCEMENT)
QUALIFICATIONS
RECRUITMENT
RETENTION
RETIREMENT BENEFITS
ROLE
SKILLS
STRATEGY
TURNOVER
UNIVERSITY LIBRARIES
USE
USERS

PERSONNEL MANAGEMENT
BT MANAGEMENT
NT JOB ANALYSIS
JOB DESIGN
LEADING
MOTIVATION
RETENTION
TRAINING
VACANCIES

PERT
UF Programme Evaluation and Review Techniques
RT APPLICATION
*CPM*
UNIVERSITY LIBRARIES

PHARMACY RESEARCH LIBRARIES
BT RESEARCH LIBRARIES
RT REFERENCE SERVICE

PHASE RELATIONS
BT IDEA PLANE
NT APPLICATION PHASE RELATIONS
BIAS PHASE RELATIONS
COMPARISON PHASE RELATION
DIFFERENCE PHASE RELATIONS
GENERAL PHASE RELATIONS
INFLUENCE PHASE RELATIONS
INTER SUBJECT PHASE RELATIONS
INTRA-ARRAY PHASE RELATIONS
INTRA-FACET PHASE RELATIONS

PHILOSOPHY
RT COLLECTION DEVELOPMENT

PHOTOCOPIED INFORMATION SOURCES
UF Xeroxed information sources
BT REPROGRAPHED INFORMATION SOURCES

PHOTOCOPYING (PRESERVATION METHOD)
RT INFORMATION SOURCES
PRESERVATION
UNIVERSITY LIBRARIES

PHOTOCOPYING SERVICES
BT REPROGRAPHIC SERVICES
RT ACADEMIC LIBRARIES
OUTSOURCING
TECHNOLOGICAL INFORMATION CENTRES

PHOTOCOPYING TECHNOLOGY
BT REPROGRAPHIC TECHNOLOGY

PHOTOGRAPHIC PAPER INFORMATION SOURCES
BT PAPER BASED INFORMATION SOURCES

PHYSICAL LAYOUT OF BUILDINGS
BT BUILDINGS

PHYSICAL LAYOUT OF TITLE PAGE
BT TITLE PAGE

RT APPLICATION
BIBLIOGRAPHIC DESCRIPTION
IDENTIFICATION

PHYSICAL PROCESSING
NT BOOK POCKETING
LABELING
STAMPING

PHYSICAL PROCESSING SECTION
BT TECHNICAL PROCESSING SECTION

PHYSICAL SCIENTISTS
BT USERS
RT INFORMATION SEEKING BEHAVIOR
SOCIAL SCIENTISTS
UNIVERSITY LIBRARIES

PHYSICIANS
BT USERS
RT MEDICAL LIBRARIES
SERVICES

PICTURES
BT INFORMATION SOURCES

PIRATED EDITIONS
BT EDITIONS

PLACE OF PUBLICATION
BT IMPRINT

PLANES OF WORK
BT CLASSIFICATION
NT IDEA PLANE
NOTATIONAL PLANE
VERBAL PLANE

PLANNING
BT MANAGEMENT
MARKETING MIX
NT STRATEGIC PLANNING
RT BUILDINGS

HUMANITIES INFORMATION CENTRES
UNIVERSITY LIBRARIES

PLANS
BT INFORMATION SOURCES

PLASTIC BOUND INFORMATION SOURCES
BT INFORMATION SOURCES

PLASTIC FURNITURE
BT FURNITURE

PLASTIC INFORMATION SOURCES
SN *Information written / printed on plastic material*
BT INFORMATION SOURCES

PLR
USE PUBLIC LENDING RIGHTS

PMEST
UF FUNDAMENTAL CATEGORIES
RT APPLICATION
AUDIO INFORMATION SOURCES
CONTROL
*ENERGY FACET*
*MATTER FACET*
*PERSONALITY FACET*
RECALL
*SPACE FACET*
*TIME FACET*

POEMS (INFORMATION SOURCES)
BT LITERARY INFORMATION SOURCES
RT SHELVING

POLICY
RT CENTRALIZED UNIVERSITY LIBRARY
COLLECTION DEVELOPMENT
DECENTRALIZED UNIVERSITY LIBRARIES
DIGITAL INFORMATION SOURCES

DIGITAL LIBRARIES
GIFTS
PERSONNEL
RECRUITMENT
STANDARDS (INFORMATION SOURCES)
UNIVERSITY LIBRARIES

POLITICAL IMPACT
BT IMPACT

POLITICAL INFORMATION SOURCES
SN *Information sources preaching political values*
BT INFORMATION SOURCES

POPLINE
SN *A cd-rom database on population.*
BT CD-ROM BIBLIOGRAPHIC DATABASES
RT INFORMATION SEEKING BEHAVIOR
USERS

POPSI
UF Postulate based Permuterm Subject Indexing
BT PRE-COORDINATE INDEXING SYSTEMS
NT COMPUTERIZED POPSI

POPULAR INFORMATION SOURCES
BT INFORMATION SOURCES

POPULAR PERIODICALS
BT PERIODICALS

POST COORDINATE INDEXING SYSTEMS
BT INDEXING SYSTEMS
NT BATTEN SYSTEM
UNITERM
RT *PRE-COORDINATE INDEXING SYSTEMS*

POSTGRADUATE COLLEGE LIBRARIES

BT COLLEGE LIBRARIES

POSTGRADUATE STUDENTS

BT STUDENTS

RT DRINKING WATER FACILITY

INFORMATION SEEKING BEHAVIOR

PUBLIC LIBRARIES

READING ROOM FACILITY

UNIVERSITY LIBRARIES

POST-MASTER (M. PHIL.) STUDENTS

BT STUDENTS

Postulate based Permuterm Subject Indexing

USE POPSI

PPBS

UF Programme Planning and Budgeting System

BT BUDGETING

PRACTICE BOOKS

BT INFORMATION SOURCES

PRECIS

UF Preserved Context Indexing System

BT PRE-COORDINATE INDEXING SYSTEMS

PRECISION

BT SEARCH

RT EVALUATION

*INFORMATION STORAGE AND RETRIEVAL*

PERFORMANCE

RECALL

*THESAURI*

PRE-COORDINATE INDEXING SYSTEMS

BT INDEXING SYSTEMS

NT CHAIN INDEXING

POPSI

PRECIS

SLIC
RT *POST COORDINATE INDEXING SYSTEMS*

PRE PRINTS
BT INFORMATION SOURCES

PRESCRIBED EDITIONS
BT EDITIONS

PRESCRIBED TEXTBOOKS
BT TEXTBOOKS
RT ACADEMIC LIBRARIES
ACCESSIBILITY
AVAILABILITY
DEMANDS

PRESERVATION
NT COOPERATIVE PRESERVATION
RT AQUEOUS DE-ACIDIFICATION
CONSERVATION
DIGITISATION
EXAMINATION PAPERS
FUMIGATION
INFORMATION SOURCES
MANUSCRIPTS
MASS DE-ACIDIFICATION
MICROFILMING (PRESERVATION METHODS)
NEWSPAPERS
PHOTOCOPYING (PRESERVATION METHODS)
PRINTED INFORMATION SOURCES
UNIVERSITY LIBRARIES

PRESERVATION SECTION
BT SECTIONS

Preserved Context
Indexing System
USE PRECIS

Press
USE NEWSPAPER

PREVENTION
RT ACADEMIC LIBRARIES

RARE BOOKS
THEFT

Price
USE COST

PRICING
UF Costing
BT MARKETING MIX
RT BIBLIOGRAPHIC SERVICES
ILL
ONLINE BIBLIOGRAPHIC SERVICES
ONLINE DOCUMENT DELIVERY SERVICES
RESEARCH LIBRARIES
SERVICES

PRIMARY SCHOOL LIBRARIES
BT SCHOOL LIBRARIES
NT GOVERNMENT PRIMARY SCHOOL LIBRARIES

PRINCIPLES
RT *SELECTION (INFORMATION SOURCES)*

PRINTED INDEXES
BT INDEXES
RT ONLINE INDEXES
RETRIEVAL PERFORMANCE

PRINTED INFORMATION SOURCES
BT INFORMATION SOURCES
RT BIOLOGICAL CAUSES
CONSERVATION
DAMAGE
DETERIORATION
FUMIGATION
MASS DE-ACIDIFICATION
NATURAL DISASTER
PRESERVATION
WATER (CAUSE OF DISASTER)

PRINTERS
BT INFORMATION TECHNOLOGY

PRINTOUT SERVICES
BT SERVICES
RT CHARGING (LEVYING MONETARY CHARGES)

PRISON LIBRARIES
BT SPECIAL LIBRARIES

PRISONERS
BT USERS

PRIVATE CIRCULATION (INFORMATION SOURCES FOR)
BT INFORMATION SOURCES

PRIVATE LIBRARIES
BT LIBRARIES

PRIVATE PUBLICATIONS
BT INFORMATION SOURCES

PRIVATE SCHOOL LIBRARIES
BT SCHOOL LIBRARIES
RT HIGHER SALARY
MEDICAL FACILITIES
MOTIVATION
PERSONNEL
PROMOTION (SERVICE ADVANCEMENT)
RETIREMENT BENEFITS

PRIVATE SECTOR
RT NATIONAL BIBLIOGRAPHY
PRODUCTION
PUBLIC SECTOR

PRIVATIZATION
RT OUTSOURCING
SERVICES

PROBLEM OF DELAYED SUPPLY
BT PROBLEMS

RT COLLECTION DEVELOPMENT
SPECIAL LIBRARIES

PROBLEM OF LACK OF CONFIRMED PRICES
BT PROBLEMS
RT COLLECTION DEVELOPMENT
SPECIAL LIBRARIES

PROBLEM OF LACK OF USER PARTICIPATION
BT PROBLEMS
RT COLLECTION DEVELOPMENT
SPECIAL LIBRARIES

PROBLEM OF LOSS IN TRANSIT
BT PROBLEMS
RT COLLECTION DEVELOPMENT
SPECIAL LIBRARIES

PROBLEMS
NT FINANCIAL PROBLEMS
PROBLEM OF DELAYED SUPPLY
PROBLEM OF LACK OF CONFIRMED PRICES
PROBLEM OF LACK OF USER PARTICIPATION
PROBLEM OF LOSS IN TRANSIT
SECURITY PROBLEMS
RT ACADEMIC LIBRARIES
APPLICATION
COLLECTION DEVELOPMENT
CONTROL
CREATION
DEVELOPMENT
DIGITAL LIBRARIES
DOCUMENT DELIVERY SERVICES
INFORMATION TECHNOLOGY
IN-HOUSE BIBLIOGRAPHIC DATABASES

MAINTENANCE
MANUSCRIPTS
PERIODICALS
PURCHASE
RECLASSIFICATION
SCHOOL LIBRARIES
SUBSCRIBING
UNIVERSITY LIBRARIES

PROCEEDINGS
BT PERIODICALS

PRODUCTION
RT NATIONAL BIBLIOGRAPHIES
PRIVATE SECTOR
PUBLIC SECTOR

PROFESSIONAL PERSONNEL
BT PERSONNEL
NT BIBLIOGRAPHERS
CATALOGUERS
CLASSIFIERS
ILL PERSONNEL
INFORMATION PERSONNEL
LIBRARIANS
NON-UNIONISED PROFESSIONAL PERSONNEL
REFERENCE PERSONNEL
UNIONISED PROFESSIONAL PERSONNEL
RT DIGITAL LIBRARIES
FUNCTIONS
INTERNET INFORMATION SOURCES
KNOWLEDGE (QUALITIES OF PERSONNEL)
NON-PROFESSIONAL PERSONNEL
PARAPROFESSIONAL PERSONNEL
REFERENCE SERVICE
SALARY

STATUS

PROFIT MAKING LIBRARIES
BT LIBRARIES

Programme Evaluation and Review Techniques
USE PERT

Programme Planning and Budgeting System
USE PPBS

PROGRAMMES
RT COLLEGE LIBRARIES
DESIGNING
EVALUATION
ORIENTATION
USER EDUCATION

PROGRAMMING LANGUAGES
BT INFORMATION TECHNOLOGY
NT CLIPPER
HTML
JAVA

PROMOTION (MARKETING MIX)
BT MARKETING MIX
NT PUBLIC RELATION
PUBLICITY
RT UNIVERSITY LIBRARIES
WWW

PROMOTION (SERVICE ADVANCEMENT)
RT GOVERNMENT SCHOOL LIBRARIES
MOTIVATION
PERSONNEL
PRIVATE SCHOOL LIBRARIES

PROMPT BOOKS
SN *The copy of a play used by a prompt,*

*showing action of a play, cues, movement of actors properties, costumes, scene and light plots.*

BT INFORMATION SOURCES

PROPER HOUSING

RT CONSERVATION
INFORMATION SOURCES

PROPOSALS

RT IMPROVEMENT
RESOURCE SHARING
SCHOOL LIBRARIES
SERVICES
UNIVERSITY LIBRARIES

PROSPECTUS

BT INFORMATION SOURCES

PROTECTION

RT ACADEMIC LIBRARIES
HOLDINGS

PRUSSIAN INSTRUCTIONS

BT CATALOGUE CODES

PUBLIC LENDING RIGHTS

SN *A subsidy paid to authors in respect of books issued from public libraries.*

UF PLR

PUBLIC LIBRARIES

BT LIBRARIES

NT BRANCH PUBLIC LIBRARIES
FEE BASED PUBLIC LIBRARIES
NETWORKED PUBLIC LIBRARIES
OPEN ACCESS PUBLIC LIBRARIES

RT APPLICATION
AUDIO CASSETTES
AUTOMATION
CD-ROM DATABASES
CONTROL
ELECTRONIC DOCUMENT

DELIVERY SERVICES
ETHNIC USERS
FINANCE
FINANCIAL IMPACT
FINANCIAL PROVISION
INFORMATION SOURCES
INFORMATION TECHNOLOGY
INTERNAL AUDIT
INTERNET BASED SERVICES
LEGISLATION
MARKETING
MINORITY USERS
MISAPPROPRIATION
NETWORKING
PERIODICALS
POSTGRADUATE STUDENTS
PUBLIC RELATION
READING HABIT
REFERENCE PERSONNEL
REFERENCE SOURCES
REFERRAL SERVICES
REGISTERED USERS
ROLE
RRRLF
SCHOOL STUDENTS
SERVICES
SOCIAL IMPACT
STUDENTS
TQM
USE
USER EDUCATION
USERS

PUBLIC RELATION
BT PROMOTION (MARKETING)
RT PUBLIC LIBRARIES

*PUBLIC RELATION MATERIALS*
UNIVERSITY LIBRARIES

PUBLIC RELATION MATERIALS
BT INFORMATION SOURCES
NT BROCHURES
CIRCULARS
NEWS RELEASE
RT *PUBLIC RELATION*

PUBLIC SECTOR
RT NATIONAL BIBLIOGRAPHY
PRIVATE SECTOR
PRODUCTION

Publications
USE INFORMATION SOURCES

PUBLICITY
BT PROMOTION (MARKETING MIX)
RT DISPLAY OF NEW ARRIVALS
EXHIBITIONS
EXTENSION ACTIVITIES
HOMEPAGES
NEWSPAPERS
UNIVERSITY LIBRARIES

PUBLISHER
BT IMPRINT

PURCHASE
BT ACQUISITION
RT MANUSCRIPTS
PAPERBACK INFORMATION SOURCES
PROBLEMS
SMALL COLLEGE LIBRARIES

PURCHASED INFORMATION SOURCES
BT INFORMATION SOURCES

PURE NOTATIONS
BT NOTATIONAL SYSTEMS

RT *MIXED NOTATIONS*

QUALIFICATIONS

RT ACADEMIC LIBRARIES
HYBRID LIBRARIES
LIBRARIANS
PERSONNEL

QUALITATIVE EVALUATION

BT EVALUATION
RT *QUANTITATIVE EVALUATION*

QUALITY

RT MEASURING
SERVICES
UNIVERSITY LIBRARIES

QUANTITATIVE EVALUATION

BT EVALUATION
RT BLANKET ORDERING
COMPUTERIZED SDI
*QUALITATIVE EVALUATION*
SCIENCE INFORMATION CENTRES

QUERY FORMULATION

BT INFORMATION STORAGE AND RETRIEVAL
RT APPLICATION
COMPUTERS

QUEUING THEORY

BT OPERATIONS RESEARCH
RT APPLICATION

Raja Rammohun Roy Library
Foundation

USE RRRLF

RARE BOOKS

BT INFORMATION SOURCES
RT ACADEMIC LIBRARIES
APPLICATION
CATALOGUING
INTERNET
PREVENTION

THEFT

RARE BOOKS BIBLIOGRAPHIC DATABASES
BT BIBLIOGRAPHIC DATABASES
RT APPLICATION
CREATION
INFORMATION TECHNOLOGY

RARE BOOKS WEBSITES
BT WEBSITES
RT EVALUATION
IMAGES
SEARCH INTERFACE
UNIVERSITY LIBRARIES

READERS ADVISORY SERVICE
BT REFERENCE SERVICE

READER'S REQUESTS
BT SELECTION TOOLS

READING ALOUD
BT EXTENSION ACTIVITIES
RT CHILDREN USERS
DEVELOPMENT
READING HABIT

READING HABIT
RT ADOLESCENT STUDENTS
BOOK REGISTERS
CHILDREN USERS
DEGREE COLLEGE LIBRARIES
DEVELOPMENT
HIGHER SECONDARY SCHOOL LIBRARIES
INTERVIEW WITH AUTHOR
PUBLIC LIBRARIES
READING ALOUD
REGISTERED USERS
RELUCTANT STUDENTS
SCHOOL LIBRARIES
STATUS

STUDENTS
TEACHERS

READING ROOM FACILITY
BT FACILITIES
RT POSTGRADUATE STUDENTS
UNIVERSITY LIBRARIES

READING ROOM INFORMATION SOURCES
BT INFORMATION SOURCES
RT ACADEMIC LIBRARIES
ROLE

READING ROOM SECTION
BT SECTIONS

READING ROOM TABLES
BT TABLES

READY REFERENCE SERVICE
BT REFERENCE SERVICE

RECALL
BT SEARCH
RT APPLICATION
CONTROL
EVALUATION
*INFORMATION STORAGE AND RETRIEVAL*
PERFORMANCE
PMEST
PRECISION
THESAURI

RECATALOGUING
BT CATALOGUING

RECLASSIFICATION
BT CLASSIFICATION
RT PROBLEMS

RECORDING OF PERIODICALS
NT KARDEX
REGISTER METHOD
THREE CARD SYSTEM

RECOVERY OF INFORMATION
SOURCES (ISSUED)
BT CIRCULATION
RT TECHNOLOGICAL INFORMATION CENTRES

RECREATIONAL LIBRARIES
BT LIBRARIES

RECRUITMENT
BT VACANCIES
NT APPOINTMENT
INTERVIEW
SELECTION (PERSONNEL)
RT MINORITY PERSONNEL
PERSONNEL
POLICY
TRAINEE PERSONNEL
UNIVERSITY LIBRARIES

REDESIGNING
BT DESIGNING
RT ACADEMIC LIBRARIES

REFERENCE INTERVIEW
NT REFERENCE INTERVIEW QUESTIONS
RT REFERENCE SERVICE

REFERENCE INTERVIEW
QUESTIONS
BT REFERENCE INTERVIEW
NT WHY QUESTIONS

REFERENCE LIBRARIES
BT LIBRARIES

REFERENCE PERSONNEL
BT PROFESSIONAL PERSONNEL
NT JUNIOR REFERENCE PERSONNEL
RT ACADEMIC LIBRARIES
BEHAVIORAL PERFORMANCE
GUIDELINES
IMPACT

INFORMATION TECHNOLOGY
NON-VERBAL COMMUNICATION
PUBLIC LIBRARIES
ROLE
SUBJECT COMPETENCIES

REFERENCE SECTION
BT SECTIONS

REFERENCE SERVICE
BT SERVICES
NT LONG RANGE REFERENCE SERVICE
ONLINE REFERENCE SERVICE
READERS ADVISORY SERVICE
READY REFERENCE SERVICE
RT ACADEMIC LIBRARIES
APPLICATION
CONJOINT ANALYSIS
CONTINGENT VALUATION
COST
DEFINITIVENESS OF ANSWERS
EVALUATION
FILL RATE
PARAPROFESSIONAL PERSONNEL
PHARMACY RESEARCH LIBRARIES
PROFESSIONAL PERSONNEL
REFERENCE INTERVIEW
THEORIES OF REFERENCE SERVICE
WAITING TIME

REFERENCE SOURCES
BT INFORMATION SOURCES
NT ALMANACS
ATLASES
BIBLIOGRAPHIES
BIOGRAPHIES
DICTIONARIES
DIRECTORIES
ENCYCLOPAEDIAS

FORMULA BOOKS
GAZETTEERS
GUIDEBOOKS
INTERNET REFERENCE SOURCES
REVIEWS
STATISTICAL INFORMATION SOURCES
YEARBOOKS
RT PUBLIC LIBRARIES

REFERRAL CENTRES
RT *REFERRAL SERVICES*

REFERRAL SERVICES
BT SERVICES
RT PUBLIC LIBRARIES
*REFERRAL CENTRES*

REGIONAL LIBRARIES
BT LIBRARIES

REGIONAL ORGANIZATION'S LIBRARIES
BT LIBRARIES

REGISTER METHOD
BT RECORDING OF PERIODICALS

REGISTERED USERS
BT USERS
RT PUBLIC LIBRARIES
READING HABIT

REGISTRATION OF MEMBERSHIP
BT CIRCULATION

RELATIVE INDEX
BT INDEX TO THE CLASSIFICATION SCHEDULE
RT *DEWEY DECIMAL CLASSIFICATION*
*SPECIFIC INDEX*
*UNIVERSAL DECIMAL CLASSIFICATION*

RELIGIOUS LIBRARIES
BT SPECIAL LIBRARIES

RELUCTANT STUDENTS
BT STUDENTS

RT BOOK REGISTERS
DEVELOPMENT
READING HABIT
SCHOOL LIBRARIES

RELUCTANT USERS
BT USERS

REMOTE USERS
BT USERS
RT ACADEMIC LIBRARIES
APPLICATION
COMPUTERS
DIGITAL LIBRARIES
DOCUMENT DELIVERY SERVICES
EXPECTATIONS
INFORMATION NEEDS
INFORMATION SEEKING BEHAVIOR
MARKETING
MEDICAL LIBRARIES
MONITORING
NEEDS
ONLINE REFERENCE SERVICE
SERVICES
UNIVERSITY LIBRARIES
WEB BASED SERVICES

REMPLOY ADHESIVE BINDING
BT ADHESIVE BINDING
RT PERIODICALS
UNIVERSITY LIBRARIES

RENEWAL (ISSUED INFORMATION SOURCES)
BT CIRCULATION

RENEWAL (SUBSCRIPTION)
BT ACQUISITIONS
RT DE-SUBSCRIBING
PERIODICALS
UNIVERSITY LIBRARIES

REPORT GENERATION CAPACITY
RT EVALUATION
InMAGIC
SOFTWARES

REPORTS
BT INFORMATION SOURCES
NT ADMINISTRATIVE REPORTS
TECHNICAL REPORTS

REPRINT EDITIONS
BT EDITIONS

REPROGRAPHED INFORMATION SOURCES
BT INFORMATION SOURCES
NT PHOTOCOPIED INFORMATION SOURCES

REPROGRAPHIC SERVICES
BT SERVICES
NT MICROFORMING SERVICES
PHOTOCOPYING SERVICES

REPROGRAPHIC TECHNOLOGY
BT INFORMATION TECHNOLOGY
NT MICROFORMING TECHNOLOGY
PHOTOCOPYING TECHNOLOGY

REPROGRAPHY SECTION
BT INFORMATION SECTION

REQUEST FORMS
BT FORMS
RT APPLICATION
DESIGNING
HTML
ILL
WEB BASED FORMS

RESEARCH
NT FEASIBILITY STUDY
USE STUDY
USER STUDY
RT CLASSIFICATION

DIGITAL INFORMATION SOURCES
DOCUMENT DELIVERY SERVICES
EVALUATION
FINANCE
INFORMATION RETRIEVAL
INTERNET
UNIVERSITY LIBRARIES

RESEARCH CUBICAL SECTION
BT SECTION

RESEARCH INFORMATION SOURCES
BT INFORMATION SOURCES

RESEARCH IN PROGRESS
BT CAS

RESEARCH INSTITUTION'S PUBLICATIONS
BT INSTITUTIONAL INFORMATION SOURCES

RESEARCH LIBRARIES
BT SPECIAL LIBRARIES
NT AERONAUTICAL RESEARCH LIBRARIES
CELL SCIENCE RESEARCH LIBRARIES
DEFENCE RESEARCH LIBRARIES
PHARMACY RESEARCH LIBRARIES
SCIENCE RESEARCH LIBRARIES
SHIP ENGINEERING RESEARCH LIBRARIES
RT ILL
MEASURING
NON-UNIONISED PROFESSIONAL PERSONNEL
ORGANIZATIONAL COMMITMENT
PERFORMANCE
PRICING
UNIONISED PROFESSIONAL PERSONNEL

RESEARCH USE

BT USE
RT INTERNET INFORMATION SOURCES

RESERVATION
BT CIRCULATION

RESERVED INFORMATION SOURCES
BT INFORMATION SOURCES

RESOURCE SHARING
NT CONSORTIUM
COOPERATION
RT ACADEMIC LIBRARIES
AGRICULTURAL UNIVERSITY LIBRARIES
APPLICATION
COST-EFFECTIVENESS
EVALUATION
INTERNET
LAN
LIBRARIAN'S ATTITUDE
MANAGEMENT LIBRARIES
NETWORKS
PERIODICALS
PROPOSALS
STATUS
UNIVERSITY LIBRARIES

RETENTION
BT PERSONNEL MANAGEMENT
RT PERSONNEL
STRATEGY
UNIVERSITY LIBRARIES

RETIREMENT BENEFITS
RT GOVERNMENT SCHOOL LIBRARIES
MOTIVATION
PERSONNEL
PRIVATE SCHOOL LIBRARIES

RETRIEVAL PERFORMANCE
BT PERFORMANCE

RT ONLINE INDEXES
PRINTED INDEXES

RETROSPECTIVE BIBLIOGRAPHIES
BT BIBLIOGRAPHIES

RETROSPECTIVE CONVERSION
BT CATALOGUING
RT APPLICATION
CDS/ISIS
CORE HOLDINGS
IDA VERSION
IDENTIFICATION
UNIVERSITY LIBRARIES

RETROSPECTIVE INFORMATION SOURCES
BT INFORMATION SOURCES

RETURN OF INFORMATION SOURCES
UF Discharging
BT CIRCULATION
RT ISSUING

REVIEWING PERIODICALS
BT PERIODICALS

REVIEWING SERVICES
BT CONSOLIDATION SERVICES

REVIEWS
BT ECONOMIC HISTORY
REFERENCE SOURCES
SURVEYS

REVISED EDITIONS
BT EDITIONS

RIGHT TEMPERATURE
RT CONSERVATION
INFORMATION SOURCES

ROLE
NT TEACHER'S ROLES
RT ACADEMIC LIBRARIES

AUDIO LIBRARIES
AUTOMATED LIBRARIES
BRAILLE LIBRARIES
INTERNET MULTIMEDIA DATABASES
JUNIOR REFERENCE PERSONNEL
LIBRARIANS
ORIENTATION
PERSONNEL
PUBLIC LIBRARIES
READING ROOM INFORMATION SOURCES
REFERENCE PERSONNEL
SENIOR LIBRARIANS
SHELF LIST
USE

ROLLING SHELVES
BT SHELVES

ROUTING OF PERIODICALS
BT CAS
CIRCULATION

RRRLF
UF Raja Rammohan Roy Library Foundation
RT FINANCE
PUBLIC LIBRARIES

RUNNING TITLE
BT TITLE

RURAL LIBRARIES
BT LIBRARIES
RT NETWORKS

RURAL USERS
BT USERS
RT INFORMATION NEEDS

SALARY
RT LIBRARIANS
NON-PROFESSIONAL PERSONNEL
PROFESSIONAL PERSONNEL

SALEABLE SERVICES
BT SERVICES
RT MARKETING
UNIVERSITY LIBRARIES
SATISFACTION
RT USERS
SCANNERS
BT INFORMATION TECHNOLOGY
SCHEDULED MNEMONICS
BT MNEMONICS
SCHOOL LIBRARIES
BT ACADEMIC LIBRARIES
GOVERNMENT SCHOOL LIBRARIES
PRIMARY SCHOOL LIBRARIES
PRIVATE SCHOOL LIBRARIES
SECONDARY SCHOOL LIBRARIES
RT ADOLESCENT STUDENTS
AVAILABILITY
BOOK REGISTERS
CD-ROM DATABASES
CHILDREN INFORMATION SOURCES
CIRCULATION
DEVELOPMENT
IMPACT
IMPROVEMENT
IN-SERVICE TRAINING
LIBRARIANS
PROBLEMS
PROPOSALS
READING HABIT
RELUCTANT STUDENTS
SERVICES
STUDENTS
USE
SCHOOL STUDENTS

BT STUDENTS
NT ELEMENTARY SCHOOL STUDENTS
SECONDARY SCHOOL STUDENTS
RT PUBLIC LIBRARIES
SERVICES

SCIENCE AND TECHNOLOGY LIBRARIES
BT SPECIAL LIBRARIES
RT FINANCE
GENERATION (FINANCE)
INDIGENOUS DATABASES
USE

SCIENCE INFORMATION CENTRES
BT INFORMATION CENTRE
RT AESTHETIC OF NOTIFICATION
CHEMICAL DATABASES
COMPUTERIZED SDI
DOCUMENT DELIVERY SERVICES
ONLINE INFORMATION RETRIEVAL
QUANTITATIVE EVALUATION
SDI

SCIENCE INFORMATION SOURCES
BT INFORMATION SOURCES
NT BENGALI INFORMATION SOURCES

SCIENCE RESEARCH LIBRARIES
BT RESEARCH LIBRARIES
RT USE STUDY

SDI
UF Selective Dissemination of Information
BT CAS
NT COMPUTERIZED SDI
RT AESTHETIC OF NOTIFICATION
DOCUMENT DELIVERY SERVICES

SCIENCE INFORMATION CENTRES

SEARCH

BT INFORMATION STORAGE AND RETRIEVAL

NT OFFLINE SEARCH

ONLINE SEARCH

PRECISION

RECALL

RT APPLICATION

CD-ROM DATABASES

CLASSIFICATION

COST

ONLINE DATABASES

OPAC

SOCIAL SCIENCE INFORMATION CENTRES

SEARCH INTERFACE

RT EVALUATION

RARE BOOKS WEBSITES

SOFTWARES

UNIVERSITY LIBRARIES

WINISIS

SEAR'S LIST OF SUBJECT HEADINGS

BT LISTS OF SUBJECT HEADINGS

RT *LIBRARY OF CONGRESS LIST OF SUBJECT HEADINGS*

SECONDARY SCHOOL LIBRARIES

BT SCHOOL LIBRARIES

NT HIGHER SECONDARY SCHOOL LIBRARIES

SECONDARY SCHOOL STUDENTS

BT SCHOOL STUDENTS

SECTIONS

NT ACCOUNTS SECTION

ACQUISITION SECTION

ADMINISTRATION SECTION

BINDING SECTION
CIRCULATION SECTION
COMPUTER SECTION
CORRESPONDENCE SECTION
EXHIBITION SECTION
INFORMATION SECTION
PERIODICAL SECTION
PRESERVATION SECTION
READING ROOM SECTION
REFERENCE SECTION
RESEARCH CUBICLES SECTION
STACK ROOM SECTION
STORE SECTION
TECHNICAL PROCESSING SECTION

SECURITY PROBLEMS
BT PROBLEMS
RT APPLICATION
BARCODES
CIRCULATION

SEE ALSO ENTRIES
BT CROSS REFERENCE ENTRIES
RT *SEE ENTRIES*

SEE ENTRIES
BT CROSS REFERENCE ENTRIES
RT *SEE ALSO ENTRIES*

SELECTION (INFORMATION SOURCES)
UF Book selection
BT COLLECTION DEVELOPMENT
RT CD-ROM
CD-ROM DATABASES
EDUCATION COLLEGE LIBRARIES
GOLF INFORMATION SOURCES
INFORMATION SOURCES
PERIODICALS
*PRINCIPLES*

*SELECTION TOOLS*
TEACHER'S ROLE
UNIVERSITY LIBRARIES

SELECTION (INFORMATION SOURCES) SECTION
UF Book selection section
BT ACQUISITION SECTION

SELECTION (PERSONNEL)
BT RECRUITMENT

SELECTION TOOLS
NT APPROVAL METHOD
BIBLIOGRAPHIES
EXPERT'S SUGGESTIONS
INTERNET
READER'S REQUESTS
RT *SELECTION (INFORMATION SOURCES)*

SELECTIONS
SN *Collection of selected works*
BT INFORMATION SOURCES

SELECTIVE CATALOGUING
BT LIMITED CATALOGUING
RT *SIMPLIFIED CATALOGUING*

Selective Dissemination of Information
USE SDI

SELECTIVE LISTING IN COMBINATION
USE SLIC

SELF-CHARGED ILL
UF Direct ILL
BT ILL
RT MEDICAL LIBRARIES
UNIVERSITY LIBRARIES

SEMINAL MNEMONICS
BT MNEMONICS

SENIOR LIBRARIANS
BT LIBRARIANS

RT JUNIOR REFERENCE PERSONNEL
ORIENTATION
ROLE

SENIOR PERSONNEL
BT PERSONNEL

Serials
USE PERIODICALS

SERIES
BT BIBLIOGRAPHIC DESCRIPTION
NT MULTIPLE SERIES
SINGLE SERIES

SERVICE LIBRARIES
BT LIBRARIES

SERVICES
NT BIBLIOGRAPHIC SERVICES
CAS
CIRCULATION
CONDENSATION SERVICES
CONSULTANCY SERVICES
DOCUMENT DELIVERY SERVICES
ILL
INFORMATION SERVICES
INTERNET BASED SERVICES
LITERATURE SEARCH SERVICES
PRINTOUT SERVICES
REFERENCE SERVICE
REFERRAL SERVICES
REPROGRAPHIC SERVICES
SALEABLE SERVICES
TRANSLATION SERVICES
RT ACADEMIC LIBRARIES
ADULT USERS
AGRICULTURAL INFORMATION SYSTEM
APPLICATION
BROADCASTING CENTRE LIBRARIES
CHARGING (LEVYING MONETARY

CHARGES)
COLLEGE LIBRARIES
DEFENCE INFORMATION CENTRES
DEVELOPMENT
DIGITAL LIBRARIES
ENGINEERING COLLEGE LIBRARIES
ENVIRONMENTAL SCIENCE
INFORMATION SYSTEM
ETHNIC USERS
EVALUATION
FEE
IMPACT
IMPROVEMENT
INFORMATION CENTRES
ISO 9000
LAN
MARKETING
MARKETING MIX
MEASURING
MEDICAL LIBRARIES
MEDIUM SIZED LIBRARIES
MINORITY USERS
NETWORKED CONTACT LIBRARIES
NURSES
OUTSOURCING
PHYSICIANS
PRICING
PRIVATIZATION
PROPOSALS
PUBLIC LIBRARIES
QUALITY
REMOTE USERS
SCHOOL LIBRARIES
SCHOOL STUDENTS
SPECIAL LIBRARIES
STRATEGY

UNIVERSITY LIBRARIES
VIRTUAL LIBRARIES

SHARED AUTHORSHIP
BT AUTHORS

SHEAF FORM CATALOGUES
BT CATALOGUES

SHELF ARRANGEMENT
BT MAINTENANCE
NT BROKEN ORDER
COMPACT SHELVING

SHELF LIST
BT CATALOGUES
RT AUTOMATED LIBRARIES
ROLE

SHELVES
BT FURNITURE
NT BOOK SHELVES
COMPACT SHELVES
PERIODICAL SHELVES
ROLLING SHELVES

SHELVING
BT MAINTENANCE
RT POEMS (INFORMATION SOURCES)

SHIP ENGINEERING RESEARCH LIBRARIES
BT RESEARCH LIBRARIES
RT ONLINE INFORMATION RETRIEVAL
USER'S ATTITUDE

SHORT COMMUNICATION
BT INFORMATION SOURCES

SHORT TITLE
BT TITLE

SHORTHAND INFORMATION SOURCES
BT INFORMATION SOURCES

SIMPLE BOOKS

BT INFORMATION SOURCES
RT *COMPOSITE BOOKS*

SIMPLIFIED CATALOGUING
BT LIMITED CATALOGUING
NT COMPUTERIZED SIMPLIFIED CATALOGUING
RT *SELECTIVE CATALOGUING*

SINGLE AUTHOR
BT AUTHORS

SINGLE SERIES
BT SERIES

SINGLE VOLUME INFORMATION SOURCES
BT INFORMATION SOURCES

SIZE (INFORMATION SOURCES)
BT COLLATION

SKILLS
RT ACADEMIC LIBRARIES
CATALOGUERS
CHIEF LIBRARIANS
COMMERCIAL LIBRARIES
DIGITAL LIBRARIES
JUNIOR CATALOGUERS
PERSONNEL

SKIN INFORMATION SOURCES
SN *Information written on animal skin*
BT INFORMATION SOURCES

SLANTED ABSTRACTS
BT ABSTRACTS

SLIC
UF Selective Listing In Combination
BT PRE-COORDINATE INDEXING SYSTEMS

SLIDES
BT NON-BOOK MATERIALS

SMALL COLLEGE LIBRARIES
BT COLLEGE LIBRARIES

RT PAPERBACK INFORMATION SOURCES
PURCHASE

SMALL LIBRARIES
SN *Up to 20000 volumes*
BT LIBRARIES

SOCIAL IMPACT
BT IMPACT
RT PUBLIC LIBRARIES

SOCIAL INFORMATION SOURCES
SN *Information sources preaching social values*
BT INFORMATION SOURCES

SOCIAL SCIENCE INFORMATION CENTRES
BT INFORMATION CENTRES
RT CD-ROM DATABASES
COST
SEARCH

SOCIAL SCIENTISTS
BT USERS
RT INFORMATION SEEKING BEHAVIOR
PHYSICAL SCIENTISTS
UNIVERSITY LIBRARIES

Soft books
USE DIGITAL BOOKS

Software for university libraries
USE SOUL

SOFTWARES
UF Library softwares
BT COMPUTERS
NT CDS/ISIS
dBASE IV
InMAGIC

LIBRATAS
LIBSYS
MINISIS
OMNIPAGE PRO
SOUL
WINISIS
RT COMPATIBILITY
EASE OF USE
EVALUATION
GUIDELINES
REPORT GENERATION CAPACITY
SEARCH INTERFACE

SOUL
UF Software for university libraries
BT SOFTWARES

SPACE
SN *Space available in the library building*
BT BUILDING
RT ONE PERSON LIBRARIES
MANAGEMENT

SPACE FACET
BT FACETS
RT *PMEST*

SPACE ISOLATES
BT COMMON ISOLATES

SPECIAL EDITIONS
BT EDITIONS

SPECIAL ISOLATES
BT ISOLATES
NT ENERGY ISOLATES
MATTER ISOLATES
PERSONALITY ISOLATES
RT *COMMON ISOLATES*

SPECIAL LIBRARIES
BT LIBRARIES
NT AGRICULTURAL LIBRARIES

AUDIO LIBRARIES
AUTOMATED LIBRARIES
BLIND USER'S LIBRARIES
BRAILLE LIBRARIES
BROADCASTING CENTRE LIBRARIES
CHILDREN LIBRARIES
COMMERCIAL LIBRARIES
DEFENCE LIBRARIES
DIGITAL LIBRARIES
HYBRID LIBRARIES
INDUSTRIAL LIBRARIES
INSURANCE LIBRARIES
LAW LIBRARIES
MANAGEMENT LIBRARIES
MAP LIBRARIES
MEDICAL LIBRARIES
MOBILE LIBRARIES
NEWSPAPER LIBRARIES
ONE PERSON LIBRARIES
PERIODICAL'S LIBRARIES
PRISON LIBRARIES
RELIGIOUS LIBRARIES
RESEARCH LIBRARIES
SCIENCE AND TECHNOLOGY LIBRARIES
TECHNOLOGICAL LIBRARIES
TWENTY FOUR HOUR OPEN LIBRARIES
WILDLIFE INSTITUTION'S LIBRARIES

RT APPLICATION
COLLECTION DEVELOPMENT
INFORMATION TECHNOLOGY
PROBLEM OF DELAYED SUPPLY
PROBLEM OF LACK OF CONFIRMED PRICES
PROBLEM OF LACK OF USER
PARTICIPATION
PROBLEM OF LOSS IN TRANSIT

SERVICES

SPECIALS
BT CLASS
RT *SYSTEMS*

SPECIALIST USERS
BT USERS

SPECIFIC INDEX
BT INDEX TO THE CLASSIFICATION SCHEDULES
RT *RELATIVE INDEX*

SPECIFICATIONS
BT STANDARDS

SPIRAL BOUND INFORMATION SOURCES
BT INFORMATION SOURCES

SPIRITUAL INFORMATION SOURCES
BT INFORMATION SOURCES

STACK ROOM SECTION
BT SECTIONS

Staff
USE PERSONNEL

STAMPING
BT PHYSICAL PROCESSING

STANDARD NUMBERS
BT BIBLIOGRAPHIC DESCRIPTION
NT ISBN
ISSN

Standard Subdivisions
USE COMMON ISOLATES

STANDARDIZATION
BT MANAGEMENT
RT ACQUISITION
ILL
UNION CATALOGUE

UNIVERSITY LIBRARIES

STANDARDS (EVALUATION CRITERIA)

SN *A statement of criteria by which a library services* can be evaluated or given library work can be carried out

NT ACRL STANDARDS

ISO STANDARDS

TECHNICAL STANDARDS

Z39.50 STANDARDS

RT ACADEMIC LIBRARIES

COLLEGE LIBRARIES

DESIGNING

EVALUATION

METADATA

STANDARDS (INFORMATION SOURCES)

BT INFORMATION SOURCES

NT SPECIFICATIONS

RT ACADEMIC LIBRARIES

CLASSIFICATION

COLLECTION DEVELOPMENT

POLICY

STANDS

BT FURNITURE

NT CASSETTE STANDS

CD STANDS

DISPLAY STANDS

NEWSPAPER STANDS

STATE BIBLIOGRAPHIES

BT BIBLIOGRAPHIES

STATE GOVERNMENT LIBRARIES

BT GOVERNMENT LIBRARIES

STATE LIBRARIES

BT LIBRARIES

STATISTICAL ANALYSIS

BT ANALYSIS

RT OVERDUE (ISSUED INFORMATION SOURCES)
UNIVERSITY LIBRARIES

STATISTICAL INFORMATION SOURCES
BT REFERENCE SOURCES
RT COLLECTION DEVELOPMENT

STATUS
NT ACADEMIC STATUS
RT HIGHER SECONDARY SCHOOL LIBRARIES
PROFESSIONAL PERSONNEL
READING HABIT
RESOURCE SHARING
STUDENTS

STOCK RECTIFICATION
RT STOCK VERIFICATION

STOCK VERIFICATION
RT APPLICATION
BARCODES
COLLEGE LIBRARIES
COMPUTERS
LIBRATAS
STOCK RECTIFICATION

STONE INFORMATION SOURCES
SN *Information written on stones*
BT INFORMATION SOURCES

STORAGE TECHNOLOGY
BT INFORMATION TECHNOLOGY
NT CD-DA
CD-I
CD-R
CD-ROM
CD-RW
CD-XA

DVD
FLOPPY DISKS
MAGNETIC DISKS
MAGNETIC TAPES

STORE SECTION
BT SECTIONS

STORY TELLING
BT EXTENSION ACTIVITIES

STRATEGIC PLANNING
BT PLANNING
RT ACADEMIC LIBRARIES
OPEN PERSON LIBRARIES

STRATEGY
RT DEVELOPMENT
MARKETING
ONLINE SEARCH
PERSONNEL
RETENTION
SERVICES
UNIVERSITY LIBRARIES

STUDENTS
BT USERS
NT ADOLESCENT STUDENTS
ARTIST STUDENTS
DOCTORAL STUDENTS
FEMALE STUDENTS
INTERNATIONAL STUDENTS
POST GRADUATE STUDENTS
POST MASTER (M. PHIL.) STUDENTS
RELUCTANT STUDENTS
SCHOOL STUDENTS
UNDER GRADUATE STUDENTS
RT HIGHER SECONDARY SCHOOL LIBRARIES
PUBLIC LIBRARIES
READING HABIT
SCHOOL LIBRARIES

STATUS

STYLE (OF WRITING)

RT INFORMATION SOURCES

OBSOLESCENCE

Subject

USE CLASS

SUBJECT ADDED ENTRIES

BT ADDED ENTRIES

SUBJECT ANALYTICAL ENTRIES

BT ANALYTICAL ENTRIES

SUBJECT CATALOGUES

BT CATALOGUES

RT *AUTHOR CATALOGUES*

*TITLE CATALOGUES*

SUBJECT CLASSIFICATION (BROWN)

BT CLASSIFICATION SCHEMES (EXAMPLES)

SUBJECT COMPETENCIES

BT COMPETENCIES

RT ACADEMIC LIBRARIES

REFERENCE PERSONNEL

SUBJECT COVERAGE

RT ELECTRONIC DOCUMENT DELIVERY SERVICES

EVALUATION

NATIONAL LIBRARIES

SUBJECT DEVICE

BT DEVICES

SUBJECT HEADINGS

UF Descriptors

RT IMPACT

TECHNOLOGICAL UNIVERSITY LIBRARIES

THESIS

USE

SUBSCRIBING
BT ACQUISITION
RT PERIODICALS
PROBLEMS
UNIVERSITY LIBRARIES

SUBSTANTIVE DIGITS
BT NOTATIONAL DIGITS

SUMMARIES
BT ABRIDGEMENTS

SUPPLEMENT NUMBERS
BT BOOK NUMBERS

SUPPLEMENTS
BT INFORMATION SOURCES

SURVEYS
BT INFORMATION SOURCES
NT REVIEWS
TREND REPORTS

SYMPOSIUMS
BT COMPOSITE BOOKS

SYNOPSIS
BT ABRIDGEMENTS

SYSTEM ANALYSIS

SYSTEMATIC BIBLIOGRAPHIES
BT BIBLIOGRAPHIES

SYSTEMATIC MNEMONICS
BT MNEMONICS

SYSTEMS
BT CLASS
RT *SPECIALS*

TABLES
BT FURNITURE
NT COMPUTER TABLES
READING ROOM TABLES

TEACHERS
BT USERS

RT DEGREE COLLEGE LIBRARIES
READING HABIT

TEACHER'S ROLE
BT ROLE
RT INFORMATION SOURCES
SELECTION (INFORMATION SOURCES)
UNIVERSITY LIBRARIES

TECHNICAL PROCESSING
NT CATALOGUING
CLASSIFICATION
RT APPLICATION
HYBRID LIBRARIES
KNOWLEDGE BASED SYSTEM
PARAPROFESSIONAL PERSONNEL

TECHNICAL PROCESSING SECTION
BT SECTIONS
NT CATALOGUING SECTION
CLASSIFICATION SECTION
PHYSICAL PROCESSING SECTION

TECHNICAL REPORTS
BT REPORTS

TECHNICAL STANDARDS
BT STANDARDS (EVALUATION CRITERIA)

TECHNOLOGICAL CHANGE
BT CHANGE
RT MANAGEMENT
MANAGEMENT LIBRARIES

TECHNOLOGICAL INFORMATION CENTRES
BT INFORMATION CENTRES
RT PHOTOCOPYING SERVICES
RECOVERY OF INFORMATION SOURCES (ISSUED)

TECHNOLOGICAL LIBRARIES
BT SPECIAL LIBRARIES

NT CENTRAL TECHNOLOGICAL LIBRARIES
RT ABSTRACTING SERVICES
BIBLIOGRAPHIC SERVICES
CD-ROM DATABASES
COMPUTERIZED SDI
DEVELOPMENT
FINANCE
GENERATION (FINANCE)
INDEXING SERVICES
WEB BASED SERVICES

TECHNOLOGICAL UNIVERSITY LIBRARIES
BT UNIVERSITY LIBRARIES
RT IMPACT
INTERNATIONAL STUDENTS
SUBJECT HEADINGS
THESIS
USE

TELE-TRANSLATIONS SERVICES
BT TRANSLATIONS SERVICES

TEMPORARY PERSONNEL
BT PERSONNEL

TERMINOLOGY
BT VERBAL PLANE

TEXINCON
BT TEXTILES BIBLIOGRAPHIC DATABASES
RT CREATION

TEXTBOOKS
BT INFORMATION SOURCES
NT FRENCH TEXTBOOKS
HUMANITIES TEXTBOOKS
PRESCRIBED TEXTBOOKS
RT ACADEMIC LIBRARIES
KANTOR METHOD
MEASURING

UNIVERSITY LIBRARIES
USE

TEXTBOOK'S AVAILABILITY
BT AVAILABILITY
RT ACADEMIC LIBRARIES
EVALUATION

TEXTILES BIBLIOGRAPHIC DATABASES
BT BIBLIOGRAPHIC DATABASES
NT TEXINCON

TEXTUAL INFORMATION RETRIEVAL
BT INFORMATION RETRIEVAL
RT APPLICATION
N-GRAM

THEFT
RT ACADEMIC LIBRARIES
PREVENTION
RARE BOOKS

THEORIES OF CLASSIFICATION
RT CLASSIFICATION

THEORIES OF INDEXING
RT INDEXING

THEORIES OF REFERENCE SERVICES
RT REFERENCE SERVICE

THESAURI
NT ALPHABETICAL THESAURI
BILINGUAL THESAURI
FICTION THESAURI
GRAPHIC THESAURI
HUMANITIES THESAURI
MONOLINGUAL THESAURI
MULTILINGUAL THESAURI
THESAUROFACET

RT CONTROL
*INFORMATION STORAGE AND RETRIEVAL*
*PRECISION*
RECALL
THESAURI CONSTRUCTION
*VOCABULARY CONTROL*

THESAURI CONSTRUCTION
RT APPLICATION
FICTION THESAURI
MULTILINGUAL THESAURI
NATURAL LANGUAGE PROCESSING
THESAURI

THESAUROFACET
BT THESAURI

THESIS
UF Dissertations
BT INFORMATION SOURCES
RT IMPACT
SUBJECT HEADINGS
TECHNOLOGICAL UNIVERSITY LIBRARIES
USE

THREE CARD SYSTEM
BT RECORDING OF PERIODICALS

TIME FACET
BT FACETS
RT *PMEST*

TIME ISOLATES
BT COMMON ISOLATES

TITLE
BT BIBLIOGRAPHIC DESCRIPTION
NT ALTERNATIVE TITLE
FANCIFUL TITLE
HALF TITLE
RUNNING TITLE
SHORT TITLE

UNIFORMED TITLE

TITLE ADDED ENTRIES

BT ADDED ENTRIES

TITLE ANALYTICAL ENTRIES

BT ANALYTICAL ENTRIES

TITLE CATALOGUES

BT CATALOGUES

RT *AUTHOR CATALOGUES*

*SUBJECT CATALOGUES*

TITLE COVERAGE

RT EVALUATION

FULL TEXT PERIODICALS DATABASES

TITLE PAGE

NT PHYSICAL LAYOUT OF TITLE PAGE

Total quality management

USE TQM

TQM

UF Total quality management

RT ACQUISITION

APPLICATION

MANAGEMENT LIBRARIES

PUBLIC LIBRARIES

UNIVERSITY LIBRARIES

TRACING AREA

BT AREAS

TRADE ASSOCIATION'S LIBRARIES

BT LIBRARIES

TRADE BIBLIOGRAPHIES

BT BIBLIOGRAPHIES

NT TRADE CATALOGUES

TRADE CATALOGUES

BT TRADE BIBLIOGRAPHIES

NT EXHIBITION CATALOGUES

TRADE LITERATURE

BT INFORMATION SOURCES

TRADE UNION'S LIBRARIES
BT LIBRARIES

TRADITIONAL CATALOGUES
BT CATALOGUES
RT OPAC

TRAINEE PERSONNEL
BT PERSONNEL
RT RECRUITMENT
UNIVERSITY LIBRARIES

TRAINING
BT PERSONNEL MANAGEMENT
NT IN-SERVICE TRAINING
RT COMPUTERS
ILL PERSONNEL
IMPACT
LIBRARIANS
LIBRARIAN'S ATTITUDE

TRANSLATION CENTRES
RT TRANSLATION SERVICES

TRANSLATION SECTION
BT INFORMATION SECTION

TRANSLATION SERVICES
BT SERVICES
NT TELE-TRANSLATION SERVICES
RT TRANSLATION CENTRES

TRANSLATIONS
BT INFORMATION SOURCES

TRANSLATORS
BT COLLABORATORS
INFORMATION PERSONNEL

TRANSPARENCIES
BT NON-BOOK MATERIALS

TRAYS
BT FURNITURE
NT CATALOGUE CARD TRAYS
CHARGING TRAYS

TREATISE

BT INFORMATION SOURCES

TREND REPORTS

BT SURVEYS

TRIBAL USERS

BT USERS

TRUST'S LIBRARIES

BT LIBRARIES

TURNOVER

RT PERSONNEL

UNIVERSITY LIBRARIES

TWENTY FOUR HOUR OPEN LIBRARIES

BT SPECIAL LIBRARIES

TYPED INFORMATION SOURCES

BT INFORMATION SOURCES

UDC

USE UNIVERSAL DECIMAL CLASSIFICATION

UNDER GRADUATE STUDENTS

BT STUDENTS

RT EFFECT

UNIVERSITY LIBRARIES

USER EDUCATION

UNDERSIZED INFORMATION SOURCES

SN *A book less than normal size*

Generally less than 3 cm height

BT INFORMATION SOURCES

UNIFORMED TITLE

BT TITLE

UNIMARC

UF Universal MARC

BT MARC

RT APPLICATION

BIBLIOGRAPHIC DATABASES

*CCF*
CREATION

UNION CATALOGUES
BT CATALOGUES
NT NUCSSI
RT STANDARDIZATION
UNIVERSITY LIBRARIES

UNIONISED PROFESSIONAL PERSONNEL
BT PROFESSIONAL PERSONNEL
RT NON-UNIONISED PROFESSIONAL PERSONNEL
ORGANIZATIONAL COMMITMENT
RESEARCH LIBRARIES

UNITERM
BT POST COORDINATE INDEXING SYSTEMS

UNIVERSAL DECIMAL CLASSIFICATION
UF UDC
BT CLASSIFICATION SCHEMES (EXAMPLES)
RT *DEWEY DECIMAL CLASSIFICATION*
*RELATIVE INDEX*

Universal MARC
USE UNIMARC

UNIVERSITY LIBRARIES
BT ACADEMIC LIBRARIES
NT AFFILIATING UNIVERSITY LIBRARIES
AGRICULTURAL UNIVERSITY LIBRARIES
AUTOMATED UNIVERSITY LIBRARIES
CENTRAL LIBRARIES OF UNIVERSITIES
CENTRAL UNIVERSITY LIBRARIES
CENTRALIZED UNIVERSITY LIBRARIES
DECENTRALIZED UNIVERSITY LIBRARIES
DEEMED UNIVERSITY LIBRARIES
OPEN UNIVERSITY LIBRARIES

TECHNOLOGICAL UNIVERSITY LIBRARIES

RT ACQUISITION
ADULT USERS
APPLICATION
ARABIZED CDS/ISIS
ARABIZED MINISIS
BACKLOG CATALOGUING
BUILDINGS
CATALOGUE
CDS/ISIS
CHARGING (LEVYING MONETARY CHARGES)
COLLECTION DEVELOPMENT
COMMITTEES
COMPUTERIZATION
COOPERATIVE ACQUISITION
COOPERATIVE CATALOGUING
DELINQUENT USERS
DE-SUBSCRIBING
DEVELOPMENT
DIGITISATION
DOCUMENT DELIVERY SERVICES
DRINKING WATER FACILITY
EFFECT
EVALUATION
EXAMINATION PAPERS
EXHIBITIONS
FEE
FEMALE STUDENTS
FINANCE
FINANCIAL PROBLEMS
FUMIGATION
HOME PAGES
ILL
IMAGES
INFORMATION NEEDS

INFORMATION SEEKING BEHAVIOR
INFORMATION SOURCES
INFORMATION TECHNOLOGY
JOB SATISFACTION
LIBRARIANS
MANAGEMENT
MANAGEMENT BY OBJECTIVES
MARKETING
MEASURING
MICROFILMING (PRESERVATION METHOD)
MINORITY PERSONNEL
MOTIVATION
NUCSSI
ORGANIZATION
OVERDUE (ISSUED INFORMATION SOURCES)
PARTICIPATIVE MANAGEMENT
PERIODICALS
PERSONNEL
PERT
PHOTOCOPYING (PRESERVATION METHOD)
PHYSICAL SCIENTISTS
PLANNING
POLICY
POSTGRADUATE STUDENTS
PRESERVATION
PROBLEMS
PROMOTION (MARKETING MIX)
PROPOSALS
PUBLIC RELATION
PUBLICITY
QUALITY
RARE BOOKS WEBSITES
READING ROOM FACILITY
RECRUITMENT
REMOTE USERS

REMPLOY ADHESIVE BINDING
RENEWAL (SUBSCRIPTION)
RESEARCH
RESOURCE SHARING
RETENTION
RETROSPECTIVE CONVERSION
SALEABLE SERVICES
SEARCH INTERFACE
SELECTION (INFORMATION SOURCES)
SELF-CHARGED ILL
SERVICES
SOCIAL SCIENTISTS
STANDARDIZATION
STATISTICAL ANALYSIS
STRATEGY
SUBSCRIBING
TEACHER'S ROLE
TEXTBOOKS
TQM
TRAINEE PERSONNEL
TURNOVER
UNDER GRADUATE STUDENTS
UNION CATALOGUES
USE
USE STUDY
USER EDUCATION
WEB BASED SERVICES
WEEDING
WWW

UNIVERSITY PUBLICATIONS
BT INSTITUTIONAL INFORMATION SOURCES

UNMARRIED USERS
BT USERS

UNPUBLISHED INFORMATION SOURCES

BT INFORMATION SOURCES

URBAN LIBRARIES

BT LIBRARIES

URBAN USERS

BT USERS

USE

NT RESEARCH USE

RT ACADEMIC LIBRARIES
AGRICULTURAL UNIVERSITY LIBRARIES
AUDIO LIBRARIES
AUTOMATED UNIVERSITY LIBRARIES
AVAILABILITY
BOOKS
BRAILLE LIBRARIES
BRANCH NATIONAL LIBRARIES
CD-ROM DATABASES
COPYRIGHT
DATABASES
FINANCIAL IMPACT
GOVERNMENT INFORMATION SOURCES
IMPACT
INDIGENOUS DATABASES
INFORMATION SOURCES
INTERNATIONAL STUDENTS
INTERNET MULTIMEDIA DATABASES
LAW LIBRARIES
LIBRARIANS
LIBRARIES
MEASURING
NETWORKS
ONLINE DATABASES
OPAC
PERIODICALS
PERSONNEL
PUBLIC LIBRARIES
ROLE

SCHOOL LIBRARIES
SCIENCE AND TECHNOLOGY LIBRARIES
SUBJECT HEADINGS
TECHNOLOGICAL UNIVERSITY LIBRARIES
TEXTBOOKS
THESIS
UNIVERSITY LIBRARIES
VETERINARY INFORMATION SOURCES

USE STUDY
BT RESEARCH
RT APPLICATION
BRANCH PUBLIC LIBRARIES
CATALOGUES
GEOGRAPHICAL INFORMATION SYSTEM
SCIENCE RESEARCH LIBRARIES
UNIVERSITY LIBRARIES
*USER STUDY*

USER EDUCATION
UF Bibliographic instructions
NT ORIENTATION
RT APPLICATION
AUDIO CASSETTES
CATALOGUES
CENTRAL LIBRARIES OF UNIVERSITIES
DESIGNING
EFFECT
EXHIBITIONS
LIBRARY HANDBOOKS
MARKETING
PROGRAMMES
PUBLIC LIBRARIES
UNDER GRADUATE STUDENTS
UNIVERSITY LIBRARIES
WWW

USER STUDY

BT RESEARCH

RT DIGITAL LIBRARIES

SCIENCE RESEARCH LIBRARIES

*USE STUDY*

USERS

NT ADOLESCENT USERS

ADULT USERS

AWARDED FARMERS

BLIND USERS

CHILDREN USERS

COUNCILLORS

DELINQUENT USERS

ETHNIC USERS

FEMALE USERS

GAZETTED OFFICERS

GENERAL USERS

ILLITERATE USERS

INTERNATIONAL USERS

INTERNET USERS

JOURNALISTS

LITERARY WRITERS

LITERATE USERS

MAJORITY USERS

MALE USERS

MINORITY USES

NEO LITERATE USERS

NON REGISTERED USERS

NURSES

PARENTS

PATIENTS

PHYSICAL SCIENTISTS

PHYSICIANS

PRISONERS

REGISTERED USERS

RELUCTANT USERS
REMOTE USERS
RURAL USERS
SOCIAL SCIENTISTS
SPECIALIST USERS
STUDENTS
TEACHERS
TRIBAL USERS
UNMARRIED USERS
URBAN USERS
USERS FROM CITY
USERS FROM METROPOLITAN CITY
USERS FROM TOWN
USERS FROM VILLAGES
RT ANXIETY
CD- ROM BIBLIOGRAPHIC DATABASES
DIGITAL INFORMATION SOURCES
FEE BASED PUBLIC LIBRARIES
IMPACT
INFORMATION DEMANDS
INFORMATION RETRIEVAL
INFORMATION SEEKING BEHAVIOR
INFORMATION TECHNOLOGY
JOB SATISFACTION
LACK OF LIBRARY AWARENESS
LIBRARY TECHNOLOGY
MEASURING
OPINION
PERSONNEL
POPLINE
PUBLIC LIBRARIES
SATISFACTION

USERS FROM CITY
BT USERS

USERS FORM METROPOLITAN CITY

BT USERS

USERS FROM TOWN

BT USERS

USERS FROM VILLAGE

BT USERS

USER'S ATTITUDE

RT ONLINE INFORMATION RETRIEVAL

SHIP ENGINEERING RESEARCH LIBRARIES

VACANCIES

BT PERSONNEL MANAGEMENT

NT RECRUITMENT

RT CATALOGUING SECTION

VALUE ADDED INFORMATION SERVICES

BT INFORMATION SERVICES

RT IMPACT

INFORMATION TECHNOLOGY

VELLUM INFORMATION SOURCES

SN *Information written on vellum*

BT INFORMATION SOURCES

VENTILATION

VERBAL COMMUNICATION

BT COMMUNICATION

NT *NON VERBAL COMMUNICATION*

VERBAL MNEMONICS

BT MNEMONICS

VERBAL PLANE

BT PLANES OF WORK

NT TERMINOLOGY

VERSIFICATIONS

SN *A poetical version of other information source*

BT INFORMATION SOURCES

VERTICAL FILES

BT FURNITURE

VETERINARY INFORMATION SOURCES
BT INFORMATION SOURCES
RT USE

VIDEO CASSETTES
BT AUDIO VISUAL INFORMATION SOURCES
RT AUDIO VISUAL TECHNOLOGY

VIRTUAL LIBRARIES
BT DIGITAL LIBRARIES
NT MANUSCRIPTS VIRTUAL LIBRARIES
RT MARKETING
SERVICES

VOCABULARY CONTROL
RT *AUTHORITY CONTROL*
*CONTROLLED LANGUAGES*
*LISTS OF SUBJECT HEADINGS*
*THESAURI*

VOLUME NUMBERS
BT BOOK NUMBERS

WAITING TIME
RT ACADEMIC LIBRARIES
EVALUATION
REFERENCE SERVICE

WAN
UF Wide Area Networks
BT NETWORKS
NT INFLIBNET
INTERNET
RT LAN

WATER (CAUSE OF DISASTER)
BT NATURAL DISASTER
RT CONSERVATION
DAMAGE
PRINTED INFORMATION SOURCES

WEB BASED FORMS
 BT FORMS
 RT APPLICATION
 DESIGNING
 HTML
 ILL
 REQUEST FORMS

WEB BASED ILL
 BT ILL

WEB BASED SERVICES
 RT ACADEMIC LIBRARIES
 REMOTE USERS
 TECHNOLOGICAL LIBRARIES
 UNIVERSITY LIBRARIES

WEBLIOGRAPHERS
 BT BIBLIOGRAPHERS

WEBPAGES
 BT WEBSITES

WEBSITES
 BT INTERNET INFORMATION SOURCE
 WWW
 NT HOMEPAGES
 WEBPAGES
 RARE BOOKS WEBSITES

WEEDING
 BT COLLECTION DEVELOPMENT
 RT DUPLICATION
 GUIDELINES
 INFORMATION SOURCE
 MUTILATION
 NON-CIRCULATION
 OBSOLESCENCE
 UNIVERSITY LIBRARIES

WHY QUESTIONS
 BT REFERENCE INTERVIEW QUESTIONS

Wide Area Networks
USE WAN

WILDLIFE INSTITUTION'S LIBRARIES
BT SPECIAL LIBRARIES
RT CLIPPING SERVICES

WINISIS
BT SOFTWARES
RT EVALUATION
SEARCH INTERFACE

WOODEN FURNITURE
BT FURNITURE

WOODEN INFORMATION SOURCES
SN *Information written on wood*
BT INFORMATION SOURCES

WORD BY WORD ALPHABETIZATION
BT ALPHABETIZATION
RT LETTER BY LETTER ALPHABETIZATION

WORKING CONDITION
RT ACADEMIC LIBRARIES
APPLICATION
IMPROVEMENT
HUMOUR

World Wide Web
USE WWW

WWW
UF World Wide Web
BT INTERNET
NT WEBSITES
RT APPLICATION
PROMOTION (MARKETING MIX)
UNIVERSITY LIBRARIES
USER EDUCATION

XEROXED INFORMATION SOURCES

USE PHOTOCOPIED INFORMATION SOURCES

YEAR OF PUBLICATION

BT BOOK NUMBERS

IMPRINT

YEARBOOKS

BT REFERENCE SOURCES

RT *ALMANACS*

ZBB

UF Zero Based Budgeting

BT BUDGETING

Zero Based Budgeting

USE ZBB

Z39.50 STANDARDS

BT STANDARDS (EVALUATION CRITERIA)

RT INFORMATION RETRIEVAL

# REFERENCES

Note:

1. The following is the list documents referred to.
2. Column 1 gives serial number.
3. Column 2 gives section number in the text where reference to the Document is made. A comma separates two section numbers.



| S/N | Section No. | |
|---|---|---|
| 1. | 3.5 | Aitchison, J. (1982). Indexing languages, classification schemes and thesauri. *In* L. J. Anthony. *Ed.* Handbook of special librarianship and information work. 5th ed. London: Aslib. P. 230. |
| 2. | 3.7.4 | Aitchison, J. (1992). Indexing languages and indexing. *In* Patti Dosset. *Ed.* Handbook of special librarianship and information work. 6th ed. London: Aslib. P. 191-233. |
| 3. | 3.9.1 | Aitchison, J. (1996). International thesaurus of refugee terminology, 2nd ed. New York: United Nations High Commissioner for Refugees. |
| 4. | 3.2 | Aitchison, J. and Gilchrist, A. (1987). Thesaurus construction: a practical manual. 2nd Ed. London: Aslib. |

| | | |
|---|---|---|
| 5. | 3.1 | Aitchison, J., Gilchrist, A. and Bawden, D. (2000). Thesaurus construction and use: a practical manual. 4th ed. London: Aslib. P.1. |
| 5a. | 3.6 | Aitchison, J., Gilchrist, A. and Bawden, D. (2000a). Ibid. P. 7. |
| 5b. | 3.7.1 | Aitchison, J., Gilchrist, A. and Bawden, D. (2000b). Ibid. P.146. |
| 5c. | 3.7.4 | Aitchison, J., Gilchrist, A. and Bawden, D. (2000c). Ibid. P. 1-218. |
| 5d. | 3.7.5 | Aitchison, J., Gilchrist, A. and Bawden, D. (2000d). Ibid. P. 82. |
| 5e. | 3.8 | Aitchison, J., Gilchrist, A. and Bawden, D. (2000e). Ibid. P. 49. |
| 5f. | 3.8.3 | Aitchison, J., Gilchrist, A. and Bawden, D. (2000f). Ibid. P. 60. |
| 5g. | 5.10.3.4 | Aitchison, J., Gilchrist, A. and Bawden, D. (2000g). Ibid. P. 55. |
| 6. | 3.9.2, 3.11.2 | Aitchison, J., Gomersall, A. and Ireland, R. (1969). Thesaurofacet: a thesaurus and faceted classification for engineering and related subjects. England: English Electric Company Ltd. |
| 7. | 3.4.1 | American (1895) Library Association. List of subject headings foruse in dictionary catalogue. Boston, Mass.: Library Bureau. |
| 8. | 3.11.2 | American (1977). Psychological Association. Thesaurus of psychological index terms 2nd ed. APA: Washington, DC. |
| 9. | 3.7.5.1 | Aptagiri, D. V. and Prasad, A. R. D. (1995). Concept grouping for thesaurus construction using NLP techniques. *Library Herald* 33(1/2). P. 38-46. |

| | | |
|---|---|---|
| 10. | 3.11.2 | Art (1994) and architecture thesaurus. 2nd ed. 5 vols. Oxford: OUP. *Review available at*: http:// shiva.pub.getty.edu/att_browser/. |
| 11. | 3.11.1 | ASIS (1998). Thesaurus of information science and librarianship. 2nd ed. Medford, NJ: Learned Information Inc. |
| 12. | 3.10 | Aslib. Current Awareness Abstract. *10 issues p.a.* London: Aslib, 1984 - . |
| 13. | 3.10 | Aslib (2002). http://www.co.uk/osis/ thesauri.html |
| 14. | 3.7.3 | Association Francaise de Normalisation (1981). Regles d'etablissement en langue francaise. NFZ 47-100. Paris: AFNOR. |
| 15. | 3.6.1 | Austin, D. (1986). Vocabulary control and information technology. *Aslib Proceedings* 38(1). P. 1-15. |
| 16. | 3.11.2 | Australian (2000) pictorial thesaurus. http:// www.picturethesaurus.gov.au/ |
| 17. | 3.7.2 | Bates, M. J. (1986). Subject access in online catalogs: a design model. *Journal of American Society for Information Science* 37(6). P. 357-376. |
| 18. | 3.4.2 | Bates, M. J. (1988). How to use controlled vocabularies more effectively in online searching. *Online* 12(6). P. 48. |
| 19. | 3.6.1 | Batty, D. (1998). WWW - Wealth, weariness or waste. http//www.dlib.org/dlib/november98/ 11/batty.html |
| 20. | 3.11.2 | Bauer, G. (1967). Anwendung des Prinzips der Facetten Klassification fur den Aufbau von Thesauri. [Use of the principles of faceted classification för the construction of thesauri]. |

*ZIID-Zeitschrift* 14(3). P.72-83.

21. 3.8.2 Bean, C. A. (1998). The semantics of hierarchy: Explicit parentchild relationships in MeSH tree structures. *In* Advances in knowledge organization, vol. 6. Structure and relations in knowledge organization. Proceedings of the 5th International ISKO Conference, Lille, 25-29 Aug. 1998. Wurzburg, Germany: Ergon Verlang. P. 133-138.

22. 3.3 Bernier, C. L. and Crane, E. J. (1948). Indexing abstracts. *Industrial and Engineering Chemistry* 40(4). P. 725-730.

23. 2.3.2 Bhattacharyya, G. (1969). Vital role of depth classification in a system for document finding: a trend report. *Library Science* 6. P. 52-70.

24. 3.2 Bhattacharyya, G. (1974). The effectiveness of natural language in science indexing and retrieval. *Journal of Documentation* 30. P. 235-254.

25. 3.7.2 Bhattacharyya, G. (1982). Classaurus: its fundamentals, design and use. *Studin zur Klassifikation* 11. P. 139-148.

26. 2.6.1 Bhattacharyya, G. and Bhattacharyya, M. (1966). Library science: depth classification. DRTC Seminar 4. Banglore: DRTC. Paper N.

27. 3.8.3 Biswas, S. C. and Smith, F. (1989). Classed thesaurus in indexing and retrieval: a literature review and critical evaluation of online alphabetical classaurus. *Library and Information Science Research* 11(2). P. 109-141.

28. 3.7.1 Blagden, J. F. (1968). Thesaurus compilation methods: a literature review. *Aslib Proceedings* 20(8). P. 345-358.

29. 3.2 Blair, D. C. and Maron, M. E. (1985). An evaluation of retrieval effectiveness for a full-text document retrieval system. *Communications for the Association for Computing Machinery* 28. P. 289-299.

30. 3 6.1 Borko, H. (1986). A note commenting on vocabulary control and information technology by Derek Austin. *Aslib Proceedings* 38(6/7). P. 219- 221.

31. 3.1 British (1979) Standards Institution. British standards 5723:1979-Guidelines for the establishment and development of monolingual thesauri. London: BSI.

32. 3.9.1 3.11.2 British (1985) Standard Institution. ROOT thesaurus. 2nd ed. 2 vols. London: BSI.

33. 3.7.3 British (1987) Standards Institution. BS 5723: Guidelines for the establishment and development of monolingual thesauri. 2nd ed. London: BSI.

34. 3.9.1 CAB (1999) thesaurus. Wallingford (UK): CAB International.

35. 2.1.2 Chan, L. M. (1995). Classification present and future. *Cataloguing & Classification Quarterly*. 21 (2). P. 5-17.

36. 3.7.5.1 Chandran, D. (1975). Candidate terms for thesaurus: A case study of sources of terms in the field of library and information science. Seminar on thesaurus in information systems. Banglore: DRTC. Paper AG.

37. 3.7.5.1 Chowdhury, G. G. (1999). Introduction to modern information retrieval. London: Library Association Publishing. P. 140.

38. 3.7.5.1 Chowdhury. G.G. Neelameghan. A. and Chowdhury. S. (1995). VOCON: Vocabulary control online in MicroIsis databases. *Knowledge Organization* 22(1). P. 18-22.

39. 3.2 Cleverdon, C. W. et.al. (1966). Factors determining the performance of index languages. 3 vols. Cranfield, (England): College of Aeronautics.

40. 3.4.3 Coates, E. J. (1960). Subject catalogues: headings and structures. London: Library Association.

41. 3.2 Coco, A. (1984). Full-text versus full-text plus editorial additions. *Legal Reference Services Quarterly* 42(2). P. 27-37.

42. 3.7.4 Craven, T. C.(2001). *http://instruct.uwo.ca/ca/gplis/677/thesaurus/main00.htm*

43. 3.7.5 Crouch, C. J. (1990). An approach to the automatic construction of global thesauri. *Information Processing and Management* 26(5). P. 624-640.

44. 3.4.1 Cutter, C. A. (1889). Rules for a dictionary catalogue. 2nd ed. Washington, D.C.: U. S. Bureau of Education.

45. 3.11.2 Dahlberg, J. (1966). Thesaurus research: Deutsche Gesselleschaft Fur Dokumentation. *EV Bulletin de l'AID*. 5(4). P. 103-104.

46. 2.6.1 Daniel, R. and Mills, J. (1975). A classification of library and information science. London: The Library Association.

47. 1.1.6 Davis, C. H. and Rush, C. L. (1979). Guide to information science.

3.1 Westport. CT: Greenwood. P. 1.

47a 3.7.5.1 Davis, C. H. and Rush. C. L. (1979a). Ibid. 5.

48. 3.7.3 Deutsches Institut fur Normung (DIN) (1987-1993). Richtlinien fur die Herstellung und Weiterentwicklung von Thesauri. DIN 1563-pt.1 1987. pt. 2 1993. Berlin: DIN.

49. 3.7.2 Devadasan, F. J. (1985). Online construction of alphabetical thesaurus: a vocabulary control and indexing tool. *Information Processing and Management* 21. P. 11-26.

50. 2.2.2 Devadasan, F. J. (1986). Ranganathan's idea of facet analysis in action. *In* T. S. Rajgopalan. *Ed.* Ranganathan's philosophy: assessment, impact and relevance. New Delhi: Vikas. P. 132-142.

51. 3.8 Dextre Clarke, S. G. (2000). Thesaural relationships. *In* C. A. Bean. and R. Green. *Eds*. Relationships in the organization of knowledge. Dordrecht: Kluwer. P. 37-52.

52. 3.7.4 Dextre Clarke, S. G. (2001). Organizing access to information by subject. *In.* A. Scammell. *Ed.* Handbook of special librarianship and information work. 8th ed. England: Aslib.

53. 2.1.2 Dhyani, P. (1999). Library classification in computer age. *DESIDOC Bulletin of Information Technology*. 19(3). P. 5-13.

54. 3.2 Dubois, C. P. R. (1987). Free text vs. controlled vocabulary: a reassessment. *Online Review* 11. P. 243-253.

55. 3.11.2 European (1991) Education Thesaurus. Luxembourg: Office for the Official Publication of the European Communities.

56. 3.11.2 FID Bulletin (1967). Comparison of UDC with descriptor systems. *FID Bulletin* 17(10). P. 106.

57. 3.2 Fidel, R. (1991). Searchers' selection of search

keys: II controlled vocabulary or free text searching. *Journal of American Society for Information Science* 42(7). P. 502-514.

58. 3.2 Fidel, R. (1992). Who needs controlled vocabulary? *Special Libraries*. 83(1). P.1-9.

59. 2.2.2.1 Foskett, D. J. (1961). Classification and integration levels. *In* Foskett, D. J. and Palmer, B. I. *Eds*. Sayers memorial volume. London: The Library Association.

60. 3.6 Foskett, D. J. (1980). Thesaurus. *In* A. Kent. *Ed*. Encyclopaedia of library and information
1.2.1 science, vol. 30. New York: Marcel Dekker Inc. P. 419.

60a. 3.7.4 Foskett, D. J. (1980a). Ibid. P. 416-463

61. 3.2 Fugmann, R. (1987). Review of second edition of vocabulary control for information retrieval by F. Lancaster. *International Classification*. 14. P. 164-166.

62. 3.7.2 Fugmann, R. (1990). An interactive classaurus on PC. *International Classification* 17(3/4). P. 133-137.

63. 3.7.5.1 Ganzmann, J. (1990). Criteria for the evaluation of thesaurus software. *International Classification*. 17(3/4). P. 148-157.

64. 3.7.4 Gilchrist, A. (1971). The thesaurus in retrieval. London: Aslib.

65. 3.7.4 Gilchrist, A. (1994). Classification and thesauri. *In* B. C. Vickery. *Ed*. Fifty years of information progress: a Journal of Documentation review. London: Aslib. P. 85-118.

66. 3.7.4 Gilchrist, A. (1997). The subject approach in managing information. *In* A. Scammell. *Ed*. Handbook of special librarianship and

information work. 7th ed. London: Aslib.

67. 3.11.1 Gilchrist, A. et.al. (1973). A compressed term index for library and information science. London: Aslib.

68. 2.3.2.1 Gopinath, M. A. (1966). DRTC research cell: a report for 1966. DRTC Seminar 4. Banglore: DRTC. P. 454.

69. 2.2 Gopinath, M. A. (1976). Colon classification. *In* A. Maltby. *Ed.* Classification in the 1970s: a second look. London: Clive Bingley. P. 64-65.

70. 2.2.1 Gopinath, M. A. (1986). Relevance of Ranganathan's postulational approach in the identification of key concepts in the newly formed subjects and its implications to intellectual organization of information. *In* T. S. Rajgopalan. *Ed.* Ranganathan's philosophy: assessment, impact and relevance. New Delhi: Vikas. P. 153-181.

71. 2.3.3, 4.1 Gopinath, M. A. (1986a). Construction of depth version of colon classification: a manual. New Delhi: Wiley Eastern Ltd.

72 3.4.2 Gopinath, M. A. and Prasad, K. N. (1975). Thesaurus and classification scheme: a study of compatibility of principles for construction of thesaurus and classification schemes. Seminar on thesaurus in information systems. Banglore: DRTC. Paper AF.

73. 2.2.2.1 Grolier, E. de. (1962). A study of general categories applicable to classification and coding in documentation. Paris: Unesco.

74. 3.1 Guinchat, C. and Menou, M. (1983). General

introduction to the techniques of information and documentation work. Paris: Unesco.

75. 3.2 Henzler, R. G. (1978). Free or controlled vocabularies: some statistical user-oriented evaluation of biomedical information system. *International Classification* 5. P. 21-26.

76. 3.2 Holst, W. (1966). Problemer ved struktuering og bruk av den polytekniske thesaurus. *Tidskrift for Ddokumentation* 22. P. 69-74.

77. 4.1 Hulme, E.W. (1911). Principle of book classification. *Library Association Record.* P. 13-14.

78. 3.11.2 Information (1968) Retrieval Thesaurus of Education terms. Cleveland, Ohio: Case Western Reserve University.

79. 3.11.2 INSPEC (1979) thesaurus. London: Institution of Electrical Engineers.

80. 3.7.3 International (1974) Organization for Standardization. ISO 2788. Guidelines for the establishment and development of monolingual thesauri. Geneva: ISO.

81. 3.7.3 International (1986) Organization for Standardization. ISO 2788.

2.2.2 Guidelines for the establishment and development of monolingual thesauri. 2nd ed. Geneva: ISO.

82. 3.10 ISKO. Knowledge Organization. Copenhagen, Denmark: International Society for Knowledge Organization. Published quarterly, Wurzzurg: ERGON-Verlag. *Each issue includes a section on knowledge organization literature including new classification systems and thesauri.*

83. 3.11.2 ITS thesaurus (2000). Intelligent Transportation System thesaurus. California: US Transportation Research Board.

84. 2.2.2 Iyer, H. (1986). Users preference of sequence of component ideas in subject representation: PMEST model. *In* T. S. Rajgopalan. *Ed.* Ranganathan's philosophy: assessment, impact and relevance. New Delhi: Vikas. P. 182-190.

85. 2.1.2 Jaiswal, B. (1999). Automatic classification. *DESIDOC Bulletin of Information Technology* 19(3). P. 23-28.

86. 3.11.2 Jaster, J. et.al. (1962). The state of the art of coordinate indexing. Washington, D.C.: Documentation Inc. P. 34-79.

87. 3.10 Johnson, E. H. and Cochrane, P. A. (1995). A hypertextual interface for a search's thesaurus. *http://www.cds.tamu.edu/DL95/papers/johncoch/johncoch/html*

88. 3.3 Joyce, T. and Needham, R. M. (1958). The thesaurus approach to information retrieval. *American Documentation* 9. P. 192-197.

89. 3.7.5.1 Karisiddappa, C. R. and Prasad, A. R. D. (1993). Declarative programming and thesaurus construction. *IASLIC Bulletin* 28(4). P. 161-165.

90. 2.2.1 Kashyap, M. M. (1986). Ranganathan's postulational approach to classification: its development and impact. *In* T. S. Rajgopalan. *Ed.* Ranganathan's philosophy: assessment, impact and relevance. New Delhi: Vikas. P. 200-215.

91. 3.2 Keen, E. M. and Digger, J. A. (1972). A report on an information science index language test. 2 vols. Aberystwyth: College of Librarianship.

92. 3.2 Knapp, S. D. (1982). Free-text searching of online databases. *Reference Librarian* 5/6. P. 143-153.

93. 3.2 Knapp, S. D., Cohen, L. B. and Juedes, R. R. (1998). A natural language thesaurus for the humanities: the need for database search aid. *Library Quarterly* 68(4). P. 406-430.

94. 3.4 Korotkin, A. L., et.al. (1965). Indexing aids, procedures and devices. Rome: Air Development Centre.

95. 3.6.1 Kosovac, B. (2000). Internet / Intranet and thesauri. *http://www.urc/ca/irc/thesaurus/* roofing/report_b.html

96. 3.7.1 Kramer, R., Nikolai, R. and Habeck, C. (1997). Thesaurus federations: loosely integrated thesauri for document retrieval in network based on Internet technologies. *Journal of Digital Libraries* 1(2). P. 122-131.

97. 3.7.3 Krooks, D. A. and Lancaster, F. W. (1993) The evolution of guidelines for thesaurus construction. *Libri* 43(4). P. 326-342.

98. 3.3 Kumar, S. K., Raghavendra Rao, M. K. and Kamath, V. A. (1975). Thesaurus: an ideal tool for vocabulary control in post-coordinate systems: INIS Thesaurus- a case study. Seminar on thesaurus in information systems. Banglore: DRTC. Paper CA.

99. 3.1.1 Lancaster, F. W. (1972). Vocabulary control for information retrieval. Washington, D.C.: Information Resources Press. P.25.

99a. 3.2 Lancaster, F. W. (1972a). Ibid. P. 135-152.

99b. 3.3 Lancaster, F. W. (1972b). Ibid. P. 23.

99c. 3.4.1 Lancaster, F. W. (1972c). Ibid. P. 24-25.

99d. 3.5 Lancaster, F. W. (1972d). Ibid. P. 22-26.

99e. 3.7.1 Lancaster, F. W. (1972e). Ibid. P. 27.

100. 3.1 Lancaster, F. W. (1985). Thesaurus construction and use: a condensed course. Paris: UNESCO. P. 5.

100a 3.7.1 Lancaster, F. W. (1985a). Ibid. P.11.

100b 3.7 4 Lancaster, F. W. (1985b). Ibid. P.1-89.

101. 3.7.4 Lancaster, F. W. (1986). Vocabulary control for information
3.7.5 retrieval. 2nd ed. Arlington: Information Resources Press.

102. 3.4.1 Library of Congress (1911). Subject headings used in the dictionary catalogs of the Library of Congress. Washington: Library of Congress.

103. 3.7.2 Lopez – Huertas, M. (1997). Thesaurus structure design: a conceptual approach for improved interaction. *Journal of Documentation* 53(2). P. 139-177.

104. 3.4.2 Lu, X. (1990). Document retrieval in a structural approach. *Information - Processing and Management* 26(2). P. 209-218.

105. 3.8 Maniez, J. (1988). Relationships in thesauri: some critical remarks. *International Classification* 15(3). P. 133-138.

106. 3.2 Markey, K. et.al. (1980). An analysis of controlled vocabulary and free-text search statements in online searches. *Online Review* 4. P. 225-236.

107. 3.11.2 Meyer. U. K. H. (1965). Klassifikation und automatische Dokumentation [Classification and

automatic documentation]. Nachrichten fur Dokumentation 16(2). P. 61-67.

108. 3.7.5.1 Miller. U. (1997). Thesaurus construction: problems and their roots. *Information Processing and Management* 33(4). P. 481-493.

109. 3.4.2 Miller, U. (2001) Thesaurus construction and new information environment. *In* A. Kent. *Ed.* Encyclopaedia of library and information science, vol. 68. New York: Marcel Dekker Inc. P. 326.

109a 3.7.1 Miller, U. (2001a). Ibid. P. 334.

110. 2.3.3 Milstead, J. (1984). Subject access to system: alternatives in design. Orlando, F.L.: Academic Press. P. 144.

111. 3.7.5.1 Milstead, J. (1991). Specifications for thesaurus software. *Information Processing and Management* 27(2/3). P. 165-175.

112. 3.2 Milstead, J. (1995). Invisible thesauri: the year 2000. *Online CD-ROM Review* 19(2) 1995. P. 93-94.

113. 3.11.2 Model, F. (1966). Thesaurus in der Dokumentation-Vielschichtigkeit des Begriffes und historische Entwicklung [Thesaurus in documentation – many aspects of the concept and its historical development]. Nachrichten fur Dokumentation 17(1/2). P. 5-13.

114. 3.8.3 Molholt, P. (1996) Standardization of inter-concept links and their usage. *In* Advances in knowledge organization, vol.5. Knowledge organization and change. Proceedings of the 4th International ISKO Conference. Washington. D.C. 15-18 July 1996. Frankfurt/Main: Indeks Verlag. P. 65-71.

115. 3.7.2, 3.7.3, 4.4 National (1994) Information Standards Organization. ANSI / NISO Z39-19: 1993. Guidelines for construction, format and management of monolingual thesauri. Bethesda: NISO Press.

116. 2.3.3 Neelameghan, A. (1969). Design of scheme for classification. *Herald of Library Science* 8(2). P. 97-110.

117. 3.8.3 Neelameghan, A. (1975). Non – hierarchical associative relationships: their types and computer generation of RT links. Seminar on thesaurus in information systems. Banglore: DRTC. Paper AA.

118. 4.7 Neelameghan, A. and Desai, A. R. (1963). Facet sequence and the law of parameter. *Annals of Library Science* 10. Paper L.

119. 2.3.3, 3.3 Neelameghan, A. and Gopinath, M. A. (1965). Pragmatic approach in the design of depth classification schedule: a case study. *Library Science* 2(1). Paper. C.

120. 2.3.3 Neelameghan, A. and Gopinath, M. A. (1965a). Productive methods in the design of a scheme for depth classification: a case study. DRTC Seminar 3. Banglore: DRTC. Paper C.

121. 2.2.4, 3.3 Neelameghan, A. and Gopinath, M. A. (1966). Grouping of quasi isolates. DRTC Seminar 4. Banglore. DRTC. Paper K.

122. 2.2.2.2 Neelameghan, A. and Gopinath, M. A. (1967). Grouping of matter (property) isolates. DRTC Seminar 5. Banglore: DRTC. Paper D.

123. 2.2.5.1 Neelameghan, A. and Gopinath, M. A. (1973).

Speciator of kind 2 with special reference to social sciences. *Library Science* 10 (3). Paper T.

124. 2.5 Neelameghan, A. and Sangameswaran. S. V (1966). Array division with packet notation: case study. DRTC Seminar 4. Banglore: DRTC. Paper L.

125. 3.6 Nestel, B. et. al. (1992). A minithesaurus as an aid to the management of agricultural research. *Quarterly Bulletin of the International Association of Agricultural Information Specialists* 27(4). P. 215-223.

126. 3.11.2 NIAAA (2000). Alcohol and other drugs thesaurus: a guide to concepts and terminology in substance abuse and addiction. 3rd ed. 4 vols. Rockville, MD: National Institute on Alcohol Abuse and Alcoholism. *Also available at:* http://www.etoh.niaaa.nih.gov/AODVolI/Aodthome.htm

127. 3.11.2 OECD (1972). A basic list of economic and social development terms. Paris: OECD.

128. 2.1 Oxford (1970) English Dictionary. Vol. 2. London: The Oxford University Press. P. 468.

129. 3.7.2 Pejtersen, A. M. (1980). Design of classification scheme for fiction based on an analysis of actual user-librarian communication and use of the scheme for control of the librarian's search strategies. *In* O. Harbo and L. Kajberg. *Eds.* International Research Forum on Information Science. London: Mansell.

130. 3.2 Perez, E. (1982). Text enhancement: controlled vocabulary vs. free text. *Special Libraries* 73. P.183-192.

131. 3.8.3 Perreault, J. (1965) Categories and relators: a new schema. *Review of International Documentation* 32(4). P. 136-144. (*Reprinted in Knowledge Organization*. 21(4) 1994 pp. 189-198).

132. 3.4.3 Pettee, J. (1946). Subject headings. New York: H. W. Wilson Co.

133. 3.3 Poole, W. F. (1878). The plan of the new Poole's index. *Library Journal* 3(3). P. 109-110.

134. 3.7.5.1 Prasad, K. N., Mahajan, S. K. and Thyagarajan, K. (1975). Work and time analysis for rendering terms in a thesaurus derived from faceted classification schedule: a case study with lathe production. Seminar on thesaurus in information systems. Banglore: DRTC. Paper BD.

135. 5.5.3, 5.10.1.1 Prytherch, R. (1990). Harrod's librarian's glossary of terms terms used in librarianship, documentation and the book craft: a reference book. 7th ed. Aldershot: Gower.

136. 3.8.3 Rajan, T. N. (1975). Related terms in thesaurus. Seminar on thesaurus in information systems. Banglore: DRTC. Paper AA.

137. 2.1.2 Ramaiah, C. K. (1998). Multimedia systems in libraries and their applications. *DESIDOC Bulletin of Information Technology* 18(6). P. 35.

138. 2.2 Ranganathan, S. R. (1933). Colon classification. Madras: Madras Library Association.

139. 3.4.3 Ranganathan, S. R. (1945). Dictionary catalogue code. Madras: Thompson.

140. 2.3.1 Ranganathan, S. R. (1957). Prolegomena to library classification. 2nd ed. London: The Library Association. P. 241.

141. 2.3.4 Ranganathan, S. R. (1960). Common property isolates. *Annals of Library Science* 7(1). P. 1-12.

142. 2.2.1 Ranganathan, S. R. (1962). Elements of library classification. 3rd ed. Bombay: Asia. P. 82.

143. 2.3.3 4.1 Ranganathan, S. R. (1964). Design of depth classification: methodology. *Library Science* 1. P.21-22.

143a 2.3.3, 4.1 Ranganathan, S. R. (1964a). Ibid. P.1-42.

143b 2.1.1 Ranganathan, S. R. (1964b). Ibid. P. 2.

143c 2.3.2.1 Ranganathan, S. R. (1964c). Ibid. P. 39.

144. 2.4 Ranganathan, S. R. (1966). Freely faceted classification and depth classification. DRTC Seminar 4. Banglore: DRTC. Paper G

145. 2.6.1 Ranganathan, S. R. (1970). Colon classification for library science. *Library Science* 7(3). Paper J.

146. 2.2.2.2 Ranganathan, S. R. (1971). Dominant area for research in classification in the immediate future. DRTC Seminar 9. Banglore: DRTC. Paper CA.

147. 2.5 Ranganathan, S. R. (1972). Colon classification: notational system-towards a plan for its productive use. *Library Science* 9. Paper A.

148. 1.3.4, 2.2, 4.0 Ranganathan, S. R. (1987). Colon classification. 7th ed. Banglore: Sarada Ranganathan Endowment for Library Science.

148a 1.3.4 Ranganathan, S. R. (1987a). Ibid. P. 273 and 288.

148b 2.2.4 Ranganathan, S. R. (1987b). Ibid. P. 323.

148c 2.2.4 Ranganathan. S. R. (1987c). Ibid. P. 282-291.

148d 2.3.4, Ranganathan, S. R. (1987d). Ibid. P. 93-103.

4.10. 4.17

148e 2.6.1. Ranganathan. S. R. (1987e). Ibid. P. 114-119.
4.0

148f 4.18. Ranganathan. S. R. (1987f). Ibid. P. 49-50.
4.23

149. 1.3.1 Ranganathan. S. R. (1989). Prolegomena to library classification. Vol.1. 3rd ed. Banglore: Sarada Ranganathan Endowment for Library Science. P.214.

149a. 1.4 Ranganathan, S. R. (1989a). Ibid. P.425.

149b. 1.4 Ranganathan, S. R. (1989b). Ibid. P.421.
4.4

149c. 1.4 Ranganathan, S. R. (1989c). Ibid. P. 399-401.

149d. 2.2.2. Ranganathan, S. R. (1989d). Ibid. P. 398-399.
4.1.3

149e. 2.2.2.1 Ranganathan, S. R. (1989e). Ibid. P. 401.

149f 2.2.2.3 Ranganathan, S. R. (1989f). Ibid. P. 400.

149g. 2.2.3.1 Ranganathan, S. R. (1989g). Ibid. P. 410-411

149h. 2.3.2 Ranganathan, S. R. (1989h). Ibid. P. 373.

149i. 2.4 Ranganathan, S. R. (1989i). Ibid. P. 1-640.

149j. 4.2. Ranganathan, S. R. (1989j). Ibid. P. 183.
4.5

149k. 4.25 Ranganathan, S. R. (1989k). Ibid. P. 232.

149*l*. 4.25.1 Ranganathan, S. R. (1989*l*). Ibid. P. 277.

149m. 4.25.2 Ranganathan, S. R. (1989m). pp. 240.

150 3.7.5 Ravichandra Rao, I. K. (1975). Semi automatic construction of thesaurus. Seminar on thesaurus in information system. Banglore: DRTC. Paper BB.

151. 3.11.2 RCHME/HE (Royal Commission on the Historical Monuments of England and English Heritage) (1997). Archaeological objects thesaurus. Sweden: RCHME/HE.

152. 3.7.1 Rees-Potter, L. K. (1991). Dynamic thesauri: the cognitive function. *In* Tools for knowledge organization and the human interface: proceedings of the first international ISKO conference, Darmastadt, Germany, Aug. 14-17, 1990. Advances in knowledge organization, vol.2, R.Fugman. *Ed.* Indeks: Frankfurt/Main. P. 145-150.

153. 3.7.5.1 Ritzler, C. (1990). Comparative study of PC-supported thesaurus software. *International Classification* 17(3/4). P. 138-147.

154. 2.2.2.1 Roberts, N. (1969). An examination of the personality concept and its relevance to colon classification. *Journal of Librarianship* 1. P. 46.

155. 3.3 Roberts, N. (1984). The pre-history of the information retrieval thesaurus. *Journal of Documentation* 40(4). P. 271-285.

156. 3.1.1 Roget, P. M. (1987). Thesaurus of English words and phrases, England: Longman.

157. 3.9.3 Rolling, L. N. (1965). The role of graphic display of concept relationships in indexing retrieval vocabularies. *In* A. Pauline. *Ed.* Classification research. Proceedings of the 2nd International Study Conference: Copenhagen, Munksgaard. P. 295-320.

158. 3.2 Rowley, J. E. (1990). A comparison between free language and controlled language indexing

and searching. *Information Searching and Use* 10(3). P. 147-155.

159. 3.1 Rowley, J. E. (1992). Organizing knowledge: an introduction to information retrieval. Aldershot: Gower.

160. 3.2 Rowley, J. E. (1994). The controlled versus natural indexing language debate revisited: a perspective on information retrieval practice and research. *Journal of Information Science* 20(2). P. 108-119.

161. 1 Rowley, J. E. and Farrow, J. (2000). Organizing knowledge: an introduction to managing access to information. 3rd ed. Aldershot: Gower. P. 125-126.

161a. 3.6 Rowley J. E. and Farrow J. (2000a). Ibid. P. 160-161.

162. 3.1 Roy, A. K. (1981). Thesaurus in information system. *In* T. N. Rajan. *Ed.* Indexing systems: concepts, models and techniques. Calcutta: IASLIC. P. 164-165.

163. 3.7.5 Salton, G. (1971). Experiments in automatic thesaurus construction for information retrieval. New York: Cornell University. P. 27.

164. 2.1.2 Satija, M. P. (1988). FID – 1988 Pre conference seminar on computer application of UDC. *International Classification* 15(3). P. 149-150.

165. 2.1.1 Sayers, W. B. C. (1955). Manual of classification for librarians and bibliographers. 3rd ed. London: Andre Deutsch. P. 1.

166. 3.11.1 Schultz, C. K. (1978). Thesaurus of information science terminology. London: Aslib.

167. 3.7.5 Schwanhausser, G. (1975). An automatically

produced thesaurus. Seminar on thesaurus in information system. Banglore: DRTC. Paper BA.

168. 3.11.2 Seattle (1996) City Clerk's Thesaurus. Seattle: Seattle City Clerk's Office. Also available at: *http: www.clerk.ci.seattle.wa.us ~public.newtoc.htm*

169. 2.2.2 Seetharama, S. (1972). Categorization of isolate ideas. *Library Science* 9. P. 491-493.

170. 3.7.5.1 Seetharama, S. (1975). Term - concept relationships in an information retrieval thesaurus. Seminar on thesaurus in information systems. Banglore: DRTC. Paper AJ.

171. 3.7.4 Soergel, D. (1974). Indexing languages and thesauri: construction and maintenance. Los Angeles: Melville Publishing Co.

172. 3.9.4 Song, M. (2000). Visualization in information retrieval: a three-level analysis. *Journal of Information Science* 26(1). P. 3-19.

173. 3.7.5, 3.3.3 Sparck Jones, K. (1971). Automatic keyword classification for information retrieval. London: Butterworths.

174. 3.9.3 . 3.11.2 SPINES (1976) thesaurus : A controlled vocabulary and structured vocabulary of science and technology for policy making, management and development. Paris: Unesco.

175. 3.7.1 Stern, A. and Rischette, N. (1991). On the construction of a super thesaurus based on existing thesauri. *In* Tools for knowledge organization and the human interface: proceedings of the first international ISKO conference, Darmastadt, Germany, Aug. 14-17, 1990. Advances in knowledge organization. vol.2

R.Fugman, ed. Indeks: Frankfurt/Main. P.134-144.

176. 3.7.5 Stevens. M. E. (1980). Automatic indexing: a state-of-the-art review. Washington, DC: National Bureau of Standards.

177. 3.4 Strater, H. H. (1969). Problem of thesaurus construction for education. *In* Council for Europe. EUDISED Technical Studies. 3. Strasbourg: Documentation Centre for Education in Europe. P. 23-51.

178. 3.7.2 Strong, G. W. and Drott, M. C. (1986). A thesaurus for end-user indexing and retrieval. *Information Processing and Management* 22(6). P. 487-492.

179. 2.1.2 Svenonius, E. (1983). Use of classification in online retrieval. *Library Resources and Technical Services* 27 (1). P. 76-80.

180. 3.7.5 Svenonius, E. (1986). Unanswered questions on the design of controlled vocabularies. *Journal of American Society for Information Science* 37(5). P. 331-340.

181. 3.7.5 Svenonius, E. (1987). Design of controlled vocabularies. *In* A. Kent. *Ed.* Encyclopaedia of library and information science, vol. 45 (supplement 10). New York: Marcel Dekker Inc. P. 82-109.

182. 3.7.4 Taylor, A. G. (1999). The organization of information. Englewood: Libraries Unlimited.

183. 3.7.1, 2.2.2 Thesaurus (1969) of Engineering and Scientific Terms: a list of scientific and engineering terms and their relationships for use as a vocabulary in indexing and retrieving technical information.

TEST. New York: Engineer's Joint Council.

184. 3.10 Thesaurus (1992) guide: an analytical directory of selected vocabularies for information retrieval. 2nd ed. prepared for the Commission of the European Communities by Eurobrokers. Luxembourg: Office for Official Publication of the European Commission.

185. 3.9.2, 3.11.2 Thesaurus (1995) of ERIC descriptors. 13th ed. Houston. Arizona: Oryx.

186. 3.2 Ulmann, W. (1967). A thesaurus of nuclear science and technology: principles of design. *Teknisk-Veteskapling Forsking (TVF)* 38. P. 46-52.

187. 3.11.2 Unesco (1977) thesaurus: a structured list of descriptors for indexing and retrieving literature in the fields of education, science, social science, culture and communication. 2 vols. Paris: Unesco.

188. 1.4 3.7.3, Unesco (1981). Guidelines for the establishment and development of monolingual thesauri for information retrieval. 2nd rev. ed. Paris: 5.4 Unesco. P. 1-64.

188a. 3.1 Unesco (1981a). Ibid. P.7.

188b. 3.8 Unesco (1981b). Ibid. P. 30.

188c. 3.8.2.1 Unesco (1981c). Ibid. P. 36.

188d. 3.8.3 Unesco (1981d). Ibid. P. 39.

188e. 3.8.3 Unesco (1981e). Ibid. P. 41.

188f. 3.9, 3.9.1, 3.9.3 Unesco (1981f). Ibid. P. 46-56.

188g. 5.2 Unesco (1981g). Ibid. P. 1-2.

188h. 5.9 Unesco (1981h). Ibid. P. 25.

189. 3.11.1 Verona, R. (1964). Posibilitati de folosire a unei liste de indici czu in indexarea coordinata. [The possibility of using a list of UDC numbers for coordinate indexing]. *Studii Cercatari de Documentare si Bibliologie* 6(2). P.137-143.

190. 2.3.3 Vickery, B. C. (1960). Faceted classification: a guide to construction and use of special schemes. London: Aslib.

191. 3.1.1 Vickery, B. C. (1960a). Thesaurus – a new word in documentation. *Journal of Documentation* 16(4). P. 182.

192. 3.11.2 Wadington, J. P. (1958). Unit concept coordinate indexing. *American Documentation* 9(2). P. 107-113.

193. 3.1.1 Wall, E. (1962). Information retrieval thesauri. New York: Engineer's Joint Council. P. 17.

194. 3.1 Webster (1987). The new lexicon Webster's dictionary of the English language. New York: Lexicon Publications Inc. P. 1026.

195. 3.4.2 Weinberg, B. H. (1995). Library classification and information retrieval thesauri: comparison and contrast. *Cataloguing & Classification Quarterly* 19(3/4). P. 23-24.

196. 3.3 Whelan, S. (1958). Library retrieval. *R.R.E. Journal* 42. P. 59-68.

197. 3.8, Willets, M. (1975). An investigation of the nature of the relations

3.3.3 between terms in thesauri. *Journal of Documentation*. 3(3). P. 158-184.

198. 3.7.3 Williamson, N. J. (1996). Standards and rules

for subject access. *Cataloguing & Classification Quarterly. 21(3/4)*. P. 155-176.

199. 3.7.5.1 Willpower (2000). Willpower.demon.co.uk/thessoft.htm

200. 3.7.1 Wooster, H. (1970). 0.46872985 square inches- a naïve look at subject access. Digest of 1970 Annual Meeting. Philadelphia, Pa.: National Federation of Science Abstracting and Indexing Services. P. 41-48.

201. 3.11.1 Yoshida, S. (1993). Construction of library and information science thesaurus. *INICAE* 12(2). P. 166-172.

# Glossary of thesaural terms

**Alphabetical display**

Display of thesaural entries in a single alphabetical sequence.

**Arrograph**

Display of thesaural terms in the form of charts representing a number of specific subjects and sub-fields.

**Broader term**

The super-ordinate term in an hierarchical relation.

**BT**

Stands for Broader Term. It is a symbol used to indicate that the terms given next to this prefix are broader terms to the heading term.

**Classaurus**

Category based faceted scheme of classification incorporating all the features of a thesaurus.

**Compound term**

A term formed by combination of two or more terms.

**Controlled indexing language**

*See* controlled vocabulary.

**Controlled language**

*See* controlled vocabulary

**Controlled vocabulary**

A controlled list of indexing terms.

**Equivalent relationship**

Relationship between the preferred and non-preferred term.

**Equivalent term**

A term that is treated as if it means the same thing as another.

**Generic relationship**

Relationship between a class and its member.

**Graphic display**

A display with two-dimensional figures indicating terms and their inter-relationships.

**Hierarchical relationship**

A relationship in which one term is strictly subordinate to other.

**Hierarchical whole-part relationship**

Relationship between whole and its parts.

**Homograph**

A term with the same spelling as that of another term but has a different meaning.

**Instance relationship**

Relationship between general category of a thing, event, expressed by a common noun and an individual instance of that category.

**Narrower term**

The subordinate term in a hierarchical relation.

**Natural language**

The language of the document indexed.

**Non –preferred term**

A term that may not be used as a indexing term.

**NT**

Stands for Narrower Term. It is a symbol used to indicate that the terms given next to this prefix are narrower terms to the heading term.

**Post coordination**

The combination of terms at the time of retrieval to form a compound term.

**Precision**

The extent to which the items retrieved in a search of database are considered relevant.

**Precision ratio**

The ratio of the number of relevant items retrieved to the total number of items retrieved.

**Pre coordination**

The combination of terms to form compound terms at or before the time of indexing.

**Preferred term**

A term that may be used as indexing term.

**Recall**

The extent to which all of the items in a database that are considered relevant and retrieved.

**Recall ratio**

The ratio of the number of relevant items retrieved to the total number of relevant items in the collection.

**Related term**

A term in a semantic relation but not in a hierarchical relation to another term.

**RT**

Stands for Related Term. It is a symbol used to indicate that the terms given next to this prefix are related terms to the heading term.

**Semantic relation**

A relation between terms that is true as a matter of general knowledge, rather than depending on what the terms refer to in some particular document.

**Syntactic relation**

A relation between terms that depends on what the terms refer to some particular document, rather than being true as a matter of general relation.

**Systematic display**

Display of thesaural terms in categories, which are arranged according to their meaning and logical inter-relationships.

**Terminograph**

Display of thesaural terms in the form of box charts.

**Thesaural relationships**

Relationships between terms in a thesaurus.

**Thesauri**

A plural of thesaurus.

**Thesaurofacet**

A thesaurus with a display of both the classification type and alphabetical type.

**Thesaurus**

A device for vocabulary control, usually for specific subject area, indicating preferred and non-preferred terms and semantic relations between terms.

**UF**

A symbol used to indicate that the following term or terms are not used in indexing and that the heading term is used instead.

**USE**

A symbol used to indicate that the heading term is not used in indexing and that the following term or terms are used instead.

**Vocabulary control**

The process of systematically selecting preferred terms for information and retrieval.

# Index

Alcohol and other drugs thesaurus 47
ASIS thesaurus of LIS 45-46
Associative relationships 42-43; 182-183
Archaeological objects thesaurus 47-48
Art and architecture thesaurus 48
Australian pictorial thesaurus 48-49
Classification 9-10
Colon Classification 10-11
Compound phrases / terms 4; 177
Depth classification
    construction methodology 18-19;56-61
    examples 22-23
    meaning 15-16
    need 16
    use 20
Depth classification schedule of LIS 23-24; 124-170
Equivalent relationships 39-40; 178-180
Hierarchical relationships 40-42; 180-182
Homonyms 3
Index to the depth classification schedule 86-124
Information retrieval thesaurus of education terms 49
IN SPEC thesaurus 49-50
Intelligent transportation system thesaurus 50
Language thesaurus and IR thesaurus 27-28
Library classification 9-10
Macrothesaurus 50-51
Natural versus controlled language 28
Plurals 3; 174
Postulational approach 11-12
ROOT thesaurus 51-52
Scattering of related terms 4-5
Seattle city clerk's thesaurus 52
Singulars 3; 174
Sources providing list of thesauri 45
Speciators 15
SPINES thesaurus 52
Synonyms 40;179

Thesaurofacct 53-54

Thesaurual relationships 39-43; 178-184

Thesaurus

and classification schemes 31

and lists of subject headings 30

and post coordinate indexing systems 32

display methods 43-45

history 28-29

management softwares 37-38

purposes 32-33

Thesaurus construction

methodologies 34-35

manuals 36-37

standards and guidelines 36

use of IT 37

Thesaurus of Engineering and Scientific Terms (TEST) 52-53

Thesaurus of ERIC descriptors 49

Thesaurus of LIS terms 45-46; 187

Thesaurus of psychological index terms 51

UNESCO thesaurus 54-55

User oriented thesaurus 35